Moral Theory and Anomaly

Aristotelian Society Monographs Series

Aristotelian Society Monograph Committee:
Martin Davies (Monograph Editor), Thomas Baldwin, Jennifer Hornsby, Mark Sainsbury, Anthony Savile

MORAL THEORY AND ANOMALY

TOM SORELL

BLACKWELL
Publishers

First published 2000

2 4 6 8 10 9 7 5 3 1

Blackwell Publishers Ltd
108 Cowley Road
Oxford OX4 1JF
UK

Blackwell Publishers Inc.
350 Main Street
Malden, Massachusetts 02148
USA

British Library Cataloguing in Publication Data

A CIP catalogue record for this book is available from the British Library.

Library of Congress Cataloging-in-Publication Data

Sorell, Tom.
  Moral theory and anomaly / Tom Sorell.
    p.   cm. — (Aristotelian Society monographs series; 18)
  Includes bibliographical references and index.
  ISBN 0-631-21833-5 (alk. paper). — ISBN 0-631-21834-3 (pbk.: alk. paper)
  1. Ethics.   2. Applied ethics.   I. Title.   II. Series.
  BJ1012.S58   2000
  170–dc21   99-16128
                                                                          CIP

Typeset in 10 on 12 pt Plantin
by Best-set Typesetter Ltd, Hong Kong
Printed in Great Britain by MPG Books, Bodmin, Cornwall

This book is printed on acid-free paper.

For Lucy, Nennie, and Mary

Contents

Preface

This book takes seriously, but also rejects, a general scepticism about moral theories that has recently been expressed by a number of philosophers writing in English. The sceptics I have in mind attack Kantianism and utilitarianism at a particularly high level of generality. They do not home in on the many deep and unresolved disputes between the two theories, or on some suspected internal incoherence in their ideas of duty and welfare. Instead, they challenge something implicit in both theories: that there are perfectly general and impersonal reasons for doing some things and omitting others, and that these can be unified under overarching values. Although the thinking behind this scepticism is sometimes profound, it can depend on too abstract a view of theory, and it reckons without the hold of utilitarianism or Kantianism on moral common sense. The theories that the sceptics worry about are sometimes the inventions of philosophers, but they do not have an existence or an influence only in philosophical books or journals. On the contrary, some of the thinking that they have pioneered is now second nature to agents in both private and public life. One need not have read Mill or Bentham to believe that actions are better the more people they benefit. And the importance of respecting people independent of their wealth or birth or race or sex – in virtue of their humanity – is widely felt, even by those who have never heard of Kant. It can seem undeniable that doing something right is a matter of benefiting people, and that doing something wrong often involves disrespect – especially when so many actions and policies that one would endorse after reflection seem to be supported by these ideas.

Again and again it is their applications to practical problems, and the plausibility of their consequences even in areas where one had not thought about them, that make the 'bad old theories' seem worthwhile.

The sceptics mistakenly stress other things: the alleged artificiality of the principles employed by the theories; the assumptions about human nature that the theories smuggle in or heroically try to do without; their devices for achieving methodological purity; the otherworldliness of their highly general accounts of value. An attack geared only or mainly to these things does not loosen the hold of moral theory very much, for the hold of theory lies in part – perhaps largely – in its colonisation of common sense and in its application to unanticipated problems and situations.

If the main moral theories often seem made for the problems and situations that are submitted to them, then a certain amount of interest attaches to apparent *failures* of application of Kantianism, utilitarianism and, for that matter, neo-Aristotelianism. The failures are particularly significant where they affect more than one of the mainstream accounts. If the theories resist a question that seems natural, or have to recast it in order to engage with it; if their answers to the question seem to miss the point or show noticeable insensitivity to what seems intuitively relevant, then that is a ground for a different and perhaps more potent kind of scepticism. This is a scepticism based not on the idea that moral theory is wrong to look for any overarching values, but on the idea that the overarching values that apply successfully to routine questions are stretched to breaking point by other moral questions that are not necessarily outlying or marginal. The overarching values here would include rationality, consistency, universalisability, the welfare of the sentient, autonomy, and human flourishing.

Cases where the mainstream theories supposedly fail to apply or apply awkwardly are reasonably well known. Ecology and gender are familiar areas of difficulty. Thus deep environmentalists complain that welfare in utilitarianism is only ever the welfare of the sentient, leaving much of the rest of nature with no moral claims on us. Radical feminists complain that apparently gender-neutral and ahistorical theories of justice are unable to recover the ways in which male oppression of women differs from other forms of oppression, or the appropriateness of, for example, separatism as a response to that oppression. These forms of narrowness in theory are supposed to stand in the way of acknowledging the scale and variety of injustices towards women, and the immorality of laying waste rain forests and polluting rivers. Or to put the criticism in Kuhn's terminology, the challenges to moral theories of properly diagnosing injustice towards women or saying what is wrong with mistreating the environment are supposed to amount to *anomaly*: meeting the challenges supposedly requires an overthrow of at any rate utilitarianism and Kantianism and the development of some entirely new theory or theories. The first two chapters in this book distinguish scepticism about moral theory in general from scepticism about particular theories based on apparent anomaly. Chapters 3 to 7 take seriously the perception of anomaly in the application of moral theories to business, political office-holding, gender, and the environment. These chapters take the scepticism seriously, but deny that all of the orthodox theories are defeated by the questions that are supposed to lead to anomaly. While no one theory is equal to all of the questions, only one of the questions – concerning the grounding of obligations to such things as islands and forests – calls for anything like a fresh start. What emerges instead is the resilience of the orthodox theories, the need for a plurality of theories, and the need for each theory to drop its claim to comprehensiveness.

Scepticism based on apparent anomaly proceeds theory-by-theory and practical question-by-practical question. Although it can be answered, the work of doing so is not straightforward, particularly where a sceptical argument is thought to apply equally to each entrenched theory, as sceptics among the environmentalists and feminists sometimes claim. One effect of responding to scepticism based on apparent anomaly is to gain a greater respect for the range of theories we actually have. I have experienced this effect myself. It once seemed to me that some version of Kantianism would prove to be an adequate, perfectly general, moral theory. Now I think that each of the standard theories – Kantian, utilitarian and neo-Aristotelian – captures part of the truth, and that if there is to be progress towards unitary theoretical understanding in ethics, it must be progress from this collection of theories, rather than the refinement of just one. It is true that in their current forms these theories conflict with one another, and that theoretical progress must partly consist in the removal of this conflict. But this is not necessarily a matter of simplification, of assimilating the approach of one to the approach of another. There are lots of good reasons for doing and omitting things, and any attempt at unifying them that makes it harder to submit practical questions to theory, or to get answers, is unwelcome. In particular, an attempt at unifying them under the master values of any one of the currently contending theories – welfare or autonomy, say – seems unlikely to succeed. Greater respect for the reasonable differences between theories as we have them is the other side of the coin of greater respect for the variety of practical questions that theories are asked to address.

Scepticism based on anomaly is never answered once and for all. There are many practical questions that I do not consider in this book that generate at least prima-facie anomaly – the question of how to respond to atrocity is one – and there is much that can be disputed in my way of showing that certain apparently anomalous questions or practices are not anomalous after all. This book is more of an attempt to broach a subject than to close it. If my approach makes sense, it tells against one kind of condescension towards applied ethics – the kind that says that while applied ethics is all very interesting, it is divorced from the real intellectual work of metaethics, and the metaphysics and philosophy of mind adjoining metaethics. Anomaly is a metaethical notion, but a discussion of the genuineness or significance of anomaly straddles the boundary between metaethics and normative ethics, and between general normative ethics and applied ethics.

From 1992 to 1996 this book existed in prototype in a paper called 'On being let down by moral theory', which has been read in different versions to nearly two dozen audiences in philosophy departments, primarily in the UK, but also in Hong Kong, and recently in the United States and Canada as well. I thank all of those audiences. During the 1996/7 academic year I was able to turn the paper into a book as a Faculty Fellow in the Ethics Program at Harvard University. The Program seminar was invaluable to me, as was the time to think and write in a stimulating environment. I wish to thank Dennis Thompson, the Director of the Program, and the other Faculty Fellows: Norm Bowie, Larry Lessig, Arti Rai, Carol Steiker and Melissa Williams. All these people read versions of four of the chapters. Norm Bowie read the whole book and discussed it often with me, for which I am very grateful. Dennis Thompson encouraged me to write about political ethics in connection with anomaly, and made extremely valuable suggestions in the seminar, and in correspondence. Among the many other people who gave me helpful criticism of drafts of the book, or material connected with it, I wish to thank Heather Draper, Sue Mendus, Ken Winston, Sophia Reibetanz, Amelie Rorty, Tom Baldwin, Robert Frazier, Catherine Wilson, and several anonymous referees. Parts of chapter 3 have appeared in M. Parker (ed.) *Ethics and Organizations* (London: Sage, 1998). An earlier version of chapter 4 is included in D. Shugarman (ed.) *Dirty Hands* (Peterborough, Ontario: Broadview, 1999).

PART **ONE**

Doubts about
Moral Theories

1

Moral Theory and Anti-theory

To what extent does behaving morally depend on having a certain kind of theory? Upright people do not act arbitrarily, but does that mean that they arrive at decisions with the help of some sort of systematic understanding? Or is doing the right thing a matter of accumulating experience or wisdom, and of using one's imagination – independent of a theory? Different answers are possible, depending on what is meant by 'theory'. A theory is sometimes thought of as a vehicle for the prediction and control of observed effects. Such a theory produces causal explanations, and if it guides action at all, it does so indirectly. It can help people to bring about effects they have already observed, if they want to, but it doesn't tell people whether they should want to. What is in question here is a different sort of theory. It is primarily practical, and it *is* concerned with what we have reason to want, intend and do. The question it typically addresses is that of whether someone should go through with some plan or intention he has already formed. A theory along these lines will tell us systematically what types of things there is always reason to do or avoid, and why. It will also tell us which general reasons for doing or avoiding things are fundamental.

Perhaps even a theory in *this* sense is unnecessary for doing the right thing: it seems that people can act morally well without being able to identify very general reasons for action, and without being able to articulate any reasons at all. If a pedestrian runs to help a child who has fallen off a bicycle in heavy traffic, the reaction may be, in a perfectly good sense, unthought out and spontaneous, and questions about reasons may leave the agent at a loss. Seeing the child fall off the bicycle by itself seems to prompt the rush to get the child off the ground and away from the cars. Perhaps the agent feels fear for the child or feels something else. If so, that might be thought to be a sentimental reaction as *opposed* to an intellectual one, a sentimental reaction as opposed to a reaction influenced by theory in particular. Even if the agent were to agree to the principle that injured people or people in danger of injury should be helped, darting into the traffic may not feel like an application of that principle, or, indeed, any principle. The child may be a person in danger, and the agent may agree that people in danger should be helped, but the person in danger may not consciously register under that description. It may not be as a *person* in danger that the child seen prompts the quick response. Perhaps it is as a *child* or as *that child* or as David or Janey or whatever. These two aspects – the immediacy of the response and the particularity of what it is a response to – do not count against saying that the pedestrian's response to the fallen child is an ethical response; but they may call in question the contribution of theory to that response. So perhaps ethical response can be untheoretical.

Other considerations point in the same direction. There is the fact that moral training starts in early childhood, and takes effect before agents are very reflective. After only a little training, infants appear to be able to do the right thing. They can say they are sorry for hurting one another or give back something they have taken against the wishes of another child. When they do the right thing, they surely don't depend on theory in the sense we are considering; and there is a certain strain in saying that they depend on theory of any kind.

Uses for Moral Theory

Unless 'theory' is understood in the very minimal sense of any pattern of belief that explains behaviour, or any mechanism that allows for the recognition of a type of situation, theory does not seem to be a requirement of all right action. It may nevertheless be a requirement of quite a *lot* of right action.

Public policy decisions; the demands of roles

The need for theory is particularly striking where the medium of right or wrong action is public policy or legislation, and where there are many goods and many agents to be taken into account, not to mention established practice, law, and the expectations of the parties affected by the policy. For everything relevant to be given weight, and for relative weights of goods to be reflected in reasoning, principles need to be devised that take one far from unreflective, everyday morality. These unobvious and complicated principles are the stuff of theory if any are.

Theory can also be required where the decisions before the agent are small-scale, for example, where there is a conflict among the demands of personal morality, or a conflict between personal morality and the demands of some more public role the agent occupies, as when the agent is a manager in a business who is under orders to make staff redundant, and yet who knows that redundancy will be disastrous for the families of the people concerned. In cases like this, agents may not know what they ought to do, and may lack resources for connecting the ethics of fulfilling a particular role with morality in general. Theory may then be indispensable.

The need for theory is often acknowledged in modern medical practice. Because it is self-consciously governed by its own ethical codes and principles, medicine is in a way pre-adapted to theory. But its codes do not seem to add up to a theory, and there are problems for which it appears that nothing less than theory will do. There is the whole range of questions concerning rationing of treatment, concerning pain-relief and euthanasia, concerning the ethics of clinical trials, which are hard to resolve with only good will, moral common sense, the law and codes of practice. No wonder that medical ethics is the best established of the branches of applied moral theory. Although health care practitioners and ethicists alike have lately begun to question the usefulness of theory in the schematic form in which it is described in the leading medical ethics textbooks, and though they have also criticised the presumption of expertise in the mainly philosophically trained formulators of theory, it is not clear that the departures they are urging from textbook models are evidence of the rejection of theory.[1] What seems to be at issue is the method of striking the right balance between particular cases and principles or other pieces of theoretical apparatus, as well as how general the theoretical apparatus should be.[2]

Rationalising and systematising pre-theoretical valuations

In indicating areas where theory may come into its own, it is natural to distinguish, as I have been doing, between, on the one hand, unreflective morality, and, on the other hand, moral theory. But the distinction may be questionable, because, in order for it to guide practice reliably, even unreflective morality may have to be grasped as a set of precepts – 'Don't lie'; 'don't steal', etc. – tied up by something. And this can be a theory or a proto-theory.[3] One traditional task of a moral theory in philosophy has been to present the various precepts and prohibitions that most of us internalise through upbringing as some sort of unity. Not the sort of unity that consists of being written on the same tablets of stone handed down from God to a prophet on a lonely mountain top, but a unity that depends on some sort of shared content of the precepts that rationalises them all. This has meant finding a principle to subsume the precepts, or, differently, identifying a human good that all the precepts could be claimed to promote. In short, moral theories in philosophy have had the dual roles of systematising and rationalising pre-existing prohibitions and prescriptions.[4] They have been concerned with identifying generally or universally acceptable reasons for action or omission and then unifying them.

Identifying the generally acceptable reasons does not necessarily involve accepting the precepts and prohibitions of conventional morality just as they are. Often they conflict with one another or run into trouble in easily thought of problem cases, and need to be revised before being rationalised. For example, a sweeping prohibition on killing human beings has consequences for some types of medical intervention, some types of punishment, and some types of military operation, consequences that many find less acceptable than the absolute prohibition itself. One familiar task of philosophical theories is to try to formulate a precept that accommodates or convincingly overrides those intuitions about punishment, medical treatment and war, or that revises both the intuitions and the principle. When many different kinds of practice are engaged by a particular prohibition, as in our example about the prohibition on killing, it is hard to make the treatment systematic without invoking principles or values more general than those connected with killing itself. It is to these overarching values that one appeals in order to justify the familiar moral precepts *en bloc* – or the versions of the principles that we would accept after reflection. So, to simplify a bit, the general welfare and respect for persons are the overarching values that, in Mill and Kant respectively, justify following the ordinary moral precepts. Similarly, according to Aristotle, one is supposed to be justified in acquiring the virtues, because one cannot flourish as a human being without them. Although it probably does some violence to Aristotle, one can say that, in the moral theories of all three of these philosophers, the overarching values can be formulated as principles enjoining people to promote something – the general welfare, autonomy, respect for persons, human flourishing – by means of rules of action or the adoption of policies or the cultivation of character traits.

It would be a mistake to see the rules or the overarching principles as supplying enough reasons for action to fill a life. Rather, a moral theory can be understood as saying that the full life an agent wants to lead should be *consistent* with the principles the theory outlines. The content of that full life does not have to be derivable from the theory.

Many courses of action will be generated by desires of the agent and by the agent's society, quite independent of moral theory. Moral theory comes into play in agents able to reflect on their desires and social influences. Even when an agent does not feel that there is a conflict between the courses of action he is inclined to follow – a conflict that may get him to reflect on the values that are driving him in opposite directions, and to choose between them – it is open to him to wonder whether something he wants to do is really worth pursuing all things considered, and this can lead him to reflect on the consistency of what he is contemplating with more impersonal, less time-bound values – such as one gets from moral theories in philosophy.

What makes sense of such reflection is the idea that actions result from choices, and that choices are good according as the reasons that support them are good or bad. If a reason is good it should be acceptable from a number of points of view. For example, it should be acceptable not just after the fact – when the best face has to be put on what has already been done – but in advance, as part of the content of reasoning that could persuade someone to do it or that could be used in deliberation. The better the reason, the less its appeal should depend on the idiosyncrasies of the agent: it ought to be acceptable to lots of agents. The better the reason, the less its appeal depends on things that interfere with choice. And so on. The overarching reasons that at least standard theories in philosophy give – 'It would satisfy the most considered preferences of all concerned'; 'It comes closest to treating everyone with equal respect'; 'It would bring out what's humanly best in the agent' – can be understood as reasons of this sort.

There are limits to how general and abstract good reasons can be if they are to influence the choice of all the agents to whom they can be addressed. In order to be serviceable in a piece of persuasion that could be directed at almost anyone or in a stretch of deliberation undertaken by almost anyone, the content of the reason has not only got to be intelligible to the great generality of agents, but it has also got to be seen as, or seen as connected with, things that most agents would regard without further argument as reasons for action. In many parts of the West at the close of the twentieth century, 'it would glorify God' would *not* qualify as a widely acceptable reason in this sense, even if the atheistic agents to whom it was directed understood it. But 'it would glorify God' might subsume an act by way of a reason that *was* generally acceptable, like 'it would relieve suffering'. Similarly, 'it would keep the peace' might provide a reason for doing something by way of a rule of behaviour like 'avoid insulting gestures' that was acceptable to people who thought that sometimes the peace might legitimately be broken. In general, for moral theory to be able to draw practical conclusions from the overarching reasons it identifies, or justify familiar precepts by reference to those overarching reasons, the overarching reasons have to be not only more general than what comes under them, but also more plausible than rivals in the light of the precepts and particular actions they seem to provide justification for.

The rationalising role of the general reasons that theories identify may make theories appear fawningly conservative or middle of the road. Not only do the overarching values of the standard theories tend to support versions of the ancient prohibitions included in, say, the Ten Commandments, but the requirement of not departing too much from what can command general assent may seem to exclude moral arguments for ways of life that would challenge or disturb a long-standing historical consensus or wide agreement at a time over how to behave. Overrationalisation is one ineradicable risk of stating generally acceptable reasons, but the danger is substantially offset by the fact that reasons have to be acceptable from many points of view. If the precepts of a theory are open to convincing interpretation as means of preventing change inconvenient to the powerful or wealthy, then the authority of the precepts may be precarious. But if it is, that is because reasons that purport to be acceptable from most points of view turn out not to be. Instead, they prove acceptable only or primarily from the point of view of the wealthy and powerful.

Rather than saying that the generality aimed at by moral theories gives them a critical edge that inhibits overrationalisation, we can say that the rationalising and systematising roles of moral theory complement one another. A unifying principle that is too general and abstract will not seem to add weight to the less general reasons it is supposed to ground; and a principle that overrationalises a particular way of life (e.g. 'Everyone deserves the advantages of their natural and fairly acquired assets.') may not be able to provide a convincing argument against public policies or actions that would bring the most advantaged down and the least advantaged up.

With their rationalising and systematising uses particularly in mind, we can return to the original question: Are moral theories necessary for right action? Since they can unify the central prohibitions and prescriptions of morality, these theories can make the part of morality covered by the central prescriptions and prohibitions look more systematic. This can heighten or reinforce the authority that any one prescription or prohibition has pre-theoretically. People who care little about lying can be appalled at the idea of killing, and a theory that finds a common source for the prohibitions on lying and killing can make the authority of the unquestioned prohibition rub off on the other. So theory can make it more probable that people will do the right thing in the area covered by the central prohibitions and prescriptions. Again, as the applied ethics literature shows, theories can provide guidance in areas *not* covered by the central prohibitions. They can do so by suggesting principles or analogies that connect the central area (everyday morality) with other areas. In this way they can in principle extend the range of right action beyond everyday situations.[5]

The oldest of the traditional theories in moral philosophy rationalise and unify the central prescriptions and prohibitions by reference to a single 'highest good'. It is controversial whether there is only one such good, and if there is, whether it has ever been identified. It is also controversial whether the prohibitions and prescriptions need to be sustained by a highest good. Kant had doubts in this connection, for example. And so must any theorist operating in a post-Rawlsian era in which the right and the good are strongly distinguished by moral theorists. Nevertheless, the *point* of positing such a good is clear enough. If each prescription of human morality is seen to promote human flourishing, for example, agents who ask why they should comply will have a general reason for following not only this or that prescription, but for being moral. The idea of a higher-order good that morality promotes has a point even where agents do not demand why they should be moral but do automatically what they think morality requires. The reason is that when agents make choices without reference to such a good, they may lack something that makes them reliable performers of right action. They do the right thing, but not knowing why it is right, they might easily do the wrong thing, or at least be brought to doubt in retrospect whether what they did was right.

If there is anything in this line of thought, then the grasp of a precept outside a theory may not yet count as moral understanding, and action prompted by it may leave something to be desired. Even if it is not required to produce actions in *keeping* with morality, theory may be required to produce actions one can *count* on being in keeping with morality. The distinction between unwittingly right action on the one hand, and, on the other, right action underpinned by a preferred sort of understanding is insisted upon by Plato and Aristotle, who both think that full-fledged virtue requires more than simply happening to do the right thing. Both Plato and Aristotle think that virtuous action has to issue from a developed moral understanding, or an explicit grasp of reasons why certain actions are right. Does either writer provide a reasonable defence of the claim that doing right depends on theory? Plato's account is too entangled with the Theory of Forms to have much initial plausibility; but Aristotle's looks much more promising.[6]

In the *Nicomachean Ethics* Aristotle holds that virtue is first acquired by habituation in the course of a good upbringing. One learns through practice and experience when and when not to flee danger, for example, and develops over time the repertoire of responses associated with courage. But this is not all there is to learn about courage; someone with the right responses can also learn from what the *Nicomachean Ethics* says about courage, in particular its connecting the possession of courage with human flourishing. Although the agent who has developed the virtues through habituation might never shrink from acting courageously, so that he does not lack the motivation to be courageous, still, according to Aristotle, he does not act courageously *with understanding* until he is able to see how courage promotes the realisation of human excellence or the flourishing life – which is where the *Nicomachean Ethics* comes in. Until the courageous person confronts these lectures, or something equivalent to them, he only sees *that* danger must be faced up to; after taking in the lectures he also has a deep reason *why* danger must be faced up to, and the understanding reinforces the habit and promotes it to true virtue.

An analogue of this argument might show that simply following a precept of ordinary morality does not amount to full-blown moral action. Thus it might be said that merely knowing that lying is wrong and acting accordingly cannot suffice for truthfulness in the full sense, that is, truthfulness with moral understanding. One needs to know why truthfulness is right, or why lying is wrong. Similarly for other types of action required by morality. Or perhaps the right way of putting it is to say that while habituation suffices for truthfulness in the full sense, moral understanding can help to anchor that truthfulness when the agent asks whether there is a good reason to make it a habit to tell the truth. Perhaps without that understanding truthfulness will seem or can be made to seem a *mere* habit. And similarly for other cases. Knowing why one should be truthful, courageous, just, and so on is plausibly said to take the form of a theory – not necessarily a theory connecting right action with virtue and human flourishing, but some theory or other connecting the precepts of morality to *some* unifying value or principle. Without being able to locate the familiar prohibitions and prescriptions of everyday morality in the context of a theory, an agent may act rightly, but the agent may lack something, for instance an awareness of something beyond habit that might make someone regularly tell the truth, or an answer to someone who does not see why anyone should generally tell the truth or face up to danger. The agent who is used to doing the right thing without being able to give a reason does not necessarily lack moral understanding altogether: even someone who knows merely *that* something is wrong understands to some extent. But the understanding can be improved upon. It lacks something.

In Aristotle, this lack is understood against the background of a theory of higher and lower principles in the soul, where reason is the pre-eminent higher principle. The idea is that until reason operates in the right way in the production of right action, the active ingredient in morality is not the higher part of the soul. Such a theory is unnecessary, however, for accepting Aristotle's point about moral understanding. Moral understanding can matter even if the soul has no higher and lower principles. It can matter because moral precepts are regularly applied in an environment in which their authority is called into question. In such an environment particular moral precepts can be challenged by defences of competing precepts, or relativistic or nihilistic positions can be introduced to undermine the authority of any and all precepts. Where moral precepts are routinely challenged or met with scepticism, proposals about their justification may be very much in order; and such proposals can come from moral theory.[7] These proposals may not be beyond controversy themselves, but that does not mean that moral precepts cannot be justified at all, or that their justifications are bound to be less plausible than challenges to them. In any case, some justification is better than none. A habituation-based morality cannot prosper if it responds with silence when challenged. At least, it cannot prosper in silence if there is a general expectation that agents should be able to defend their practices. It cannot prosper in silence even if moral scepticism is uncalled for. For in a climate even of unjustified moral scepticism, silence will look like moral blindness or smugness. Moral theories can be the antidote to this smugness or blindness. They can be used to defend habits like truthfulness and promise-keeping from several quite distinct starting points. The defences that these theories provide may not be ideal; but it is the attempt to defend one's actions morally that rebuts the charge of blindness and smugness, not the perfection of one's weapons of defence. And an established practice of accounting for one's actions is itself one of the best practical antidotes to a facile nihilism or relativism.

Does theoretical moral understanding matter *only* in a climate of moral scepticism or moral controversy? No. It has a use even in an atmosphere of moral acceptance or moral conservatism, and its use in this atmosphere is the same as its use in the other, namely for justification. This may seem paradoxical: in an atmosphere in which there is wide agreement at a time over what it is right to do (moral acceptance) or wide agreement over time (moral conservatism), the authority of precepts is not generally in doubt; so where does the need for justification come from? The answer is, from the clash there is always likely to be between moral precept and inclination. Here as elsewhere in the assessment of the role of moral theory, it is very important to remember what Kant made so much of: that for ordinary mortals as opposed to holy beings, morality presents itself as constraint, as a counterpoise to inclination. Its requirements characteristically go against the grain, getting us to do or omit things we would not do or omit if nature were allowed to take its course. Morality tells us how we ought to behave; not how we do behave or feel like behaving. If this is right, morality must often cope with a relatively weak natural motivation for doing what it asks and sometimes a strong natural motivation for not doing what it asks. If morality is to motivate us it must do so by giving us reasons *not* supplied by inclination for doing what it tells us to do. Reasons for what it tells us to do are reasons for following its particular precepts, which brings us back to the justificatory role of moral theory.

If one task of moral theories is to make up for deficiencies of motivation, and to alert us to cases where even normally legitimate interest may be outweighed, how is it that doing right can *ever* fail to depend on theory? The answer is that theory is not the only thing that makes up for motivational deficiency. There is also, as we have seen, habit-formation or habituation. Habituation rather than theory is plausibly said to explain why infants can do the right thing. Habituation can also explain how the pedestrian's reaction to the fallen cyclist can be automatic and unthinking and yet still be a case of doing right: because helping people who are in danger, or children in danger, or a particular child in danger, is right, and because in a certain agent giving that help has become second nature. But habituation is geared to the normal or near-normal and repeatable case, and something more may be required to rise to the morally complicated, the morally unusual, the morally subtle, the morally controversial – in short, the morally challenging. Moral understanding in the form of theory is part of the more that is needed. (I do not claim it is all.)[8]

In my view, then, moral understanding in the form of theory works alongside habituation. It does not take its place; and it is not required, as Aristotle and Plato held, for the non-accidental production of right action. More explicitly, we can think in the following way about the connection between habituation and theory. As children we are weaned away from doing what we like. Norms of the family and of the wider society are made children's norms. Our elders tell us after we have done a thing prohibited by a norm that we mustn't do it again, perhaps enforcing that message with some corporal punishment. Eventually we get a sense of a range of things that are standardly prohibited. The next step is forming the ability to ask whether something not known to be on the prohibited list is also prohibited and why. At that stage we can be told that something new is prohibited because it is another case of something already known to be. This is where a proto-theory starts to operate. We are able to think about what we do and ask that some sort of pattern be imposed on prohibitions, when they are added to in moral theory. Suggestions about why all of the so-far-prohibited things are wrong, or why bunches of them are, is a proto-theory. Out and out theory is developed where there is consciousness of different ways in which bunches of prohibitions (and, indirectly, permissions and prescriptions) can be justified, and when the different methods of justification are themselves reflected upon.

If this story is right – I assume it is at least plausible – then 'May I do this?' rather than 'What should I do?' may be the most primitive question for theory, and theory starts to get a hold on us as an extension of a kind of child-rearing. Again if this story is right, the basic method of extension of moral thought is by connecting unanticipated prohibited action to previously encountered prohibited action. On the account I am putting forward habituation can be enough for much non-accidentally right action, though if circumstances throw up surprises and complexities for an agent, and rhetorical challenges, it is unlikely to suffice for *all* non-accidentally produced right action. Unlike Plato and Aristotle I do not associate full-blown morality only with acting correctly for conscious reasons, since right action can be produced, and produced reliably, by conditioning alone. Acting correctly for reasons – doing the right thing in the light of theory – is not what makes the difference between accidental right action and non-accidental right action; rather, it is what makes the difference between knowing that and knowing why ordinary prescribed acts are right; between knowing and not knowing what to do in circumstances that are out of the ordinary; and between being motivated to act and not being motivated to act according to the precepts of morality when the inclination to do so is weak or absent. Theory need not be regarded as an antidote to weakness of will, though it may well make available unsuspected general reasons for doing the right thing. Theory need not disarm all misleading moral rhetoric either. It does, however, challenge the rhetorician to match the general reasons given by theory for a particular action or omission with ones of his own.

Scepticism about Moral Theory

As I have been describing it, a moral theory operates to begin with on the familiar prohibitions and prescriptions handed down to us in ordinary moral training. It identifies a value or a principle that unifies the prescriptions and prohibitions, perhaps after they have been revised in the light of counterexamples, and it justifies adherence to those prohibitions and prescriptions by reference to that value or principle. On this account, moral theories are not free-standing philosophical constructions. They take as raw material a shared lore about right and wrong, a lore that is not timeless and unchanging, and that is often developed for ever day life, and domestic life at that. Often this lore presupposes a modicum of background social peace and modest abundance. Extreme hardships are catered for by special precepts or by escape clauses in ordinary precepts. The norms taken for granted in ordinary moral training sometimes pass unnoticed into moral theories as background assumptions, and when they are unsettled or lapse, theories, too, can fall into disarray. (This fact will assume considerable significance by the end of the book.)

One moral theory is distinguished from another chiefly by the unifying material. Other differences derive from the arguments for the particular values selected, the metaphysical arguments about the nature of those values and about human nature and the casuistical methods that enable the unifying goods and the prohibitions and prescriptions to engage with particular cases. Thus Kantianism and utilitarianism differ in the principles that they select to unify the prohibitions and prescriptions of conventional morality; and Kant's Kantianism differs from Nagel's or Rawls's not so much at the level of unifying values, as in their assumptions about the nature of agency and authoritative practical reasoning.

Even where there is broad *agreement* between theories about unifying values, moral theory as I conceive it is not monolithic. The literature shows that there is considerable variety even among those who follow the same general approach, whether it be utilitarian, Kantian, neo-Aristotelian, or something else. Despite that, and perhaps surprisingly, moral theory *in general* has increasingly attracted criticism and scepticism. Writers have looked beyond the failings of particular versions of Kantianism and utilitarianism and have thought they have seen problems in the very enterprise of giving higher-order justification for action or omission. The main varieties of recent scepticism about theory in general are sampled in the remainder of this chapter.[9] Although the sceptical onslaught has considerable depth and sophistication, it seems to me to go wrong precisely by being expressed at the level of generality it so often condemns in theory itself. In my view there is nothing wrong with the very idea of moral theory, though there are many imperfect embodiments of that idea. That is, there is nothing wrong with the very idea of identifying higher-order justifications for whole classes of action and omission, though there are striking difficulties for the major normative ethical theories in accommodating some of these classes of action and omission. Some of these difficulties I call 'anomalies'. After trying in this chapter and the next to argue against wholesale dismissals of moral theory and in favour of criticism of particular moral theories based on particular prima-facie anomalies, I shall give several chapter-length examples of would-be anomaly, and suggest how they might be addressed by particular theories.

Six theses of anti-theory

I begin with 'anti-theory', that is, with scepticism about moral theory in general. It is remarkably difficult to recast the claims of various anti-theorists as a single line of thought, or even as a list of common assumptions.[10] There appears to be a consensus among at least the anti-theorists writing in English that Aristotle's ethics does not amount to a theory in the required sense, and that Kant's and utilitarian ethics do. In general, the anti-theorists recognise a connection between modernity or the biases of the Enlightenment and the sort of theory that they are against.[11] It should already be clear, however, that the anti-theorist's interpretation of Aristotle's ethics as a non-theory is disputable. Not only can Aristotle be understood as rationalising a certain sort of personal and role morality by reference to a highest good of flourishing, which the virtues each and together promote; he can also be read as saying that ethical development and the practice of the virtues is incomplete if the agent lacks theoretical insight into the common features of the virtues and the contribution of each to flourishing.[12] What is more, Aristotle's appropriators in our own day are just as capable as undoubted theorists – the Kantians and utilitarians – of applying the doctrine of the virtues to the rationalisation of unselfish business practice or to the humane treatment of animals. It is unclear why this counts any less as the application of moral theory than utilitarian or Kantian treatments of similar topics. As for the idea that we inherit from the Enlightenment an unfortunate general appetite for theory that is catered for in Anglo-American moral philosophy by utilitarianism and Kantianism, that is hard to cut down to a discussible size. I shall concentrate on six theses which are supposed to tell against theory in the following sense of 'theory': a set of precepts of personal and role morality all unified by some overarching principle that rationalises the precepts, together with metaethical arguments about the nature of moral value and the way human beings recognise and act upon it.

(1) *Moral theory is no substitute for a historically evolved set of practices and customs as a guide to action.* Annette Baier,[13] Alasdair MacIntyre[14] and Stuart Hampshire[15] all make use of this claim in arriving at versions of an anti-theory position. Part of what is at issue is what makes a morality take hold of people in practice. For the critics, a self-conscious theory is rarely made of the right stuff. According to Baier it is not the intellectual impact of moral precepts or a system of them that is decisive. It is how examples are set in moral training and how one kind of behaviour elicits a pattern of behaviour and emotion in response. Much of this action and reaction proceeds independently of the articulation of precepts, and the result is an induction into a way of life, not a conversion to a set of principles. Even when a way of life is established enough to be reflected upon and exposed to criticism in the light of theory, the way of life exercises a hold on us and has a legitimacy even in the face of criticism. The reason is that for a way of life to be a subject of reflection and criticism at all, it has to have been able to have survived long enough to have been workable; that is, it has to have shown itself to be a possible channelling of collective effort, desire, intelligence and need in the face of the demands of growing up, mating, ageing, learning, trading and protecting oneself against natural disasters and human incursions. Workability is compatible with inconsistency, unfairness and many other things that moral theory exposes to criticism. But so long as the workability of a way of life is not owed wholly to these criticisable practices, the way of life should not be an object of contempt, or seen as something primitive in comparison to a theory, especially when theories so often fall at the hurdle of being put into practice.

(2) *The habits of thought of philosophy can produce relativism and scepticism when applied to moral problems.* Like (1), this thesis puts pressure on the claim of theory to guide practice or to motivate agents. According to some anti-theorists, the details of theories and the methods of argument of the theorists, far from making people more upright, actually give people reason to distrust the authority of theory, and the authority of morality. The theories can seem outlandish. By the standards of Quinean naturalism at least, some theories go to extreme lengths to show that one cannot fail to have a motivation for being moral. They find themselves invoking otherworldly eternal standards, or otherworldly rational faculties, things that are harder to believe in than the unexplicated necessity of refraining from killing the innocent or the untheorised rightness of keeping one's promises.[16] Again, there are the habits of mind routinely inculcated when philosophers teach moral theory and its application to students. Often the aim of such teaching is to disturb the unthinkingness of some moral reactions and views. Students hear the

teacher playing devil's advocate and suggesting arguments for any moral position students might readily reject. When devil's advocacy extends to contriving arguments for improbable moral views, students can be left with the impression that one or another moral theory can produce a good argument for virtually *any* practical conclusion. This impression can be morally disabling.[17]

(3) *Moral theories ask too much of us and hold up as exemplary figures people who are not wholly admirable.* When moral theory justifies precepts by calling attention to values like respect for persons or the good of general human welfare, it often puts one in one's place. Theory deflates the importance of one's personal projects, likes and dislikes, passions and aversions, and starts to make them look more or less comparable in urgency and weight to those of anyone else.[18] Often the effect of theory's putting one in one's place is more than a revaluation downwards of the things one *selfishly* and immorally pursues. Often it is a revaluation downward of one's otherwise defensible interests, when these are in the balance alongside the severe deprivations and misfortunes of other persons. Not only selfish motivation but also self-interested motivation starts to look like morally deficient motivation, or at least challengeable motivation. For example, doing a thing because it advances one's career, or because it improves the lot of those who are close to the agent, can be represented by theory as suspect. Not only is defensible self-interest denigrated, but extreme self-sacrifice and saint-liness are over-valued, or at least presented in an unbalanced way, without regard to the things that make saints hard to live with and hard to like.[19]

(4) *Moral theories produce idealisations that are too far removed from the real world of unaltruistically motivated agents, inequality and scarcity to be of any use. What is more, they draw their illustrations and test cases not from life but from far-fetched thought-experiments. When they base arguments on concepts allegedly shared with pre-theoretical thought, they often mangle those concepts.* Consider the idealisations that have been used in ensuring that theories of justice arrive at their principles impartially. Rawls's veil of ignorance, which is supposed to conceal from authors of principles of justice any information that would make them choose principles advantageous to themselves, leaves them with a very sketchy conception of their or their society's place in history, complete ignorance of their economic, intellectual and other assets, and entirely in the dark about their conception of the good. Bruce Ackerman draws principles of justice from the decisions some newcomers to a planet might make about the use of a substance convertible into anything they might like.[20] Critics sometimes pillory these theoretical devices for assuming the impossible:

a choice of principles of justice influenced by no point of view or particular information at all. Annette Baier complains about the limitations of Rawls's strict compliance theory of justice, and argues that there are very formidable difficulties with the mechanisms she thinks might be needed to bring a theory of justice into contact with a world in which not everyone complies.[21] A broadly analogous point comes up with respect to the artificiality of examples. In the abortion literature there is Thomson's violinist example[22] or her example of the house in which people-seeds can take root.[23] These things often put off non-philosophers, leaving them with the impression that theory is not sufficiently attuned to the forms in which abortion confronts medical practitioners or teenagers who are unprepared for pregnancy. Again, and differently, there is the complaint from within the philosophical community that certain concepts with very rich connotations have been denatured and impoverished by the applications made of them in the bioethics literature, and in philosophical feminism.[24]

(5) *The precepts that make up normative moral theories are too general and unqualified to improve moral understanding, and arguments from them are open to the charge that it is not for philosophers to tell the rest of humanity what to do.* Bernard Williams has criticised the tendency of theory to recast a whole variety of reasons for action as considerations about well-being or considerations that flow from the freedom, equality and rationality of persons. According to Williams, since theory tries to get a wide variety of precepts and prohibitions covered by a single overarching principle or value, the overarching principle or value is going to be relatively schematic, and therefore of relatively little help to agents who want to make their decisions and choices sensitive to more considerations rather than fewer.[25] Baier points out that when precepts that moral theory offers to bear out, such as 'Do not kill', are understood with all of the usual qualifications, they become relatively empty.[26] Again, there are many critics who say that theory is no help to agents because the same theory can give conflicting advice, or because different theories can give conflicting advice.[27] These critics are encouraged by the fact that some pro-theory writers themselves are uneasy at the possibility of genuine moral dilemmas.[28] Still others think that to read a grasp of general precepts into right action is to miss the sensitivity of moral response to the irreducibly particular, as in the example of the response to the child who falls off the bicycle in heavy traffic. No set of precepts could entirely capture what a virtuous person is disposed to do or how he is disposed to live.[29]

Not only do the contents of moral theory leave something to be desired if what they purport to do is help agents to decide what to do and to give weight to the wide variety of considerations right action should be sensitive to; it can also seem presumptuous of philosophers, who may have very little experience of the world, to offer their services as moral advisers to those who have much more such experience. Familiarity with theory and a skill in argument or analysis can give the illusion of something that only exists in the form of wisdom – namely, moral expertise.[30] Again, Baier has questioned the value of any philosophically formulated normative theory, but has seen a role for empirical studies of moral behaviour and social institutions. Anthropology, psychology, history – all have a stronger claim to tell us something we can hope to make use of than philosophy on its own.[31]

(6) *Knowing what one ought to do is not natural scientific knowledge, and its content and methods of compensating for error are not to be modelled on those of natural science.* This thesis belongs to an anti-theory position because a number of moral theories have pretensions to objectivity and universality that the anti-theorists trace to an aspiration to be scientific, or to an excessive rationalism. Among the anti-theorists who lay considerable emphasis on the asymmetry between science and ethics Williams, in *Ethics and the Limits of Philosophy*, is perhaps foremost. Fastening on the devices in moral theory which he thinks give the theorist the illusion of reaching perfectly objective conclusions, Williams insists that the hankering after a conception of the world devoid of subjective elements, however appropriate it is as an ideal of natural scientific enquiry, is radically out of place in ethics. So is any aspiration to a type of understanding that is truly cosmopolitan, that gets beyond the point of view of a particular culture. A similar conclusion, albeit connected to a different and far more deflationary view of natural science, is arrived at by Richard Rorty,[32] who not only denies the possibility of a cosmopolitan perspective, but doubts that there is any need to apologise for a frankly ethnocentric approach to morality. However much liberal practices, for example, seem to be endorsed by reason and not mere historical accident, the authority may be no more deep than our entanglement with one way of life rather than another. The practices are no worse for that, according to Rorty.

Countering Anti-theory

What theory does not exclude: inarticulateness and the influence of ways of life

Perhaps the first thing to say in response to anti-theory is that it saddles the theorist with claims he does not have to make. According to the picture built up earlier in the chapter, theory organises, but does not supply, most of the material that guides action. What supplies most of the material is moral training, which (to respond to theses (1) and (6)) can be as culture-bound and tradition-bound as one wants. Theory is supposed to present some of the content introduced by moral training in a form in which it can be argued about, argued for and argued from, but it need not be assumed that all moral content can be articulated, or that every moral conclusion can be represented as the conclusion of a good argument from some very general set of precepts. Nor have even the arch-theorists ever claimed as much. Kant famously insists on a role for judgement in the application of all principles, and in utilitarianism some things are worth doing because they promote goods that most people recognise without argument. So here the anti-theory position is likely to exaggerate the rationalism and cognitivism of a pro-theory position.

That is not the only exaggeration in this area. Another crops up in appeals to the idea of tradition. When Baier insists that tradition as opposed to explicit theory supplies most of the convictions that people bring to their study of moral philosophy, she is both right and wrong. She is right because the medium of moral training is not only, and perhaps not mainly, explicit precept; but she is wrong also, because some of the moral commonplaces of life in, say, America or Britain, have historical roots in traditions of thought, including philosophical traditions, as much as in non-intellectualist practice. When a late twentieth-century American or British child makes the entirely unremarkable protest that a certain form of treatment by her parent is unfair because it is not the same as the treatment another child gets from another parent or a sibling gets from the very same parent, that sounds like an argument from equality whose intellectual roots are philosophical. Many readers of this book live in a culture in which argument (and to that extent rationalism) is as much a part of the way of life as other inchoate, uncodifiable practices. And this quasi-rationalist culture has a world-wide influence. Even when its moral standards are dismissed as parochially western, and not necessarily better than other traditions, that is itself an implicit argument from equality – equality of different cultures – owed to the West and to the theories of westerners. So to say that theory is puny compared to tradition in its practical effects is to beg the question of how free from the influence of theory tradition has to be.

There is an upshot for the anti-theorist's theses (2) and (5). Whether or not people are aware of it, philosophers have long been successfully influencing the rest of humanity, or transforming their moral concepts,[33] though it has sometimes taken centuries for a given influence to be widely felt. In a sense there is a long and respectable tradition of philosophers telling other people what to do, and this tradition does not seem to deserve less respect than the religious traditions that Baier contrasts with the practice of moral theorising. Nor, coming to thesis (2), must the doubt-sowing techniques that Baier rightly associates with the teaching of moral philosophy in the English-speaking world be regarded as more typical of philosophy than straightforwardly moralistic engagement with issues of great moment. Kant's lectures on ethics are not in the least exercises in inducing a kind of intellectual vertigo: they take up a range of practical questions and use a single theory to arrive at definite conclusions. Mill's arguments about the subjection of women and capital punishment are no less engaged. And in the twentieth century there has been a very great body of morally committed, unsceptical and unrelativistic philosophical argument to definite moral conclusions.

As for the fact that a theory can offer arguments on both sides in a controversy, that does not by itself show that the theory applies unsatisfactorily. On the contrary, it may show that the theory is morally sensitive. Moral sensitivity is precisely a matter of seeing what is morally relevant to a moral question. And relevant considerations can support each side of, for example, the abortion debate. On the other hand, it does not follow from the fact that there are considerations on both sides that they are equally strong, or that the arguments they generate are equally weighty. The arguments may be of quite unequal weight, and yet the supporters of the weaker arguments happen to be stubborn or persistent or politically powerful. If a controversy turns out to be interminable for reasons like this, then that is no embarrassment to the theory that generates arguments on both sides.

Do things stand differently where the arguments generated by a theory pro and con are more evenly balanced? Not necessarily. If the theory generates arguments both ways because it gives reasonable weight to considerations on both sides, and the considerations seem relevant and genuine, how is this to the discredit of the theory? By hypothesis, the theory would leave something relevant and genuine out if it did not take account of all the things it takes account of. It is true that the purpose of a moral theory is to guide practice in some sense, and that when its arguments for and against are evenly balanced there is no clear indication what to do. But this does not mean that according to the theory the agent can and should do nothing, but that that there are good reasons (from the angle of the theory) for doing either of two conflicting things. Expecting a moral theory always to narrow down the advisable course of action in a conflict to one may be like expecting the rules of chess to say which of exactly two legal ways of moving out of check is the right one. The rules of chess require one to move out of check, but there is no getting the *rules* to require just one of the moves. A *strategy* might exclude one of the two moves. But a strategy is a plan of action consistent with the rules rather than dictated by them. And even strategies can underdetermine the moves required to carry them out. No one would say that when strategies fail to determine moves or when rules fail to tell one which legal move to make they fail to guide practice. They guide but not always determinately.

Overdemandingness and questionable ideals

The third thesis of anti-theory is that moral theories are overdemanding, and in ways that are morally objectionable. They oblige human beings to act on impersonal reasons while suppressing the force of reasons geared to local attachments to people or projects. Thus critics of utilitarianism or Kantianism sometimes say that those theories require one to think twice about certain actions that one's personal relations give one perfectly adequate reasons for doing *without* thinking twice. When utilitarianism makes us consider seriously saving three strangers rather than a single loved one, it is utilitarianism rather than the inclination to save the loved one that has to be thrown out. The practical deliberation of the agent who hesitates to save the loved one contains 'one thought too many', in Williams's famous phrase. In the case of the three strangers versus the loved one it is hard to disagree. But when the number of strangers is increased significantly, say to a million, and an agent is in a position to save the million, say because he leads a government, things are not so clear intuitively. Why? Perhaps because it is hard to divorce the role of leader of government from one in which numbers do count, and personal ties count for less than in private life. Or perhaps there is unclarity because, whatever one's role, numbers count *and* freedom to cultivate and maintain a personal life counts. An impersonal morality can acknowledge that both things generate objective reasons.[34] It is not as if the reasons generated by one's personal ties are necessarily puny or essentially outweighable. If they seem to be undervalued by theory in comparison to pre-theoretical morality, that may be because pre-theoretical morality and moral training highlight the ethics of private life, and also because utilitarianism can be seen as fundamentally an ethics of public life and only derivatively an ethics of private life. Perhaps an ethics of private life derived from an ethics of public life is always going to suffer from the kind of implausibility Williams complains of. But as a Kantian theory of private life works quite differently, perhaps there can't be a single set of misgivings about the improprieties of impersonal morality. Morality needs to tell us how to live, and to give reasons why this rather than another way of life is to be led; but the reasons why need not always count *against* strong personal attachments and projects, any more than in their favour.

There is a moral in this for those who claim that to accept the message of moral theory we have to accept its saints and heroes as people we or our children ought to aspire to be. The fact that such models are daunting and that saints and heroes can be unhappy and unloved does not show that they are not worth imitating; but in any case saints and heroes are not the only ideals presented by standard theories. Moral decency is a moral ideal, even though it requires much less than saintliness, and there is every reason to hold that it is a much more central ideal in moral training, and therefore in a moral theory parasitic on moral training, than the ideal of saintliness or heroism.

Naturalised ethics and its limitations

Coming now to thesis (5), what are we to make of the idea that when moral theory is taken to be the source of moral guidance, morality is made to seem too much the preserve of *philosophy* and not influenced enough by the rest of the sciences, including the human sciences, and literature? Baier is not alone among critics in disliking the apriorism of philosophy, especially in respect of how human agents form and apply moral concepts.[35] There are also the naturalistic critics of moral theory.[36]

According to Flanagan,[37] for example, traditional utilitarianism goes wrong in trying to define the good in a unitary way (p. 22). Other traditional theories, not necessarily naturalistic ones, invest the idea of something's being *really* right or *really* good with a transcendental source or basis for moral claims: a mysterious faculty of pure practical reason, for example, or correspondence with a transcendental Form of the Good. This transcendentalism Flanagan also repudiates (p. 22). He admits that sense can be made of talk of the really good or the really right, but it must be deflationary sense along pragmatist lines: what is really good or really right is what passes the pragmatist test of doing justice to the moral complexities of real life in a real time and place, or what passes the pragmatist test of winning social acceptance from critical fellow agents (pp. 31f.). It is too much to associate the really good or the really right with what would win universal human acceptance, or what would do justice to moral complexities in a view from nowhere. Whatever is discovered to be really good or really right is discovered relative to a time or place and an individual and social experience: a picture of ethical knowledge as local knowledge takes the place for Flanagan of the traditional philosophical picture of ethical knowledge as universally valid.

There are two important problems facing Flanagan's idea that the really right or really good is a matter of what critical social feedback would allow to pass as really right or good. The first, which he and other naturalists acknowledge,[38] is that social feedback, even when it is critical, can amount to mere 'socialisation': it can be mere pressure to conform to a way of life or not to depart from it, rather than reasons for falling in with the way of life or not departing from it. Mere socialisation can sometimes add nothing to moral knowledge; but the appropriate social feedback, especially when it is itself sustained by reliable truth-sensitive mechanisms or techniques, *can* be enlightening. So what distinguishes socialisation from the critical reception of action needed for moral knowledge? According to Flanagan, it is the same thing that distinguishes the acquisition of natural science from slavish obedience to a research tradition: namely, the existence of public learning networks, networks existing in societies that 'are under pressure to refine [their] categories of social and moral perception.'[39] This is a question-begging account, however, since the pressures for 'refinement' in society can be immoral as well as moral, reactionary as well as progressive. The growth of a body of accepted results, experiments and tried and tested theories need not have an exact ethical counterpart, for example in the growth of an accepted body of ethical principles, court decisions, and legislation, since many of these are reversible or open to debunking in ways that the accepted results, experiments and so on are not within a scientific research tradition. It is true that the debunkers may not have it all their own way. They can meet opposition that keeps alive or current what is being debunked or discredited. But the opposition can be overcome, and a new orthodoxy arise that is more similar to what preceded the debunked view than the debunked view itself. Think of how 'liberal' values have come to be repudiated in the USA by conservatives, some of them in the mainstream. Is it clear that when people use the word 'liberal' as if it were an obscenity – calling it the 'L'-word – they represent pressure for the *refinement* of moral perception? Surely this is not obvious. Yet whatever pressure is represented by this rhetoric is certainly pressure for moral change, pressure that is supposed to promote increases in moral knowledge, according to Flanagan's account. In fact, not all pressure appears to work this way. Which leaves us with an analogue of the problem of socialisation, not a solution to it. The analogue may be put by asking which pressures for change in moral thinking and practice count as refining and improving that thought and practice; and which are merely questionably motivated attempts to discredit a sound or defensible way of thinking and acting.

The second problem with Flanagan's approach is that it understates the motivation for the transcendentalist view in moral philosophy. It is not just a taste for the metaphysically exotic or a casualness about multiplying entities that leads a Plato or a Kant to posit a Form of the Good or a pure practical reason. Transcendentalism or non-naturalism can also be morally motivated: it can be motivated by the idea that human beings and human behaviour are not in perfect order just as they are; so that the standard of how they ought to be cannot be drawn from nature or actuality but from some other source, on pain otherwise of acquiescing in what is bad about human beings. One does not have to be a philosopher in the metaphysical tradition to see the point of keeping the ideal and the actual, including the natural, apart. In a way Flanagan agrees, for he endorses an institution of social criticism: and what is this but a faculty for seeing departures from how things ought to be, or fallings short with respect to ideals? On the other hand, he subscribes to a Principle of Minimal Psychological Realism: 'Make sure, when constructing a moral theory or projecting a moral ideal, that the character, decision processing, and behaviour prescribed are possible, or are perceived to be possible, for creatures like us.'[40] Like other appeals to realism in moral philosophy, it needs to be approached with questions about its moral implications in mind. For example, what does Flanagan's principle require of theory in a world in which only the worst of the current human beings survive? Must the theory speak the language of thugs? A refusal to be 'realistic' when doing moral theory for such a world seems perfectly defensible morally. Such a refusal might even be defensible morally where the world was the actual one, and the theory was urging the richest of us to settle for much less so that the rest could have much more. Moralising, I am suggesting, may require a certain amount of unrealism, and moralising may be one of the jobs of theory or one of the ways in which theory is most familiarly applied.

So far the problems with the naturalistic position centre on its apparent failure to capture the normativity of moral theory. Advocates of naturalistic ethics can also be criticised for exaggerating the ignorance or neglect or exclusion of empirical considerations in moral theory. Even Kant, who believes that the *foundations* of moral philosophy need to be divorced from anything empirical, in particular what he calls 'anthropology', does not think that the empirical has no place at all in moral philosophy. On the contrary, he holds that moral philosophy needs to draw on empirical information in its doctrine of how the observance of duty comes to be second nature, and that observing some of the moral duties of public life depends on empirical information about what makes other individuals happy. Not only does Kant's, among the traditional moral theories, have an important place for the empirical; it is not clear that the empirical hypothesis suggested by Flanagan is itself inconsistent with or excluded by traditional theories, the ancient Greek ones possibly excepted. Just how far it gets beyond a pre-scientific view of moral agents is also a question. Flanagan considers what he calls 'moral network theory', according to which

> there is a straightforward analogy between the way a submarine sonar device that needs to learn to distinguish rocks from mines might acquire the competence to do so and the way a human might acquire moral sensitivities and sensibilities. (p. 25)

Using connectionist networks, the mine/rock detector's correct guesses about which things it tracks are in fact mines and which are in fact rocks selects out a small number of perceptible features as reliable indicators of whether a thing detected is mine or rock. Situations in which one ought to tell the truth might similarly be distinguished from situations where it only appears one ought to tell the truth – by a small set of indicators found out over time to be particularly relevant, for example, that the truth will hurt someone in the audience; that the truth will be used to hurt me, and so on. This account does not quite reduce to the truistic 'children learn by a kind of trial and error when and when not to tell the truth'. But it comes close. It is saved from triviality by the implication that there might be some structure in the child's brain analogous to the structure of whatever is the brains of the mine/rock detector. The analogy between visual discrimination and moral discrimination by itself is a commonplace of the aprioristic philosophical literature, and has been since ancient times.

Finally, just what is the relation of scientific psychology to moral theory supposed to be? Flanagan's fellow naturalist, Mark Johnson, argues[41] for the incorporation of the former into the latter, on the grounds that

> our morality is a human morality . . . directed to our human concerns, realisable by human creatures like ourselves, and applicable to the kinds of situations we encounter in our lives. This means that we cannot do good moral theory without knowing a tremendous amount about human motivation, the nature of the self, the nature of human concepts, how our reason works, how we are socially constituted, and a host of other facts about who we are and how the mind operates. Moreover, we cannot know

how best to act unless we know something about the details of mental activity, such as how concepts are formed, what their structure is, what constrains our inferences, what limits there are on how we understand a given situation, how we frame moral problems, and so forth.

The claim that a grasp of scientific psychology is a necessary condition of acting for the best would, if true, be a good ground for supposing that moral theory must contain scientific psychology. But it seems wildly implausible. The fact that our morality is a human morality implies that knowledge of human beings is necessary for moral theory, not that scientific knowledge of human beings is. If the knowledge of human beings is pre-scientific, that does not disable it for moral theory. The incorporation thesis is in any case stronger than a naturalist needs. It is enough to say that scientific moral psychology is *relevant* to moral theory. One does not have to insist on the containment of one by the other. There is a good analogy between history and psychology in this respect. History can certainly be useful to moral theory; but no one would claim that it is a *branch* of moral theory.[42]

Conceptual loss, artificiality and idealisation

One does not have to be a naturalistic philosopher to have doubts about traditional theory. On the contrary, one can have doubts about traditional theory that extend to naturalism. Virginia Held has objected to the scientistic inspiration of the kind of naturalism promoted by the Churchlands, Johnson and Flanagan,[43] but she has objected more generally to a gender bias in traditional moral theory, which she thinks a naturalised moral philosophy simply reinforces. In downgrading moral experience and subjectivity, a theory in keeping with cognitive psychology simply continues the tendency to associate morality with reason rather than emotion and to model moral agents on the sort of person who is independent rather than interdependent. A moral theory that compensates for gender bias is different from either naturalistic or traditional moral theory. It is not neutral or non-committal about the unequal treatment and domination that women have endured historically. And just as important, it finds a place for moral experience in the very words that women use to describe it, not in a preferred scientific vocabulary.[44]

The claim that the concepts of traditional and newfangled moral theory alike are biased against women is important, and I shall return to it more than once in this book. But I shall consider first the more radical claim, implicit in the anti-theorists' thesis (3), that when the medium of moral thought involves a theoretical concept of *any* kind, for example a feminist conception of the person or a Kantian concept, moral thought or imagination suffers a kind of loss or distortion. A line of thought that appears to have this implication has been developed by Cora Diamond,[45] and she locates her misgivings in a tradition going back at least as far as Miss Anscombe's 'Modern moral philosophy' via such writers as MacIntyre, Cavell and Iris Murdoch. For example, Diamond objects to some pointed uses of the term 'human being' in philosophical arguments alleging speciesism, and she objects to the use of a gender-neutral concept of a 'person' in the writings of at least one feminist philosopher.

Diamond's method is to remind us, sometimes with the help of great literature, how much in human life that matters to ethics, that matters in particular to knowing what it is to be human, is not expressed in words. Sometimes, as she points out, a look can convey a great deal. When what matters *is* expressed in words, the words can be drained of some of their valuable content by the contortions of philosophers. The source of this tendency, she thinks, is a certain pernicious philosophy of language, which is encapsulated in the belief that the descriptive content of morally valuable vocabulary can be adequately captured by stating its classificatory content. But this objection seems to me to misunderstand what happens in moral theory. No one who uses 'human being' inter-changeably with 'rational agent' or even 'adult member of the species *Homo sapiens*', or in some other theoretically pointed way, purports to be doing descriptive semantics and recovering all of the connotations, even the morally relevant connotations, of the term. The pointed use can perfectly well be admitted to be idiosyncratic. It has some connection with the term 'person' or 'human being' in ordinary language, but the definition or explication of the term in its pointed use does not capture everything, and should not be expected to. That's why talk of a *pointed* use is in order. It may be true that pointed uses are unrepresentative uses and leave out a lot; but for purposes other than descriptive semantics this may not matter. Diamond's objection is a little like the objection Aristotelian physicists made against explaining some of the earth's behaviour by imagining it had the properties of a geometrical sphere: the earth is not a geometrical sphere: it has ridges and so on; but taking it to be a sphere can have explanatory value. Similarly, focusing only on the aspect of a person that consists of being a locus of responsibility, and leaving out other things about persons, such as that they are historically situated, can advance a sound argument to the conclusion that something is right or wrong.

It might be objected that there are special reasons why the schematising tendency of *moral* theorists is objectionable, even if the schematising tendency of other theorists is unworrying. Moral theory is supposed to affect the practice of ordinary agents, whose concepts are not schematised; perhaps any schematisation prevents moral theory from affecting practice; or perhaps it only gives the illusion of affecting practice; perhaps in order to be influenced, ordinary agents have to reinvest the schematised talk with all the content that the schematisation leaves out. Perhaps. It seems to me just as plausible to say that the schematisation is no more an obstacle to understanding in morals than the schematisation of the earth as a perfect sphere is an obstacle to recognising that physicist's demonstration about the sphere applies to the earth. In any case, it is not as if the schematised talk makes inaccessible the unschematised talk of everyday life or the unschematised talk of great literature. It is not as if readers or writers of moral philosophy books or journals are unable to turn (with relief even) to the fully nuanced writing that Diamond approves of. Unless she is claiming that after doing moral philosophy this literature means less than it does before one has done moral philosophy, the loss of the concepts of the fully nuanced language may only be a local and temporary loss, like the loss we experience when we see the earth as a geometrical circle or sphere, and not as it is in life.

This is not yet a defence of the pointed use by theorists of vocabulary that has a use outside theory. But it *is* a way of questioning whether the departure from the fully nuanced language known outside theory really involves a *loss* of concepts expressed by the nuanced language. Talking about persons as abstract loci of responsibility is a further way of speaking, not one which replaces the old way of speaking. And the two ways of speaking can be taken in at once. Otherwise it would not be possible to criticise theory for its infidelity to experience as ordinarily described, which is Held's objection against traditional moral theory when it ignores the unschematised description of women's experience.[46]

Insisting on the theorist's right to a pointed use of 'person' or 'human being' is not to deny every charge of artificiality or idealisation against theory, and the anti-theorist's thesis (4) made several such charges. Are any of these charges defensible? As said earlier, there are some famous idealisations in moral theory that are increasingly dismissed as misleading – Rawls's veil of ignorance, for example, or Ackerman's fiction of the manna. Can these theoretical devices be rejected for assuming the impossible: a choice of principles of justice influenced by no point of view or particular information at all? This objection is certainly well taken if the devices banish information ignorance of which leads to no choice of principles or no intelligible choice of principles, or to principles that do not treat people equally. But the objection is irrelevant if it is to the effect that no one could credibly ignore the information that it requires be ignored.[47] This is irrelevant because the point of the devices is not to say what is possible or not for human beings involved in a process of choosing principles but to say what is morally irrelevant and biasing if it is allowed to affect the principles chosen. The fact that certain people could not help thinking about certain would-be voters as blacks and as women, and therefore as undesirable voters, does not overturn the claim that race or gender is morally irrelevant to whether one can vote. Nor need a Rawls or an Ackerman say that anyone of us would find it perfectly easy to imagine our way into the folds of the veil of ignorance or into the crew of the space ship deciding on what to do with the manna.

Rawls's and Ackerman's idealisations may alienate some of the audience for a moral theory; and so perhaps their rhetorical utility is limited; but in this respect they are no different from (and therefore no more sinister than) countless other thought-experimental devices that abound in the philosophical literature. These devices are never supposed to be true to life: their construction is dictated by the philosophical principles that they are meant to test. In the philosophical literature on the analysis of knowledge, for example, there are many improbable and entirely artificial counterexamples to a whole series of suggested necessary and sufficient conditions for having factual knowledge. The whole point of these examples is to show that knowledge can be present though a suggested necessary condition fails to be satisfied, or that knowledge can be absent when an alleged sufficient condition is fulfilled. The fact that these examples can involve big coincidences or wild implausibilities does not keep them from being counterexamples. It is the same in the ethics literature.

Summary

I have been trying to argue against anti-theory and in favour of theory. The argument in favour has identified a use for theory where moral training gives out. Moral training imparts understanding that can partly be summarised in the form of precepts of personal morality. What counts as a theory in moral philosophy is something that unifies the precepts, and connects those with other demands it offers to formulate, the demands of role morality, for example. A theory also produces accounts of the authority of the values it uses to organise pre-theoretical morality, and produces arguments from some of the precepts it articulates to different practical conclusions. Although theories have certain common features on my account (all aspire to present the best-entrenched parts of conventional morality as a unity; all can be pressed into service in the justification of decisions that might otherwise be regarded as arbitrary; all offer to stand back from the values they think are fundamental and give an account of why we should be guided by them and how we can be) there is no unified target of anti-theory. Even when some of the theories offered by philosophers are viewed as specimens of 'modern' thought or post-Enlightenment thought, 'theory' is still a term for a plurality of approaches.

I have tried to show that anti-theory arguments often overstate the pretensions of theories to guide practice. Moral training is mainly responsible for guiding practice, and that is largely untheoretical. But training is not necessarily equal to situations in which personal and role morality conflict, or in which individual decisions of conventional morality or its assumptions are subject to sceptical or nihilistic criticism. Here theory takes over from, rather than takes the place of, moral training. In taking over it does not always deliver us from indecision, but it does give us a much more systematic and sometimes deeper appreciation of what competing values make the indecision reasonable. At other times, moral theory wakes us from our dogmatic slumbers. It shows that the values that may help to organise the content of moral training may be at odds with some of the practices that have usually co-existed with moral training, but that may not be consistent with it, such as a high level of consumption or a low level of aid to the worst off.

We have not seen the last of anti-theory. In the next chapter I consider some criticisms from Bernard Williams that, while also rebuttable, lead us to a different doubt about theory, the kind that arises when problems that moral philosophy has tried to solve using utilitarianism, Kantianism and neo-Aristotelianism appear to defeat all of these theories.

2

Theory versus Theories

Williams on Moral Theory

An account that powerfully combines many of the elements of scepticism about moral theory that we have already reviewed is Bernard Williams's.[1] Williams objects to the abstractness, impersonality and generality of moral theory, in particular to the idea that theory – a system of prescriptions and prohibitions tied up by some high-order good or prescription – might be a good medium of moral guidance. Theory tells us that we ought to be engaged in actions that are in keeping with principle. But this form of advice, according to Williams, gives a very blank conception of what human activity at its best can be. Indeed, the blankness is indicative of a certain objectionable turning away from the traditional concerns of moral philosophy. In the hands of Socrates, Plato and Aristotle ethics focused on the question of how to live, or how to live well. The utilitarians and Kantians, the modern moral philosophers, have hijacked the subject, and given it a new set of preoccupations. For one thing, they have entrenched a very narrow conception of ethical experience, one that focuses on moral beliefs to the exclusion of emotion.[2] For another, they have tended to take a very abstract view of what matters morally about and to human beings. The satisfaction of rational preferences, the more the better, matters crucially in utilitarianism and is the basis of utilitarian obligations; the joint and mutual promotion of autonomy matters crucially to Kantians. Obligations based on these values can conflict very sharply with the requirements of living well. Modern moral philosophy can even denigrate the requirements of living well by regarding the felt costs of not meeting them as a kind selfishness or squeamishness: Williams's well-known critique of utilitarianism and Kantianism emphasises this unreasonable exactingness.[3]

Although the exactingness can be questioned, it has a source in an idea we find hard to dispense with: namely, that we have to be able to expose the way we live to reflection and criticism. One form the reflection and criticism can take is that of utilitarian or Kantian theory. But if Williams is right, there is no *need* for reflection to issue in theory, that is, a system of justificatory reasons that is acceptable perfectly impersonally, from the 'point of view of the universe'. After all, Williams says, not all reflection naturally encourages theory:

> There is reflection that asks for understanding of our motives, psychological or social insight into our ethical practices, and while this may call for some kinds of theory, ethical theory is not among them. Nor is it merely that this kind of reflection is explanatory, while that which calls for ethical theory is critical. Much explanatory reflection is itself critical, simply in revealing that certain practices or sentiments are not what they are taken to be. This is one of the most effective kinds of critical reflection.[4]

Williams seems to be gesturing towards the benign sort of reflection he has in mind when he considers racial and sexual discrimination in employment:

> The investigation of what someone who discriminates is really doing is all the more forceful, and still more removed from ethical theory, in the more usual case where the person practising it does not admit that 'he's black' or 'she's a woman' is his reason. Rationalisation takes the form of overt discrimination, and some reason will be proffered that may well be relevant but is believed solely because it suits the purpose. This once more is irrationality, and of a deep form, but it is an irrationality of belief, self-deception, of social deceit, rather than any that lies in resisting the drive of an ethical theory. It is in such areas that the study of irrationality in social practice should lie, and it demands inquiries more detailed and substantive than the schematic considerations of philosophical theory.[5]

If the point of critical reflection is to make sure that one is not living in ways that contribute to self-deception or social deceit, then anthropology or sociology, even psychoanalysis, may be of greater service than moral philosophy, according to Williams.

Still, it is hard not to be left with the impression that the question is being begged. For even if there is plenty of room for theory to illuminate the practices and thoughts that mask racial and sexual discrimination, there is still the question of what makes such discrimination wrong. To this question Williams has a preferred answer: 'It is wrong, because unjust, to treat blacks or women unfavourably in comparison to whites or men, and when the practices are enforced, it is often cruel as well.'[6] Presumably this answer is untheoretical: the concepts of justice and cruelty are available to those who are unacquainted with a Kantian or utilitarian system, and presumably they suffice to say why discrimination is wrong. Nevertheless, might it not take a theory to connect this form of injustice with others, or to connect cruelty in the form of sex discrimination with cruelty in the form of battering or cruelty in the form of bullying and baiting? Williams's answer is 'No', because at the place at which he brings up discriminatory practice he is associating theory with the assumption that if something is wrong, it is irrational. The way in which he thinks the wrongness of discrimination can be traced to irrationality is by thinking of discrimination as a kind of inconsistency, and he denies that discrimination need be a matter of inconsistency or irrationality. But why can't there be a connection between wrongness and irrationality through the concept of injustice? And why anyway must it be through a connection between wrongness of action and irrationality that theory gets a purchase on wrong practices? It is true that if 'theory' has to be neutral between utilitarianism and Kantianism, then the assumptions of theory will assume the highly schematic character that Williams rightly claims may not do full justice to discriminatory practices. But there is no reason why 'theory' needs to be characterised in this way. Kantianism can talk about the wrongness of racial and sexual discrimination very readily, by saying that the characteristics of people that merit their being treated with equal respect are independent of biology; utilitarianism can talk about the disutility to women, blacks and the rest of society of singling them out for worse treatment than other people get. These diagnoses of the wrongness of discrimination are not only less schematic and more informative than the connection between wrongness and irrationality: they are much more characteristic of the types of diagnosis of wrongness given by 'theory'.

Of course, Williams's attack on theory goes beyond claims about the approaches to moral problems that are likely to be most fruitful. He believes that the appeal of 'theory' in ethics is borrowed from the appeal of natural science, and that moral theorists tend to boil down moral experience to just those elements that have close counterparts in the experience explained by natural science. He is critical of Kant for implying that theoretical and practical thought each admit of a high degree of detachment,[7] and he claims repeatedly that practical thought is radically first-personal, unlike factual thought.[8] In general, Williams is inclined to insist on a sharp asymmetry between the factual and scientific on the one hand, and the practical on the other. But at times, and when he is developing what I have already claimed is a problematic line of criticism against moral theory in the form of the belief that everything moral stands to reason and everything immoral is a kind of unreason, he seems prepared to countenance more of an analogy between ethics and science. The analogy becomes available when a certain, primitive foundationalist philosophy of science is given up in favour of a holistic one:

> In theoretical connections, the foundationalist enterprise, of resting the structure of knowledge on some favoured class of statements, has now generally been displaced in favour of a holistic type of model, in which some beliefs can be questioned, justified or adjusted while others are kept constant, but there is no process by which they can all be questioned at once, or all justified in terms of (almost nothing) . . .
>
> When we have given up the linear model, we might still be left with the possibility that for every practice there is some reason; what we shall have lost is the possibility that there should be some one reason for everything. In the case of ethics, however, even the weaker requirement, that there should be some reason or other for each practice, will have to be taken in some very undemanding way if we expect it to be met. We may be able to show how a given practice hangs together with other practices in a way that makes social and psychological sense. But we may not be able to find anything that will meet a demand for justification made by someone standing outside those practices.[9]

The analogy between ethics and science holds only up to a point, according to Williams, because, while every bit of factual thought is supposed to be open to question and justification if other things are held constant, there are some practices that are extremely hard to put into question and impossible to support with considerations more compelling than the practices themselves.

But it is unclear that the analogy *does* break down at this point, because it is plausible to hold that in the justification of factual beliefs we also reach bedrock and limits to detachment. As Wittgenstein observes in the notes published as *On Certainty*, there are some pieces of factual thought that are as much indicative of our world-picture as descriptions of the world, and it is hard to detach ourselves from them and question them if we are to describe the world at all. Once the holistic model is introduced, Williams's insistence elsewhere on a sharp distinction between ethics and science starts to sound a little hollow. In the passage just quoted Williams claims that the holistic model is inconsistent with the moral theorist's belief that every belief or practice, if moral, has to be justified by reason, specifically by one kind of reason. But the attribution of this sort of rationalism to theorists is as suspect as talk of 'theory' that applies equally to Kantianism as to utilitarianism. Many different kinds of reason are recognised by different Kantians and utilitarians, and not every moral claim is assumed by every theorist to stand as much in need of justification as any other. On the contrary, and as Williams himself acknowledges,[10] the relative obviousness of certain beliefs is often registered in the recent literature by labeling them 'intuitions', as in the Rawlsian methodology of seeking to achieve 'reflective equilibrium'. The writer Williams quotes in defence of his contention that theorists expect reasons for everything ethical is not Kant or a Kantian nor again a utilitarian. It is Locke.[11]

Part of what goes wrong with Williams's account is that he tries to explain the hold of theory-in-general in ethics by reference to a belief in reason-in-general in ethics. But the hold of theory consists of the hold of Kantianism, utilitarianism and (latterly, at least) neo-Aristotelianism, and while these theories have some family resemblances, it is hard to represent them as the products of a single philosophical impulse, like the craving for a reason for everything. Things are no better for Williams if only Kantianism and utilitarianism are regarded as out-and-out theories. While versions of both theories assume that the bases for obligations are objective in the sense of being acceptable from a point of view drained of sources of moral blindness and bias, they differ over which obligations we have, and over the sources of moral bias and blindness. It is true that they are both philosophers' systematisations of precepts that are supposed to guide the practices of everyone, or at least everyone who subscribes to the precepts in a pre-systematised state. But is this fact enough of a target for a critique of theory that bypasses the details of Kantianism and utilitarianism in their several versions and in the wide variety of applications to problem cases and problem policies? Reading *Ethics and the Limits of Philosophy*, one gets the impression that for Williams the answer is 'Yes'. It looks as if he thinks that 'theory', whether utilitarian or Kantian, is always too distant from the point of view of those who are supposed to be guided by it to be acceptable.

According to Williams, the tension between theory and audience either arises from theory's relative disregard for widely shared intuitions or its aspirations to objectivity (utilitarianism), or the fact that its 'natural constituency' extends beyond the set of people who share an intellectual and cultural background or a society with the theorist (Rawlsian contractualism). It is not easy for theory to maintain its intended audience while retaining its aspirations to objectivity. The more that theory is on the same wavelength as fellow members of society, the more its authority may only be local and its precepts open to relativistic criticism; on the other hand, if its precepts are designed for the perfectly rational who find them inescapable, that leaves the question of how they are supposed to apply to less than rational creatures like us.

There are problems with Williams's argument, and they are clearest in connection with Rawlsian contractualism. Here his criticism turns crucially on the ambiguous idea of the 'constituency' natural to a particular 'style' of moral theory. 'The natural constituency for contractualism', he says, 'consists of those to whom you could conceivably justify your actions – in the simplest interpretation, other moral agents.'[12] And Rawlsian contractualism collapses because the constituency that makes best sense of the theory is far narrower than the natural constituency of contractualism. The constituency that gives Rawls's contractualism maximum plausibility (though even so, not very great plausibility, according to Williams) is a society of people who are committed to living together, and who generally want to resolve moral disagreements by reference to binding principles, principles that will enable them to preserve some but not all of their pre-theoretical institutions.[13] This understanding of the constituency will do for questions of social justice for one society at a time, Williams says, but for a full-scale ethics, the natural constituency will expand outwards beyond the members of a given society, and far beyond the members of a given society at a given time:

> and when we turn our attention beyond a possible political order, any concrete conception of society dissolves: the theory reaches out to that 'natural constituency,' as I have called it, of everyone who might be subject to an ethical agreement: any moral agent, as the theory might put it.[14]

As soon as the constituency expands outward, the intuitions that could soundly be relied upon for reaching a resolution to one society's disagreements look too local to have much authority, and principles geared to them will lack authority in turn.

Williams's argument works only if 'intuitions' in the relevant sense have to be peculiar to one society. If one society's intuitions have counterparts in another, or if the values of one society can colonise another's, or if international campaigning groups can successfully promote a set of values with no particular national identity in a number of different nations, then the fact that the natural constituency for an ethic is wider than one society does not mean that the authority of principles worked out in one society will evaporate at border crossings. The slogan 'Egalité, liberté, fraternité' proved catchy outside eighteenth-century France, and a current worldwide campaign against capital punishment uses the language of the American constitution in saying it must be prohibited because it is 'cruel and unusual'. As for temporal distance, that is no more unbridgeable, necessarily, than the difference between cultures at a given time. It is not as if the very significant differences between western democracies now and the Athenian polis several centuries before Christ mean that Aristotle's ethics or Plato's ethics have no intuitive appeal to Americans or British people twenty-odd centuries later. Besides, when contractualism is associated with a methodology of wide reflective equilibrium, 'intuitions' alone (that is, widely shared spontaneous reactions to moral claims) are not the only things constraining the choice of principles for resolving disagreements. Background theories and arguments from them will up to a point give support independent of 'intuitions' for choices of principles.[15]

The claim that a Rawlsian contractualism must have an appeal narrower than its natural constituency is questionable, then. So is the more general claim that theory, so long as it is self-consciously theory, with aspirations to universality and objectivity, must be mismatched with an audience of agents with parochial beliefs and irremediably local attachments. Admittedly, the claim of mismatch is more plausible when directed against utilitarianism than when directed at either contractualism or theory in general. For, as Williams points out, utilitarianism does not see itself obliged to defer to intuitions. That many utilitarians have vindicated large portions of common-sense morality is not due to a utilitarian respect for common sense, but to the apparent consistency of many common-sense moral precepts with a scientifically attractive basis for morality in the maximisation of welfare. Identifying that scientific basis was not necessary to make people behave any better: people did not need to believe that not killing contributed to the general good in order not to kill. It was necessary mainly for the purpose of being able to locate morals among the intellectually respectable branches of learning, that is to say, among the sciences. Mill and Sidgwick both were anxious to put morals on a footing of principles, and this meant, in Mill's case, showing how precepts like 'Don't kill' could be reconstructed as 'secondary principles' guiding the application of the 'greatest happiness principle'. In Sidgwick's case, as Williams points out, it meant showing that utilitarianism uncomplicatedly harmonised with the self-evident truth that no one's good mattered more than any one else's – that it was the good, impersonally speaking, that had to be pursued.

Now when Williams comes to shortcomings of utilitarianism that are traceable to its status as a self-conscious theory, he focuses on two things: its condescension towards ordinary agents, and its association, through

Sidgwick's phrase 'from the point of view of the universe' with the deeply philosophical hankering to see everything *sub specie aeternitatis*. The second sort of complaint is important to bearing out Williams's claim that there is some motivation for theory – a belief in reason, say – that underlies the motivations for particular moral theories, and that perhaps even underlies the motivations for theories as different as ethical theories and scientific theories. Rationalism is supposed to account for a number of features of philosophical writing in ethics: its artificiality, the meagreness of its explanatory and descriptive resources, and its relatively weak appeal to agents.

Rationalism is reflected in ethical theory by the search for justification rather than, say, antidotes to false consciousness. 'Reflective criticism,' Williams says,

> should basically go in a direction opposite to that encouraged by ethical theory. Theory looks characteristically for considerations that are very general and have as little distinctive content as possible, because it is trying to systematise and because it wants to represent as many reasons as possible as applications of other reasons. But critical reflection should seek for as much shared understanding as it can find on any issue, and use any ethical material that, in the context of reflective discussion, makes some sense and commands some loyalty. Of course that will take things for granted, but as serious reflection it must know it will do that. The only serious enterprise is living, and we have to live after reflection; moreover (though the distinction of theory and practice makes us forget it), we have to live during it as well. Theory typically uses the assumption that we have too many ethical ideas, some of which may well turn out to be mere prejudices. Our major problem now is actually that we have not too many but too few, and we need to cherish as many as we can.[16]

This line of thought seems to me to be confused in its talk of quantities of ethical material. According to Williams, theory drives us in the direction of fewer reasons for action, representing an apparent variety of reasons as special cases of a few very general reasons, while non-theoretical critical reflection conserves the variety and maximises the number of reasons or ethical considerations. In fact, however, there are many different theories and many different versions of similar theories, invoking a wide variety of ideas. It is true that theory refers decisions to principles, and principles to overarching principles or overarching conceptions of the good. But the intermediate principles are not typically held to be special cases of the ultimate ones. For example, the principle that one should not kill is not supposed to be a special case of the greatest happiness principle, though it may indicate a means of satisfying the greatest happiness principle. On the other hand, the greatest happiness principle may go some way towards capturing the good that the principle of not killing promotes, and that justifies not killing. Similarly with other lower-order principles. The overarching principles systematise a variety of ethical material; but to systematise is not necessarily to reduce the amount of material.

A second problem with Williams's line of thought, and one that helps me to introduce a positive account of my own, is that it underestimates the variety of differences that systematic thought can and does tolerate. In other words, it makes out the domain of theory as one in which there is hostility to the multiplication of ethical ideas. It also makes out theory as concerned only with general morality, and addressed to ordinary agents, who are depicted as passive recipients of it. In fact, theory often focuses only on a section of general morality, and often it develops arguments for only a subclass of agents. Again, theory has an important and non-passive audience among theorists, some of whom, as we have seen, explicitly constrain theory to tailor what it says and how it says it to what agents are like. Many theorists seem to be reconciled to the existence of a plurality of theories. There is no reason, therefore, why theory cannot be a site and a source for many rather than few ethical ideas. On the contrary, there is good reason to think that theory is a natural setting for the multiplication of ethical ideas.

If Williams misses this, the reason may be that he identifies theory with the contents of the canonical books in moral philosophy, rather than seeing it as an activity in which the contents of the canonical books are elaborately controverted by critics and substantially revised even by sympathisers. A passage that is revealing of the significant one-sidedness of his account of theory concerns the

> attempts of theorists to replace the categories that give us reasons with others that are supposed to have better systematic credentials. Thus Michael Tooley, the theorist who wants to get us used to the idea of infanticide, urges the notion of *person* as the operative notion in these kinds of questions: infants fall out of the favoured class at one end, and the senile fall out at the other. This engaging proposal is investing in a deceptive concept. The category of a person, though a lot has been made of it in some moral philosophy, is a poor foundation for ethical thought, in particular because it looks like a classificatory concept while in fact it signals characteristics that almost all come in degrees – responsibility, self-consciousness, capacity for reflection, and so on . . .
>
> The defects of *person* as a theoretical category represent a failing in that particular proposal, but they also illustrate the failings in the theoretical enterprise more generally. How can we come to see the weaknesses of a

theoretical concept except by reference to the everyday distinctions it is supposed to justify, and by a sense of the life it is supposed to lead? So far from having some special authority because of their belonging to a theory, these conceptions . . . are likely to be more arbitrary than those they are supposed to replace.[17]

As if one had to be an anti-theorist to think arbitrariness and artificiality were two of the problems with Tooley's arguments about infanticide.[18]

Williams is right to say that the concepts and distinctions introduced by theory have no special authority; but this is something theorists can agree with him about. Williams is also right to say that theoretical concepts and arguments employing them have to have a sense of the life they are supposed to have a bearing on. But this, too, can be conceded by theorists. It is only when the theorist is saddled with the wholly unreal assumption that the concepts and the arguments have to be the products of reason alone or reason itself[19] that these observations are tantamount to scepticism about theory. One reason why theory can be expected to be a site for the multiplication of ideas and for proposals of ideas less blank than Tooley's is that theorists can take seriously the reservations Williams has and try to make their solution a condition of adequacy on a successor theory that is still normative, still general, and that still implies that infanticide may be permissible. To put it another way, theorists can recognise the existence of puzzles and anomalies in moral theory, that is, problems which do not yield readily to solution by reference to the principles or concepts of established moral theories, but which may be open to solution by some theoretical approach or other. Puzzles and anomalies change ideas within theories and encourage people to develop new theories. They do not need to generate second thoughts, as Tooley's concept of the *person* generates second thoughts in Williams, about theory itself.[20]

A Rough Parallel: Normal Science and Standard Normative Ethical Theory

The idea of anomaly is familiar from the work of Thomas Kuhn,[21] where it is used to identify the sort of problem in science whose stubbornness can lead to the overthrow of one theory by another. In transferring talk of anomaly to the sphere of moral theory I do not want to imply that there is much of a parallel between say, utilitarianism and the germ theory of disease, or Rawls's theory of justice and the theory of continental drift. I do, however, want to maintain that there is a counterpart of what Kuhn calls 'normal science' in organised reflection about how to live and how to act.

'Normal science' is Kuhn's term for the doctrine and activity that occupies scientists in the (usually long) periods between revolutionary episodes – times when anomalies become recognisable and a scientific revolution or 'paradigm-shift' results. Normal science is typically a matter of refining and incrementally increasing the application of a received theory. It is the stuff textbooks keep track of, and the subject-matter of most of the articles in most latter-day scientific journals. It is not necessarily uncreative, but received theory sets the terms in which it is conducted and the problems it works on. Some of these problems are what Kuhn calls 'puzzles': there is a known result or observation and an established theory that ought to encompass the result; the puzzle consists of getting the theory and the result satisfyingly connected. Such activity is not a world apart from the activity of solving textbook problems, where the problems are devised specially to get novices to see just what the applications of the theory are. In that case the theory is given; a method of generating a standard type of result from the theory is also given; and the student's job is to apply the method so as to get the right instance of the standard result, i.e. one that matches the answer at the back of the textbook. In the case of puzzles, one is given the theory and the result, and the task is to show how the latter comes from the former. This means either coming up with an analogue of a textbook method of application, or elaborating the content of the theory for a special subject-matter.

Normal science proceeds apace so long as puzzle-solving does. But some puzzles can refuse to be solved; and such recalcitrance is an early warning of anomaly. Puzzles begin by being treated as invitations to apply a theory, and, after repeated failures, they raise the question of whether the theory is applicable at all. For example, puzzles in medieval astronomy led gradually to the ousting of Aristotelianism in celestial physics. Sunspots and supernovae had either to be explained as meteorological illusions in order to preserve the Aristotelian theory; or else the Aristotelian idea that objects in the spheres of the heavens were unchanging had to be given up. In the end the Aristotelian idea *was* given up, and sunspots and supernovae, which began by being puzzle phenomena, turned out to be anomalous.[22]

The counterpart of a piece of normal science is a standard moral theory. A standard moral theory brings together standard or conventional prohibitions and prescriptions, perhaps qualified or refined in certain ways, under either a single general principle or a small number of unifying principles. The principles can be taken to indicate or express a practical ideal: something that human action ought to aim at or at least not conflict with. Thus a moral theory can bring versions of the prohibitions on lying, killing, breaking promises, and so on, under a greatest happiness principle, or a principle of respect for persons, or perhaps under a greatest happiness principle constrained by some other principle,[23] or under a mutually reinforcing set of Kantian principles. Even an Aristotelian theory can be organised under the principle that one ought to promote human flourishing, or perhaps under a principle that one should benefit others within limits set by a sense of self-worth, that is, without going to the extremes of self-effacement or self-sacrifice.[24] When a standard theory is successful, its unifying principle or set of principles is also able to ground judgements about the rightness or wrongness of actions that are not standardly prescribed or prohibited. Thus the principle of respect for persons might be used to justify a prohibition on invasions of privacy by newspapers, or the greatest happiness principle might be used to justify the prohibition in some legal systems on profiting by insider knowledge as trader or investor. The ideal of human flourishing might provide arguments against ways of life that would exclude the development of a family or friendships, or that would subordinate those things to undertakings, such as getting as rich as possible, that are not essential to prospering as a human being. The ideal of benevolence compatible with self-worth might be sensitive to the possibilities of servility and masochism in certain types of otherwise admirable devotion, and they might provide arguments against those types of devotion, based on the possibilities.

Except when described at a very high level of generality, moral theories differ from scientific theories much more than they resemble them. It is true that the overarching principles of scientific and moral theories alike are general, but the type of generality is different in the two cases, and the reasoning leading to the two types of general principle is answerable to different constraints. The contrast is clearest where the principles belong to physics on the one hand and an ethical theory on the other. In the case of physics, inference aims at the identification of a pattern or regularity that is causally explanatory of an observed effect. The general principle is usually mathematical, and the relationships it postulates, for example between energy and mass, or force and acceleration, are supposed to obtain independently of the physiological and psychological peculiarities of human observers. Accordingly, there can be a big discrepancy between the concepts used by the explanatory principle and the concepts that, for instance, register observations of a cannon ball falling from a tower: the explanation is not required to be intelligible to most or all of the people who can make the observations or understand them when reported. In ethics, reasoning also aims to arrive at a general truth, but the truth concerns what ought to be done, the generality is not mathematical, the reasoning does not arrive at a causal explanation, and it does not correct for the peculiarities of human perception. Instead it corrects for the undue weight human agents give to the self, the present, the pleasurable and other things in their practical deliberations. Typically, ethical reasoning aims at establishing whether something an agent is thinking of doing for some private end is consistent with other ends that are authoritative for *any* agent, ends that everybody has reason to promote and that moral principles state. Reasoning seeks to determine the consistency of a course of action with a principle whose application in the case is not in question, or else it investigates whether a principle that appears to apply really does. This is not reasoning to the best explanation, except in as much as principles that would tell in favour or against doing things also explain why in particular cases we *think* actions of those types are right or wrong. Instead, it is reasoning to a possible authorisation of action or intention. And the *content* of practical reasoning and practical principles is of a piece with this. The principles are normative, and they make use of concepts that if not entirely pre-theoretical (e.g. the concept of welfare) are at least closely connected with widely grasped concepts, such as the concepts of pain and pleasure. The principles could not guide action if they went over the heads of most agents. In both of these respects – being non-esoteric and normative – moral principles and theories are unlike scientific principles and theories.

What about puzzles? These can arise when a standard moral theory fails to deliver a clear verdict of rightness or wrongness on an action, and yet, pre-theoretically, the action is not morally neutral. They can also arise when a theory does deliver a verdict, but does so while ignoring, perhaps having to ignore, something that seems to constitute the problem as a moral problem. When puzzles resist solution after repeated attempts to solve them by theorists, they qualify as prima-facie *anomalies*. Now the existence of prima-facie anomalies is a reason for feeling let down by particular moral theories, but not, I want to insist, a reason for writing off moral theory. Examples of recalcitrant puzzles can be readily found in the applied ethics literature, and I shall discuss two in a moment. My claim is that puzzles and anomalies can and have led to the introduction of new material into moral theory, and problems that some philosophers would respond to by abandoning theory altogether may be met instead by revising standard theories, by inventing non-standard theories, and by rehabilitating theories which have been pushed out of the mainstream, but which were once standard theories.

Once again, the parallel between the response to a recalcitrant puzzle in science and the response to a recalcitrant puzzle in morals should not be exaggerated. I am not convinced that the response to a recalcitrant puzzle in morals is likely to be outright theory replacement: I believe that, as in philosophy generally, lots of incompatible theories are likely to co-exist in moral philosophy, the new ones, whose formulation has been stimulated by a recalcitrant puzzle, taking their place alongside the very long-lived. I believe also that theories embarrassed by a recalcitrant puzzle now are capable of rehabilitation later, as in other areas of philosophy. So I do not believe there is a strict analogy between a recalcitrant puzzle in the case of a piece of normal science and a recalcitrant puzzle in the case of a standard moral theory. A further difference is that a recalcitrant puzzle or prima-facie anomaly is as likely to come from the collision of philosophical theory with extra-philosophical theory and practice, including pre-philosophical theory and practice, as it is likely to come from a failure to solve problems it sets for itself. Apparent anomaly can come from the failure of moral theory to engage with ways of life that are unusual but that seem to have moral content, such as the ways of life of some religious or ecological groups or experiments in marriage and child-rearing that consciously reject conventional ways of life. It can also come from the clash of philosophical theory with very prevalent opinion, the clash of philosophical theory with the line of a political party or broadly based interest group, or with the inability of a theory to encompass the enormity of current events, or to keep up with sea changes in popular opinion or popular culture. By contrast, there do not seem to be many pre-scientifically inspired anomalies in current natural science. These differences apart, it remains that recalcitrant puzzles in moral theory can provoke precisely the variety of ideas familiar from natural science, i.e. the variety of ethical ideas that Williams claims theory discourages.

Puzzles in Moral Theory

If we confined attention to puzzles for standard moral theory constructed in the academic textbooks and journals of Anglo-American moral philosophy and social theory, the analogy with puzzles in normal science would perhaps be quite exact. But, as already implied, moral theory is both more messy and more exposed than this analogy would suggest. First, there is no one standard moral theory or general framework that would command as wide a following as a piece of normal science might in its sphere. Instead, there is a variety of standard theories, each with significant followings. Second, these theories do not have a presence in academic literature alone. Many have migrated over centuries into popular thought. Or at least parts of them have. Thus it is not just the phrase, 'the greatest happiness for the greatest number' that has a familiar ring to people who have never heard of Bentham or Mill. Some of the thinking behind the phrase has also become second nature. Large sections of the public, especially in the English-speaking world, are used to asking how many people benefit before they decide which of two policies is the better. And just as a certain moral theory can be in circulation, so can consciousness of puzzles. People who are used to forming moral preferences among policies by reference to hunches about the general welfare often recognise that decisions between policies on these grounds can be delicately balanced. This can get people to think about such puzzles as how the values of safety and architectural conservation are to be weighed; or how far the value of religious freedom should be reflected in an educational curriculum that can conflict with some religious teaching.

Although the range of puzzles for moral theory is wide, I shall often be considering puzzles of exactly the kind that do withstand comparison to the puzzles of scientific theory, namely those drawn from the academic literature concerned with theory and its application. This literature is often highly explicit about the questions that a satisfactory theory has to answer, and highly explicit about the ways in which existing theories fall short. The literature is also sophisticated about weighing the relative merits of various would-be acceptable theories. In this chapter I take up two recalcitrant puzzles that come from the academic literature, and I proceed to distinguish them and their ilk from what are supposed to be anomalies for moral theories. In the cases I consider, one knows what one would like from a satisfactory theory and the conditions of adequacy seem satisfiable in principle, but known attempts to meet these constraints fail to do so or exhibit such strain in doing so, that one seeks something better. On the other hand, the apparent anomalies I shall concentrate on are all cases where, allegedly, there is some difficulty in principle about trying to apply moral theory to a sector of human activity or in trying to extend it so that it can be applicable to something outside human activity.

A puzzle about hunger and poverty: O'Neill

My first example of a recalcitrant puzzle in moral theory comes from the branch of normative ethics dealing with poverty, hunger and development, and the obligations of those in the richer parts of the world to do something for the vast numbers in the world who have very little and often less than they need to survive. The shortcomings of standard moral theories in this area have been surveyed recently in Onora O'Neill's book, *Faces of Hunger*.[25] O'Neill suggests that both utilitarianism and rights theory fail to satisfy the very exacting conditions that any adequate normative ethics of poverty and development must satisfy, but she thinks that a Kantian theory can do better, specifically a Kantian theory of justice and beneficence. Let me briefly outline what I take to be her argument.

Utilitarianism is at first sight well suited to the gravity of problems of poverty and development, for the great distress of great numbers of people is taken seriously by the theory, and the sympathetic and cultural distance of the ones in distress from those in a position to relieve the distress is not regarded as a moral but only a psychological obstacle to action. On the other hand, utilitarianism is at the mercy of disagreements about the consequences of different actions to relieve poverty. Even if there were a social science that could tell us authoritatively what the consequences of different actions would be, utilitarianism would still be faced with disagreements about which consequences were beneficial in the sense of being subjectively preferred. The donors' subjective preferences might not coincide with those of recipients. And yet there is no provision in utilitarianism for a non-subjective theory of value, according to O'Neill. Actually, this claim of O'Neill's may have been overtaken by refinements in utilitarian theory, since recent work suggests that a non-subjective theory of value may indeed be possible.[26] On the other hand, the liberal politics that utilitarians sometimes embrace might forbid the adoption of a theory that overruled subjective preferences. Further tensions in utilitarianism arise from the demand that moral theory be able to achieve a critical distance from the established theory and practice of development and aid, while using concepts that can be understood by, and guide the action of, institutions and agencies.

The difficulties for utilitarianism, then, are significant; and rights theories face problems in their turn. Rights theories use an appealing and widely accessible rhetoric in addressing problems of poverty and development, but they do not necessarily leave any individual or institution responsible for alleviating poverty, and rights theories geared to liberty rights may even deny that the poor have rights to improved welfare at all. Even rights theories that collapse the distinction between liberty rights and welfare rights and that appeal instead to basic rights do not take us far, for these theories may leave unspecified what action is to be taken in the service of basic rights, and which agents are to undertake it.

It is against this background that O'Neill urges the benefits of a Kantian theory, in the first place a theory of justice, and, secondarily, a theory of beneficence. Kant's theory of justice specifies duties binding on individuals as well as agencies and institutions, to prevent coercion and deception. Those with least are particularly vulnerable to coercion and deception. So a Kantian theory of justice implies that there are special reasons for taking practical measures to alleviate the vulnerability of the poor. If this involves undoing established economic and legal arrangements between nations, or altering aid-giving institutions or policies, then there are arguments from justice for taking these steps, not just arguments from beneficence. To be sure, judgement may be needed in interpreting both how the duties of non-deception and non-coercion are to be met in the real world, and in interpreting which arrangements that disadvantage the developing world are subject to change in the name of preventing coercion or deception, but at least the Kantian theory applies to development issues, and is capable of being anti-establishment. At least it makes its practical recommendations accessible, and grounds them in duties that are genuinely binding. At least it directs its prescriptions to identifiable agents. Not only that, but it recognises grounds for individuals to act from beneficence, especially during the time that the demands of justice are being imperfectly met.

I am attracted to Kantian theories in ethics, and so I am in sympathy with O'Neill's general approach to the ethics of poverty and development; but I do not think that a theory of justice geared to preventing deception or coercion captures one's sense of what is wrong with poverty and hunger and why it needs to be combated. What is wrong with poverty and hunger must be more closely connected with the badness of pain and incapacitation than with the harm of being deceived or coerced, and the source of the wrong ought to be addressed by principles of justice. Now a Kantian theory can make it an injustice not to try and prevent extreme pain and incapacitation where possible. But I doubt that the Kantian theory O'Neill outlines in *The Faces of Hunger*, which is close to Kant's own version, does make this an injustice. Worse, there are problems with its strict duties of non-deception and non-coercion outside development ethics. Perhaps some cases of deception are morally permissible, either because they are arguably cases of beneficence, or because they prevent much worse things than deception. As for the principle of non-coercion, perhaps it is inconsistent with any form of penal system, or any form of state. This much is already material for an *ad hominem* against Kant. Returning to development ethics, arguments from justice are likely to be in conflict with certain doctrines about the economic realities of capitalism that have a special authority in the aftermath of the collapse of Communism in Europe. The doctrines may be refutable, but perhaps only by reference to considerations that would be too far from the categories of aid agencies to affect their practice, or too far from the categories of capitalism to weigh with those in charge of development funding. If this objection is sound, then Kantianism is open to a version of the problem that, according to O'Neill, utilitarianism faces. It, too, must be formulated in ways that are either faithful to its message and unintelligible or unimpressive to its audience; or persuasive to this audience but not necessarily Kantian. Further problems may arise for a Kantian theory that is close to Kant's own theory when it comes to giving due value to the traditional cultures of the developing world. Perhaps Kant himself was too much under the sway of Enlightenment values to suppose that a culture with no semblance of European fine art and science, and with no aspiration to any, say the culture of a rain-forest tribe, was worth preserving.

The upshot is not that a Kantian theory has no future, or that principles about coercion and deception do not carry any weight.[27] It is that, when judged in relation to the problem of grounding obligations to the poor, O'Neill's version of Kantian theory runs into difficulty. Might the theory be amended to overcome the difficulty? There are reasons to think the work of amendment would not be straightforward. The principles about deception and coercion that I have been claiming do not engage the badness of poverty directly enough co-exist in O'Neill's work with complicated views about what is required in a moral theory. Principles about deception and coercion recommend themselves to O'Neill because they root particular kinds of obligation in conditions of agency itself, and she believes that a satisfactory moral theory, especially one that runs along Kantian lines, has to concentrate on obligations rather than rights, and has to hold on to universalisability as a test of policies rather than acceptability under a Rawlsian veil of ignorance.[28] Coercion and deception undermine agency itself, and so there is a sense in which no agent could will the universalisation of policies involving deception and coercion.

In her latest work, O'Neill has argued for the universalisability of an institutional policy of rejecting injury,[29] and has put forward an interpretation of injury that extends to indirect injury. This principle promises to mesh much more satisfyingly with the pain and incapacitation involved in extreme poverty and hunger than principles about non-deception and non-coercion, and it may well count by itself as a partial solution to the problems with O'Neill's approach in *The Faces of Hunger* that I have been reviewing up to now. But the rejection-of-injury principle, too, has its problems, as O'Neill acknowledges. The rejection by agents of injury seems compulsory where injury would amount to total disablement; for there is a kind of incoherence in agents willing the conditions for the loss of agency. Not all injury is this severe, however; and so it isn't clear that rejecting a policy of injury on a very small scale would be compulsory. Again, O'Neill distinguishes between a policy of rejecting injury, and a no-injury policy.[30] The latter favours pacifism and non-retaliation even for acts of injustice; while the former does not. Thus the rejection-of-injury principle would presumably permit retaliation against the aggressors in a just war. Even if we agree that such retaliation is not itself injury, it is hard to deny that a just war can involve unavoidable injury. O'Neill indeed recognises the category of unavoidable injury.[31] But this category is precisely the one that might be invoked by those who think that poverty and hunger are unavoidable if economic development is to take place reasonably quickly, and that even just institutions designed to hasten economic development and more generalised prosperity cannot but permit both. Isn't there, then, too much scope in O'Neill's theory for someone in charge of unjust institutions to plead that some of the injuries they foresee coming from their policies are unavoidable? It would be over-hasty to conclude as much. O'Neill's theory is far from lacking resources to challenge unjust appropriations of the idea of the unavoidable injury, since the theory implies that evidence of gratuitous or systematic injury is evidence of the absence of a policy of rejecting injury. Again, the theory is able to exploit properties of the rejection of injury as an *underlying* institutional policy. To be an underlying policy it must unify a lot of institutional actions, not just be an idle, added extra.

Even if the apparatus introduced in *Towards Justice and Virtue* does not equip Kantianism to deal with central obligations in development ethics, O'Neill is evidently moving towards that goal, and the impression of progress already keeps our puzzle about development ethics from amounting to anomaly. Nor is O'Neill's the only Kantian theory in the field. The broad outlines of another theory are discernible in Nagel's *Equality and Impartiality*.[32] And there are other writers with work in the same area.[33]

A puzzle about the basis of the right to health care: Daniels

The question of how to apply a theory of justice to health care is another example of what I am calling a puzzle. Norman Daniels has tried to solve this puzzle. In his book, *Just Health Care,* he notes that debates about health insurance use concepts, such as the concept of a right to health care, that a theory of justice can be expected to make precise; yet it is no straightforward matter to get the theory to engage the peculiarities of the good of health and its uneasy relation to wants and needs. Daniels tries to get Rawls's theory of justice to engage the peculiarities, but the manner of the engagement, I am going to suggest, is unsatisfactory.

There *ought* to be a way of getting a theory of justice to engage with the distribution of health care. Daniels's way is to work with the familiar conviction that health care is a special sort of good.[34] For example, it is widely believed that access to health care should not depend on ability to pay, even when it is agreed that health care has to be paid for, and that health care is expensive. What helps to make sense of this set of attitudes is the belief that people *need* health care. According to Daniels, this means more than that health care is important to people: it means that having or not having health care can make the difference between being able and not being able to do things a member of the species normally does. Maintaining the species ability range is important because it maximises opportunities, which in turn are crucial to carrying out life-plans, which in turn help to define the good for each person:

> Life plans for which we are otherwise suited and which we have a reasonable expectation of finding satisfying or happiness-producing are rendered unreasonable by impairments of normal functioning. Consequently, if persons have a fundamental interest in preserving the opportunity to revise their conception of the good through time, then they will have a pressing interest in maintaining normal species functioning . . . by establishing institutions, such as health care systems, which do just that. So the kinds of needs picked out by reference to normal species functioning are objectively important because they meet this fundamental interest people have in maintaining a normal range of opportunities.[35]

Daniels goes on to refine this proposal in various ways, and I shall come to the details in a moment. But there is reason to think that the account has already got off to an unsatisfactory start. For in the passage quoted the good of health care is tied to the importance of keeping one's options in life open, and to the extent that health care is a need, it may have more to do with keeping one alive and free of pain than changing course in life. The ability to change course in life is of course promoted by health but why should that be the purpose of health or the thing that makes health care necessary? It is not as if in the absence of a life-plan, still less in the absence of the ability to revise one, health would be pointless or health care unnecessary. On the contrary, some illnesses might be serious, treatable and yet keep people from forming or pursuing life-plans. And health care could be needed at times in life when a person was not yet able to form a life-plan, or at a time at which most or all of the plan had been carried out and yet the person was still alive. Someone who has done everything they want to and who has no real life-plan any more can still have health care needs, including needs we recognise as urgent ones.

Daniels is not unaware of these points, or of the conflict between them and his own account. But he tends to associate with utilitarianism any attempt to locate what is special about health care in the relief of suffering,[36] and in working with Rawls's theory he has turned his back on utilitarianism. He also thinks that utilitarianism is unstable in its treatment of what makes health care special, since it could turn out that the relief of pain actually mattered less to the satisfaction of the whole range of preferences than other things. If it came to matter less, then the special status of health care would not only not be explained but would be denied.[37] Daniels takes the view (reasonably enough) that whatever makes health care special does so independent of shifting or temporary preferences and shifting or temporary requirements of happiness. Hence the attractions for him of normal species functioning: this does enjoy the sort of independence he is looking for.

There are other attractions of the normal species functioning account, this time inspired by theory rather than intuition. Because there is a straightforward connection between this sort of functioning and opportunity, and because equality of opportunity is a recognised good in a theory of justice and a good with a certain kind of priority in Rawls's theory of justice, there is a chance, using Rawls's theory, of reflecting the intuitive *need* for health care in its helping to secure a good with a certain *primacy* among all the other primary goods, namely equality of opportunity. Equality of opportunity has 'lexical priority' in that nothing can justify departures from it, not even material rewards for the worst off. (Such rewards *can* justify inequalities in wealth, status, and so on.) Again, the fact that one's entitlement to health care is relativised to what Daniels calls a 'normal opportunity range' keeps the account from falling prey to a 'hijacking' problem: health resources cannot be mobilised on a gargantuan scale to bring people with very low levels of natural skills and talents up to the same level of opportunity as those with very great skills and talents; the relevant level is the one that would have been reached on the strength of pre-existing skills if disease or illness had not intervened.[38] On the other hand, Daniels's theory is able to discern injustice in the loss of opportunities even when there are very few opportunities to begin with, so that the loss of some makes a bad situation only a little worse. Like its parent theory in Rawls, Daniels's theory implies that people should be protected from ill effects of disadvantages that are beyond their control just as they shouldn't be rewarded for the benefits of a natural advantage. Finally, Daniels's theory implies that health, like education, is a good that helps to secure equal opportunity, rather than a good that equal opportunity helps to secure, like wealth and status. This way of thinking gives preventive health institutions particular importance: they are means of assuring that each person is fully functioning and has a normal life-span in which to pursue and revise his or her life-plans.[39] Reactive health institutions, such as hospitals offering acute care and emergency clinics, are in a certain sense secondary: they correct for unavoidable departures from full functioning.

The way in which Daniels's theory distinguishes between preventive and reactive health care is a key to how far it has departed from any *intuition* about health care being special because necessary. Surely reactive health care, particularly the sort one gets from acute hospitals, is much closer to the intuitive idea of special because a more necessary health care than counseling about diet and smoking, useful as those forms of preventive health care are. The reason that acute treatment is so effective at showing medical care under the aspect of need, is that lives and not just life-plans can depend on it. The treatment of acute pain, even when not life-threatening, also has a very strong claim to be necessary. The reason is that it blights life at its most immediate – life at the level of moment-to-moment experience – not because it disrupts or requires the elimination of certain life-plans. The life-plan perspective is more important to goods like a long-term career than to health care that cries out its necessity. This is not to say that no forms of health care are bound up with life-plans; the claim is rather that there is no particular connection between life-plans and forms of health care that are most likely to appear necessary. Nor does one have to be a utilitarian to connect the necessity of health care with the strength of reasons for action provided by the badness of pain.[40]

Although it is hard to provide a knock-down argument in this area, my hunch is that Daniels has worked out his conception of just health care from deep within the machinery of a certain theory of distributive justice, rather than, as he purports to do, from some starting point in the 'widely held judgements that there is something especially important about health care and that some kinds of health care are more important than others'.[41] This may not be the most important objection against Daniels: the suspicion that because the theory emphasises life-plans it discriminates against those with little life left may be more telling morally. So might the objection that, in Daniels's theory, those who lose great natural gifts seem to lose more of a fair share of the normal opportunity range, and presumably have more of a claim to restorative health care, than those who lose some of the very few skills and talents they start with: in general, there is a suspicion that natural advantage inflates the unfairness of a loss in Daniels's theory. But the objection that the phenomenon – health care or the necessity of health care – has been tailored to the theory rather than the other way round is the more indicative of failed puzzle-solving. It recalls the trouble with O'Neill.

Nothing that has been said so far suggests that the puzzle of bringing health care within the scope of a theory of distributive justice is insoluble. And I have not been arguing that the claimed starting point of Daniels's theory is the wrong starting point, or that a theory that both bears out and explains our convictions about the importance of health care in general and the relative importance of different forms of health care is an inappropriate form of theory. Even the difficult question of how inclusive the concept of health care is should not be unanswerable, if the relevant concept of health care is supposed to bear out the judgement that health care is a need. So we do not have here the makings of the claim that the question of the just distribution of health care constitutes an anomaly. As with O'Neill all we have is a case where a reasonable question fails to be answered by a working moral theory that can reasonably be expected to answer it.

Puzzles versus Anomalies

The failure to find solutions to our puzzles seems to go back to an insensitivity of certain theories to the intuitive source of an obligation: in one case, the badness of pain and incapacitation; in the other, the badness of pain and loss of life. In neither case does the insensitivity seem irremediable: the discussion of O'Neill showed that reformulating principles relevant to justice can itself constitute an important advance towards a solution. Even if O'Neill's neo-Kantianism were entirely defeated by the problem of how to ground obligations to relieve global poverty; even if Rawls's theory of justice could not begin to generate principles for the just distribution of health care, we would still be far from showing that moral theory in general was defeated by these problems. As has already been implied, utilitarianism applies to the ethics of relieving poverty and distributing health care, though it is not without problems of its own. And perhaps there are other theories – theories of the social virtues – that would get a purchase in the areas we have been considering.

It is different with would-be anomalies. In their case the standard theories are supposed to be silenced by the questions addressed to them, or thrown into disarray by the task of assessing practices whose rightness or wrongness is controversial. Thus, the claim that there can be no utilitarian or Kantian or Aristotelian theory of our obligations to mountains can be treated as the claim that questions about the commercial uses of mountains are anomalous. Or it might be said that the legitimate norms of a certain activity – conducting a large-scale war, say – elude both the concepts of justice and utility. A claim of anomaly is distinct from an endorsement of anti-theory. It does not have to be the claim that for answering most moral questions, the use of theory misleads us about what is at stake. It does not have to be the claim that no normative moral theory at all can deal with a particularly troublesome question, still less the claim that no metaethical theory can deal with it. At most, claims of anomaly are implicit rejections of one or more normative theories, and *standard* normative theories at that – Kantianism and utilitarianism typically. The claim of anomaly can even be accompanied by the *proposal* of a normative theory, so long as it is not a standard theory of this kind.

Now one way of expressing one's support for the enterprise of moral theorising is by saying that anomalies – if they exist at all – are rare, and this is the conclusion towards which I will be heading. In order to reach it, however, I propose to investigate different lines of criticism of traditional theories that might be thought to identify anomalies. Two lines of criticism in particular will be prominent in subsequent chapters.

(1)   The first accuses the traditional theories of being unworldly. It takes certain sharp practices in business and politics and says that they are excusable or legitimate, because business and politics have to be judged by their own moral standards. Traditional moral theories, the criticism runs, attempt to extend the scruples of ordinary morality to business and politics, but should not. The reason a distinctive morality governs some activities and not others is they are subject to extraordinary pressures or extraordinary constraints. For example, in some activities the participants routinely stand to one another as enemies or at least adversaries who are willing to confront one another aggressively and

even violently. Ordinary morality treats these pressures and constraints as exceptional; and so does a utilitarianism or Kantianism geared to ordinary morality. So they are less understanding of sharp practices in response to these pressures than perhaps they should be.

(2) The main types of normative moral theory discount certain differences between agents as morally irrelevant. Theories are supposed to be blind to gender, race, nationality, religious conviction, or to one's age once one has reached adulthood. But according to the critics, theories that disregard these differences leave out both too little and too much. On the one hand, theory leaves out too little. It has cultivated a *selective* blindness to difference, disregarding differences between human beings – and only the adult and rational ones at that – while taking account of differences between human beings and members of other species and inanimate elements of the wider natural world. As a result, the non-humans have not always been considered to have rights or interests that humans are obliged to defend. On the other hand, the critics go on to say, difference-blindness *within* the class of human beings may stand in the way of appropriate treatment of groups that, historically, have suffered because of their race, gender, religion and so on. In order to undo the accumulated disadvantage to these groups, the features that make them different may need to weigh in the distribution of compensating benefit.

It is important that the highly general arguments that are used to establish would-be anomalies are not arguments in the abstract, like Williams's argument. They are arguments inspired by practical matters. Thus, to take a version of argument (1) considered later, the ethics of holding high political office seems to disclose a category of reasons – reasons of state – that justify politicians in doing what morality condemns. How can these reasons trump moral reasons? And if they cannot, doesn't that show that morality is too unworldly to guide the practice of necessarily worldly people who occupy political office? Something similar may be asked about morality and business, as we shall see in chapter 3. In business, reasons of state have a loose counterpart in reasons of business survival. If these reasons are held to be of no account when they conflict with the precepts of ordinary morality, then isn't business also being held – unreasonably – to count for nothing, or not much? Argument (1) implies as much. People who put it forward hope for revised but more 'realistic' moral theories, theories which show understanding for the distinctive pressures facing those involved in business or politics – or if not understanding, then outright exemption for politicians and businessmen from the demands of ordinary morality.

Makers of argument (2) are after something different. They look for the abandonment of 'working' theories and the creation of an entirely new theory. For example, the conviction that there is something unjust about the way the burden of work in the family throughout the world falls mainly upon women is hard to bear out using a standard theory of justice, if the theory says that questions about justice arise only in the public sphere, and if the family is excluded from that sphere. On the other hand, a demand for a more equal distribution of this work between men and women – which a standard theory supports – may be too minimal morally, even if it is coupled with a demand that women have more of the agreeable work outside the home. The reason these demands may ask too little is that, historically, men have determined the type of work that is to be done outside the home, and their preferences have also defined what work is agreeable. It may be that far more reconsideration is required of the types of work that are desirable and have status, before inequalities and injustices can be recognised for the fundamental ones they are. But this may be difficult or impossible using a gender-neutral moral theory (which also turns out to be a male artifact). It may be that to be fair, moral theory has to express solidarity with, by incorporating the viewpoint of, the oppressed. According to the line of thought that sets chapter 5 into motion, this may mean abandoning traditional moral theory as it has come down to us in favour of something new.

The clear moral questions raised by women's work, as by many other practical questions, are at the source of many apparent anomalies. Not only do some standard theories appear to falter when these questions are asked, or to exclude these questions for the sake of simplicity or some other intra-theoretic reason; the faltering or the exclusion can itself appear to be a case of moral insensitivity, as if the question of women's work or factory farming were too trivial to bother theory with, or as if theory were implying that in these areas one can do what one likes. One important goal of those who insist on the moral insensitivity of these theoretical exclusions and omissions is to find a theory in which the accompanying overtones of moral unimportance are strongly challenged, and this can mean looking for a systematic source for these exclusions in different versions of orthodox moral theory.

The Argument of the Rest of the Book

In the face of claims of anomaly different responses are open to the supporter of theory. One is to say that all or some traditional theories do address, albeit inadequately, the practices emphasised by their critics, so that the task of correction does not consist of overcoming anomaly but of solving a puzzle. Another is to say that one at least of the traditional theories applies reasonably well, and that while the others do not, that does not show they are without useful applications in other areas; perhaps it is a mistake to expect each theory to have the same scope as the next. A third response can be put by saying that while traditional theories fail to apply, there is no reason why they should apply, and that the areas to which the critics want them applied are not areas to which moral theories *should* be applied. Finally, one can say that while no application has yet been devised and a new theory would be required to meet the case, there is no reason why such a theory couldn't be constructed.

For the most part in what follows, I make use of the first form of response. That is, I try to show that the large-scale problems that are supposed to defeat all of the standard normative moral theories do not in fact do so: versions of one or another standard theory, and someimes more than one, can usually cope. The exceptional case – the one that really does call for something like a fresh theoretical start – is that of environmental ethics. With the exception of that case most of the *big* supposed anomalies – the ones that arguments (1) and (2) illustrate – are really only puzzles. But the book does concede that here and there in business ethics and political ethics, as well as in the ethics of gender-relations, there appear to be candidates for the role of *minor* anomaly – a marginal problem that cannot apparently be dealt with using the apparatus effective for the *central* problems of business, political office-holding and gender.

If minor anomalies exist, doesn't that show that there is something wrong with the theoretical impulse in ethics, even if what is wrong is not as serious as arguments (1) and (2) suggested? Not necessarily. At the end of the book I argue that some problems for theory arise from its connection with the circumstances and content of the ordinary moral training that it is primarily designed to rationalise, and not from any impulse to make everything stand to reason or to show all moral phenomena to be specimens of just a few main types. The theoretical impulse may in a certain sense be less narrow and parochial than the moral tradition that theory tries to square with. The moral tradition, rather than theory, may leave us unprepared for unusual moral choices or challenges, and may blind us to the merits of certain unusual ways of life, or reasons for rejecting conventional ways of life.

Can this sort of pro-theory approach possibly do justice to arguments (1) and (2)? At first sight each seems to identify a supposed failing of theory connected with the two tasks of theory identified in chapter 1: the rationalising and systematising ones. Argument (1), if sound, shows that that there are some practices that cannot be rationalised except by reference to standards internal to those practices. In other words, the good reasons that there are for those practices will not necessarily seem good from anybody's or most people's point of view, still less from a point of view that makes them cohere with the nostrums of a conventional personal morality. They will only make sense to insiders, or to outsiders who give excusing weight to the morally undesirable background conditions in which the activities are pursued, for example cut-throat competition for profit in business and terrorist or military threats in political office-holding at the national level.

Not only is it naïve for anyone to disregard these conditions, the critics of theory might suggest; there is something unreal in the idea that everything that has legitimacy derives it from lofty reasons or principles. In the case of business and politics, we are confronted with complex practices that have many different manifestations in different parts of the world, and that have been thrown up over a long period of time in different places. The fact that these practices exist and have been widely participated in for ages, almost always against the background of morally unsavoury pressures, itself gives the institutions legitimacy, it might be said, whether or not everything done by agents involved with them can be justified by reference to moral principle. The line of thought does not stop there. There is a limit to rationalisation not only when people involved in business or politics feel forced to do things that conflict with their ideals, but also, it might be thought, where ideals alone or mainly seem to be inspiring public policy or business practice. Enterprises that are experiments in worker democracy have been known to produce unmarketable goods, and public policies that have plausible principled justifications – such as policies of racial integration – have sometimes broken down because people who had benefited by segregationist policies have been unwilling to give up the ways of life those policies permitted. Not to take account of the resistance in a local culture to what is eminently justifiable in theory; not to make concessions to a recalcitrant human nature in pieces of more general social engineering; not to put the horse of making saleable products before the cart of democratising the enterprise that makes them, can look like foolishness if there are significant limits to rationalisation.

Rationalisation is one task of theory; systematisation is another. And just as argument (1) can be understood to point to the limits of rationalisation that is possible in moral theory, so argument (2) can be understood to point to the limits of systematisation. Whatever the attractions

for system-builders of a homogeneous category of human being not
further specified, the problems of racial injustice and sexual injustice, it
might be said by the critic, are not properly understood as offences
against raceless and sexless human beings. It overabstracts from what is
at stake in these matters to suppose that the injustices are offences
against human beings primarily, and against women and non-whites only
secondarily; it overabstracts to say that the *perpetrators* of these injustices
are human beings primarily, and men and whites only by the way. But,
the criticism goes on, the pressure is on for the abstract view as soon as
one goes in for theory. No one who confronted the injustices head on
as they arise in life, or who experienced them, would naturally reinter-
pret them in terms that left out race or gender. And the abstract human
being so beloved of theory, argument (2) continues, is at the same time
hard to locate in a continuum that includes other animals or organisms
or as a part of nature.

I reject argument (2). Plausible as it is to say that abstraction has a
distorting effect and that highly general concepts such as that of human
being fail to capture what is distinctive about certain types of injustice,
it is also plausible to say that abstraction *aids* thought and action
about these injustices. Sameness and likeness can matter as much as difference in these areas. Thus, it can be a goal of members of a group that
is routinely exploited to be treated the *same* as another, better treated,
group, and for the burden of proof to be put on their exploiters or
others to say why the differences for which they suffer justify their being
treated worse. It can help a group that everyone mistreats that other
people say or think that no one – no human being – should suffer such-
and-such treatment. And members of groups who suffer different types
of oppression can be helped by the recognition of analogies between the
types of oppression, by the recognition that they are in the same in
important respects as some other group. As will emerge in chapter 5,
feminist arguments routinely exploit analogies between the mistreatment
of racial minorities and the mistreatment of women. And as will emerge
in chapter 6, environmentalists compare discrimination in favour of
one's own species to discrimination in favour of one's racial group. These
arguments make use of the generality one finds in moral theory, but in
pursuit of justice for a special group, sometimes not even a specifically
human one.

The case of feminism, discussed in detail in chapter 5, reveals that,
contrary to argument (2), there is *no* deep tension between the craving
for generality in the form of principles, or systems of principles, and even
the partisan defence of an oppressed group. The case of environmentalism, discussed in chapter 6, shows, again contrary to argument (2), that

theory does not need to cling to an unecological category of the person or of the human being to generate reasons for caring about islands or forests: the fact that things other than persons can be damaged, and damaged gratuitously, may be enough of a basis for environmental ethics. It will turn out, in fact, that many of the objections that have dominated the feminist and environmentalist critiques of traditional moral theory in the philosophical literature can be met. It is true that challenges to moral theory do exist in the areas of feminism and environmentalism, but these arise more convincingly in my view from radical *practice* rather than from the radical criticism of theory, or from the radicals' attempt to formulate new theory. Radical practice of the kind I consider in chapters 5 and 6 is usually only loosely grounded even by the theories of radical feminists and environmentalists. Although some of it seems to me to be straightforwardly immoral, some seems to have a positive value that is hard to articulate, which may be the stuff of an outlying but still interesting sort of anomaly for moral theory.

As for business and politics, they may also throw up anomalies, but not on the large scale that argument (1) from the previous section suggested. Or so I am going to argue. I reject the claim that even sharp practices in business or dirty hands in politics are no-go areas for moral theory. On the contrary, they are natural areas of application, though not always perfectly satisfactory application, for utilitarianism, and perhaps also virtue theory. Utilitarianism is hard to accuse of utopianism, and so argument (1) is not even initially plausible when directed at all standard or traditional moral theories. Argument (1) is wrong in another way, according to me, for it tries to identify an anomaly in political ethics and business ethics by focusing on what politics and business have in common, and such would-be anomalies as I think might emerge in the two areas lie elsewhere. In politics, the politics of representative democracies particularly, partisanship may point to a possible anomaly. Politicians are guardians and promoters of a public good that may conflict with the effective and also obligatory defence of constituency interests. This is just one example of the way the demands of impartiality conflict with the apparent right of constituencies and individuals to pursue or preserve their ways of life. In business, there may be the stuff of anomaly in the very indefiniteness of the role of business person: some ways of playing this role seem to effect an unlikely fusion of exemplary uprightness and commercial success. These ways of playing the role are troubling because traditional moral theories, even utilitarianism, say that the business role has a contingent moral value, if a moral value at all, while other roles have a moral value that rubs off on their occupants.

The exemplary business people seem to do things that are morally better than humdrum lawyers or judges, but legal institutions having the moral value they have, exemplary business people seem to be morally under-rated. Perhaps there is more to the business person's role, or more indefiniteness to the role, than is allowed by the usual moral conde-scension of theory to business, and perhaps the condescension is hard to undo.

If there is an anomaly at all in the area of exemplary business people, however, it is a small one. All of the claims of *large*-scale anomaly that I discuss, I eventually reject. That said, I do not think that arguing for their rejection is easy or straightforward. Arguments (1) and (2) have considerable complexity when applied, and although they should not deter anyone from trying to extend the scope of current mainstream theories, they should make us less confident that these theories will occupy the mainstream in even the forseeable future. On the other hand, if the current trio of Kantian, utilitarian and neo-Aristotelian theory-types is displaced, what supplants them cannot afford to ignore their insights. In any case, whether these theories deserve replacement or revision is a question it will be necessary to pursue theory by theory – and application by application – not by reference to what might be meant by theory in the abstract. There is too much to be said for and against theory from the angle of their success or failure in answering specific practical questions for aprioristic criticisms of theory to have much authority on their own.

PART **TWO**

Some Sources of Anomaly?

3

Business, the Ethical and Self-interest

'Greed is good', says the stock market speculator in Oliver Stone's film *Wall Street*. He makes the remark in a speech at a meeting of shareholders of a firm that is not as vigorous as it might be in maximising returns. Although it is not morally outrageous in the context in which it is uttered, it is put in the mouth of a morally outrageous character. Gordon Gecko buys companies whose asset values exceed their stock market values, and he breaks them up and sells them, regardless of the consequences for employees and others connected with the firm. To make his deals he illegally uses inside information collected from a young broker whom he nearly corrupts. In the end, Gecko is ruined by his protégé, whom he accuses, in a burst of something like moral indignation, of ingratitude. Stone's film showed his 1980s audiences the business ethics of the then burgeoning financial services markets. But it is hard to be given this description without hearing heavy irony in the phrase 'business ethics'. Some cynical people say that the phrase is a contradiction in terms, an oxymoron, even when applied to business practice outside the scandal-ridden investment houses. The widely perceived tension in the idea of business ethics is the subject of this chapter. If the idea makes no sense, then perhaps business cannot be colonised by moral theory either.

Two Sources of Prima-facie Anomaly

Why, if at all, should the application of moral principle to business practice seem futile or naïve or even incoherent? The most straightforward answer, and the one which explains why the term 'business ethics' strikes some people as oxymoronic, is the uninteresting one that business practice is often dishonest or greedy or morally unsavoury in other respects. This is an uninteresting answer, because the same could be said of much human activity generally, and yet no one claims that 'human ethics' is a contradiction in terms. Again, if some business activity or much business activity is agreed to be unsavoury, that does not show that the idea of business ethics is incoherent: it shows, on the contrary, that ethical standards can be and are applied to business, and that business is found wanting when measured by those standards. If the same standards are adopted in moral theory, then moral theory applies in turn, and there is not even a prima-facie case for business being anomalous. I believe the matter is actually less clear cut than this conclusion would suggest. As we shall see in the present chapter, business people and their spokesmen say two things that suggest that moral theory does not apply.

Separate spheres

First, they sometimes say that everyday morality and the morality of business are different and separate, and that there is no judging the behaviour of people who are in business by the standards they would observe when at home or in their private lives. Since moral theory often incorporates and justifies the precepts for the conduct of private life that are being alluded to here, moral theory, too, may be being expected to open a separate moral account for life in business. And this is problematic. Moral theory is the theory of right and wrong, and when it says that a particular type of action is wrong full stop, it does not appear to be making an exception for actions of that type performed in the course of commercial life. It looks as if the plea for keeping the morality of home and business separate is a plea for double standards; and this is outlawed by moral theory. So perhaps it is the connection between morality and consistency that unsuits moral theory to business, when business is regarded (as it often is) as a separate sphere.

Moral reasons and business reasons

A second source of prima-facie anomaly is a line of thought to the effect that moral theory is bad at recognising ethical business activity for what is, because it tends to denigrate the self-interest in business, and to imply that self-interest taints even business activity that has social benefits. According to the supposedly objectionable outlook adopted by theorists, business activity is typically pursued to benefit those who own an enterprise or who manage it, and benefiting these people significantly or to the greatest extent possible can be at odds with benefiting others: not just the public but also those close to the business who are not managers and owners. When there is a convergence of benefits for the business with benefits for the public that is not because benefits to the public are aimed at by business, but at best because they are foreseen as by-products of policies which, above all, must somehow affect the bottom line. Motivated in these ways, the relevant policies can hardly be regarded as having moral value. Businesses that go in for them are merely going through the motions of being ethical, according to some theorists, which makes some business people and some business ethicists say that theory is hopelessly condescending or unreal in its treatment of the efforts of business to be ethical. Moral theory loses touch with business in this connection, it is claimed: it is unduly Utopian.

I shall argue that a deep tension between ethical and business motivation is undeniable, and that this makes sense of the condescension by theory towards the role of business person, when theory gives moral weight to motivation. The tension is not incoherence, however, and it is not by itself the stuff of anomaly. On the other hand, anomaly *can* arise when the role of business person or firm is played abnormally. There are exceptional cases in which someone in business manages to make business and ethics fuse: a business policy or a business decision that looks wildly generous by the normal standards of business may not look either overgenerous or unbusinesslike for that particular business or that particular business person. The normal tension between being businesslike and being generous is overcome without it looking as if the decision or policy in question has ceased to be recognisable as commercial. But anomaly along these lines is a relatively outlying case of an anomaly for moral theory, because moral theory is first and foremost addressed to people – regardless of their roles. Moral precepts do not fail to apply and to have overriding authority over the people who are in business, even if in order to follow them one has to invent a new style of business.

The Utopianism of Business Ethics

Not all theorists – not all academic business ethicists – are purists about the motivation that makes business behaviour ethical. On the contrary, much academic business ethics consists of parlaying the fact that commercial self-interest does sometimes converge with promoting the public good into a rationale for the philanthropy and enlightened industrial relations of certain exemplary profitable companies. The example of these companies is then commended to profitable but ethically unenlightened or ethically aspiring companies. However effective this strategy is with business people, it is questionable. For it consists of arguing that it is profitable to be ethical, and so concedes a great deal – perhaps too much – to the view that in the final analysis reasons for doing things in business have to be business reasons. On this view whatever is done in a firm has to promote the survival of the business, and even humane or generous decisions that significantly weaken commercial prospects have to be avoided. Thus a donation of a company's profits to famine relief or a postponement of the day when employees will be fired may be impermissible, if it hastens the failure of the firm. In short, much of the business ethics that tries to reconcile self-interest with moral motivation says that, while always having to be taken into account, moral reasons may be overridden or ignored. They may be overridden or ignored if the effects on a business are particularly bad, or if acting on them would mean ceasing to give due weight to commercial considerations.

This view is problematic. If moral reasons are subordinated to other reasons, or if they are ignored altogether, then that seems to be *wrong*, even if acting in accordance with them is inconvenient, or financially costly, or stomach-turning. A near-relation of the idea that moral reasons are unignorable and non-overridable is the idea that moral reasons promote the *highest* sort of value, not just some sort of positive value or other. This idea tells against another nostrum of worldly business ethics, to the effect that if business people do what morality asks, even if they do so for business reasons, that action is morally right. It is possible to dispute what worldly business ethics has to say in this connection. For how can meeting a requirement of morality for business reasons be as good as doing what morality asks just because it is right? And if the business-motivated right action is not as good, so that there is something better that could be done, how can what's done for business reasons have the highest value, i.e. moral value? Perhaps the answer is to challenge the idea that moral value is the highest value and that moral value is unignorable and unoverridable.[1] If so, then business ethics seems to revise the pre-theoretical conception of morality.

People, business people included, *want* distinctively moral reasons to have weight. Even ruthless financiers would prefer their children to refrain from fighting for the sake of one another rather than for the sake of some money or sweets, and if the children only refrain from fighting as long as they get the money or sweets, children are not developing morally. Why should it be different in business itself? Unless material rewards make one go in for a fair or just or benevolent business practice that one eventually sees as valuable in itself, so that one would try to keep up the practice if the material reward disappeared, it is hard to see how philanthropy or benevolent industrial relations motivated by self-interest is ethical. Yet the moral theorist's wish to get not just generally beneficial outcomes into business, but also authentically disinterested motivations for those outcomes, is often seen by business people as ivory towerism and utopianism at its worst. Can moral theory come up with more than a business ethics geared to self-interest and yet not sound like preaching from the ivory tower? It can. One way is by arguing that the non-self-interested parts of a people's *personal* morality do not lose their force in their business life except out of a certain kind of selective blindness or a disputable view of business activity as a kind of stage activity in which actions are traceable to a mere persona rather than the actor himself.

Utopianism and the rhetorical difficulties of business ethics

Now the rhetorical task of finding reasons to be ethical that will be acceptable in business is not the only task of academic business ethics. There is also the more theoretical one of specifying systematically the metaethics and normative ethics appropriate to, for example, human resource management, marketing and advertising; competition; and financial reporting. The most general questions that arise in this connection include those to do with whether businesses or business people are the agents on whom ethical responsibilities fall; whether the ethical responsibilities of businesses can conflict; whether responsibilities vary according to local standards of business and ethics in different parts of the world; whether carrying out these responsibilities requires a motivation consistent with or at odds with self-interest. These are important questions, and they connect the theory of business ethics to normative ethical theory and metaethics in general as well as to other areas of applied ethics. But answering these questions may not be as urgent as finding arguments that business people will accept for improving their treatment of employees, customers and the local community. The reason is that the distance between academic ethicists and business people is much greater than the distance between academic ethicists and practitioners of medicine, legal advocacy, police work or public administration. Not only means but also ends in business can seem morally problematic to ethicists, whereas there seems to be wide agreement that many of the purposes of lawyering, doctoring, administration, even political office-holding are morally valuable.

Let us call what I am describing 'the problem of the alienation of ethicists from practitioners' or the *alienation problem* for short. Unless it is solved the goal of affecting practice is in danger of being compromised in business ethics as it hardly ever is elsewhere in applied ethics. Business ethics is in danger of making itself seem entirely irrelevant. This may not amount to wholesale inapplicability or to incoherence in the project of business ethics: a wholly ineffectual business ethics is not self-contradictory. There may even be an intellectual point to systematising the normative ethical justification for certain business practices and to answering the metaethical questions already listed. Still, the *moral* point of doing so when no business people are listening is surely obscure. Yet the alienation problem is not easy to overcome. Worse, those who would solve it have to avoid a corresponding problem. There are business ethicists who, perhaps for the sake of gaining credibility with the business community, are overzealous in arguing for the primacy of the obligation of maximising share-holder return.[2] Call this the *overrationalisation problem*. In order to overcome the alienation problem without succumbing to the overrationalisation problem, business ethics has to tailor its standards not to business as usual, but to businesses that manage to be both morally out of the ordinary and profitable at the same time. This is the form of the rhetorical task that I have been suggesting is central to any business ethics that wishes to affect the practice it deals with. I shall argue that this rhetorical task can be discharged, and that moral philosophy, far from getting in the way, can actually help.

Rhetoric without moral philosophy?

To get clearer on what the rhetorical task might involve, we need to look more closely at the ingredients of the alienation and overrationalisation problems. A good guide to the alienation problem comes in a recent article by Andrew Stark:

> Far too many business ethicists have occupied a rarefied moral high ground, removed from the real concerns of and real-world problems of the vast majority of managers. They have been too preoccupied with absolutist notions of what it means for managers to be ethical, with overly general criticisms of capitalism as an economic system, with dense and abstract theorising, and with prescriptions that apply only remotely to managerial practice. Such trends are all the more disappointing in contrast to the success that ethicists in other professions – medicine, law, and government – have had in providing real and welcome assistance to their practitioners.[3]

Stark backs up this claim with many effective quotations from the recent literature of business ethics. He traces the problem he is describing to a number of different factors, not the least of which is the dominance of

American academic business ethics by moral philosophers. According to Stark, the moral philosophers have tended to emphasise the wrong question – 'Why should business be ethical?' – and have ignored or dissented unreasonably from the perfectly good answer that business people were giving to this question long before the moral philosophers came on the scene: namely, that it *pays* business to be ethical, or that it is in the enlightened self-interest of business to be ethical. Not all business ethicists, not even all moral philosophers among the business ethicists, are tarred with the brush that Stark applies to the purists. He has praise for the virtue theorist Robert Solomon.[4] But he wishes that philosophers would turn from the question of the motivation of ethical practice to the principles that should guide it in the face of competing considerations, like the need to get more business, the need to pay off debt, and the need to pay dividends.

Elsewhere,[5] I have expressed sympathy for Stark's view, agreeing that some business ethics is too far removed from business to be any good. I went further, suggesting that there is a whole genre of applied ethics – 'armchair applied ethics' – that extends in an objectionable way the method of arguing a priori and by abstract counterexample that is justifiable in most of the rest of philosophy. In applied ethics there is an obvious value to leg-work – to leaving one's armchair and finding out about the actual practice of business, medicine and law, including the questions that seem natural to practitioners, or urgent to them at different times. The value of the leg-work is that it increases the chances of a piece of applied ethics appearing relevant to practitioners, who are part of the natural audience of applied ethics. Resorting to leg-work, however, is not the same thing as going native, and there is no reason why applied ethicists should desert the role of moral critic when they get closer to the practices and practitioners they write about, substituting the norms of business people for their own wherever there is a discrepancy.[6] There is no reason, in other words, why the principles proposed by business ethicists who are knowledgeable about business practice should not conflict with and imply the need for the reform of, that very business practice. The reason why this last claim does not necessarily reintroduce utopianism is the very straightforward one that many business people are themselves self-critical and see that some standard business practices are, if not in fact dubious themselves, then like dubious practices. One reason why they are prepared to say that their business practices are prima-facie dubious is that they can involve departures from practices they would find normal in personal morality. This is a very important piece of common ground between academic business ethics and business, and in my view one of the reasons why the rhetorical task of business ethics is practicable at all. The existence of such common ground also helps to explain why the problem of overrationalising business practice is avoidable: because business people do not themselves think that everything they do is all right. To meet them on their own ground it is not necessary to deny that all practices that seem questionable to outsiders *are* in fact questionable. What is required is some understanding of and respect for the reasons that make some of these practices seem legitimate or unavoidable.

Stark gestures at what he thinks is another piece of common ground in repeated references, throughout his article, to the parallels between, on the one hand, a profession of business or management and, on the other hand, other professions, such as government, law and medicine, which in Stark's view are not alienated, or are less alienated, from the corresponding branches of professional ethics. For example, enlarging on the impracticality of business ethics, Stark says that

> it is concerned with prescriptions that, however morally respectable, run so contrary to existing managerial roles and responsibilities that they become untenable. As a result, such work in business ethics hasn't 'taken' in the world of practice, especially when compared with the work of ethicists in other professions such as government, medicine or law.[7]

He goes on to call attention to some parallels between legal and business ethics: both generate moral demands that put particular strain on the relevant professionals in ways that, say, ethics for governments does not. The strategy of modelling business ethics on some more congenial branch of professional ethics strikes me as doubly ill-conceived. First, it is not at all clear that business is a 'profession' at all, let alone a profession in the sense that law and medicine are. Second, to ask for the same treatment for business as government gets from ethics sounds like a plea for permissiveness, and one of the things at issue when one claims that there is something wrong with business ethics is whether business ethics is or is not permissive enough. The fact, if it is one, that professional ethics lets politicians off the hook more readily than business people may not be a reason for agreeing that business ethics ought to be like ethics for politicians, or that political ethics *should* let politicians off the hook.

As for the claim that business is one more profession like law or medicine, that is disputable in a number of ways. First, the status of law or medicine as a profession is based on, among other things, the existence of an agreed body of specialised medical and legal doctrine, which has been part of the university curriculum since before the Renaissance. To enter the profession it is usually necessary but not sufficient to have university qualifications. It is usually also necessary to pass examinations set and marked by current members of the profession. To be a member of the profession is usually to be on a publicly available list of practitioners recognised by the profession, from which one can have one's name taken off and so be excluded from the profession. Not all of the traditional professions – architecture or engineering, for example – follow the pattern of law and medicine in every particular, but they conform more closely than the would-be profession of business. Partly this is because business is so varied an activity. One can be in business shining shoes or in business manufacturing sixty different types of automobile. One can be in business with very little, sometimes no, education, and certainly without business school training. Indeed this is how most business has always been carried out. Even big business, which arguably demands more specialised knowledge than at any rate some small business, is open to the self-taught. There is no real analogue of being struck off a professional list, indeed no list in the first place. Not even bankruptcy excludes one from business for long in most countries, and there is a vast amount of business conducted entirely clandestinely and out of the reach of law in black and grey markets. Only the finicky would deny the status of business to the building firm in the grey economy with two sets of books and more transactions in cash than through the banking system. The people who run the firm are certainly business people. But are they professionals? Not in the sense spelt out above, even though they may have specialised knowledge and have direct dealings with customers.

Again, many professions are in principle able to be practised solo. This means that in principle one practices in person and deals directly with clients, who know one personally, not just the firm one works for. One can be directly liable for negligence or error. One reason why the microlevel of legal and medical ethics – the level of one-to-one client dealings – is open to codification and requires codification is that it is to do with one-to-one relationships. These are professional relationships often carried out personally, and so test the limit between professional and personal, which is at the heart of much professional ethics. Clients of medical professionals are often ill or in trouble and therefore possibly vulnerable and dependent, and they standardly require trust and confidentiality, even some kinds of intimate contact. All of this is background for moral risk as well as moral responsibility. In business it is also possible for professional relationships to be personal, and to involve trust. Standardly, however, being vulnerable or in trouble is not quite the factor in being a customer that it is in being a lawyer's or doctor's client. Not that they can never be standard factors: they may be in the funeral business, for example. But an ethics for business in general would not have to cater for them in quite the same way as a code for lawyers and doctors, and a would-be ethics for business in general is what is under discussion.

The differences go on. Doctors and lawyers are often reimbursed according to a scale of rates fixed by fellow practitioners. There is no standard 'business person's' fee, still less one that is fixed by a body of business people. Doctors and lawyers practice in institutions – hospitals and law courts – that have a public identity of their own and can be run by the state rather than privately. Businesses are not public institutions in the same way even when they are state-owned.

Moral Sensibility and Insensibility in Business

The idea of business as a profession seems an unpromising, even a pretentious, beginning for a business ethics that aims to overcome the alienation problem. A better place to start is with a sense of moral problems derived from business itself. This sense may be acquired by talking to business people or joining their ranks, but it is also available in print. One such public source, perhaps a little notorious in American business ethics, is an article dating to 1968. This is Albert Z. Carr's 'Is business bluffing ethical?',[8] an essay belonging to the dawn or early history of academic business ethics, or perhaps even its prehistory, since its author was not an academic. The foreword to the article says that

> Mr. Carr became interested in this subject when he was a member of a New York firm of consultants to large corporations in many fields. The confidences of many stress-ridden executives made him aware of the extent to which tensions can arise from conflicts between a firm's ethical sense and the realities of business. He was struck also by the similarity of the special ethical attitude shown by many successful and stress-free businesspersons in their work to that of good poker players.[9]

Carr argues that certain forms of deception in business are just as permissible as bluffing is within a card game. It is all right to bluff in poker, although it is not all right to do other things. Some of the other things are simply against the rules, such as playing with cards up one's sleeve or in secret partnership with another player. Others are ethically wrong, as when one gets one's opponent drunk or distracts him with loud talk when it's his turn to bet. Although these things are wrong, bluffing is permissible. In the same way, it is permissible in business to sell a product that one knows one could make to last longer, or to exert certain kinds of influence on politicians who can introduce legislation advantageous to one's business.[10] It is permissible to do these things, but wrong to do other things, such as fix prices or spread malicious rumours about one's competitors. One reason why the things indicated are permissible, according to Carr, is that they are in keeping with people's expectations. Everyone who plays poker is prepared for bluffing, and the practices of lobbying legislatures and designing products not to last forever are to be expected in business as well.

Carr realises that deception is not permissible in every context, even though everyone with even a little experience knows that other people lie. But then he thinks that not all kinds of human relations are the same, morally speaking. Thus he insists on 'a sharp distinction between the ethical systems of the home and the office'.[11] The action of a businessman that looks tawdry or compromising from the standpoint of private morality can be seen as a matter of 'game strategy' when viewed from a position within business itself. Or so Carr claims. What gives this sort of position a use as a starting point for the rhetorical task of business ethics is that it was put forward by Carr himself with some sense of its appearing controversial, even to other business people. The article did in fact generate a large and mostly hostile correspondence from readers of *Harvard Business Review*, which is evidence that Carr was drawing the line between permissible and impermissible behaviour in a way that could be challenged by those inside as well as those outside business.

A natural point of entry is Carr's assumption that private morality and business morality belong to separate areas of activity that work by distinct rules. There are a number of straightforward ways of questioning this that are open to elaboration by a usable yet critical academic business ethics. First, how can the spheres be separate if the business person is the same as the person who has a family life and who engages in business activity? Second, and more important, both spheres are known to matter enormously to people who occupy them; so much so that there is often serious competition from each sphere for the same person's time. Connected with the time spent in both spheres is what one might call the investment of one's self in each sphere: the extent to which one identifies oneself with one's job or one's home life. If one's identification with both one's job and one's home life is significant, then it is plausible to hold that following rules in one sphere that one cannot follow in the other is not just a psychological but a moral problem, since one cannot occupy both spheres with integrity, and integrity may be part

of living life honestly or flourishingly – where both honesty and flourishing have moral content. The fact that it may be possible for business
people to keep the two spheres separate in the sense that activity in one
is kept out of sight of the other sphere does not mean that they *are*
separate or that one sphere does not have consequences with moral
significance for the other. A person may manage to lead two quite
separate lives (say by conducting a love affair, or through an occupation
that requires very sustained play-acting) and yet still be morally responsible for betrayal in the one role and deception in the other. And this
may be true though people enter marriage nowadays knowing that affairs
are quite common, for example, and though the play-acting part of
one's life remains unknown to people in the other part of one's life.
Finally, the fact that a certain activity comes to be expected does not
necessarily alter its moral character. Someone who is known as a con-
genital liar does not cease to act wrongly in telling lies just because no
one expects him to tell the truth; and the fact that stealing is epidemic
in a certain neighbourhood of town does not mean that when you
enter that neighbourhood the normal prohibition on stealing lapses
and you can take what you like, because the people there find stealing
commonplace.

Not only virtue theory but also utilitarianism can develop these
points, and in ways that do not begin to impugn business activity *per se*.
Virtue theory represents certain difficult-to-acquire but cultivatable
characteristics, such as courage, justice and self-control, as good to
acquire because of the way they contribute to something else that is
uncontroversially good: namely a flourishing human life. The person who
approaches business activity as if it were a game like poker might experience strains on integrity, and these strains might be thought to interfere with flourishing. This line of thought is compatible with thinking
that both business and its material rewards are part of the flourishing
life. Utilitarianism represents as morally obligatory whatever practicable
policy or action tends to increase the most the welfare of sentient beings.
The theory lends itself to arguments that say that the split life of the
Carr-approved businessman is psychologically harmful if generalised
and therefore better avoided on moral grounds.

Again, there is nothing in the *role* of business person that requires
there to be the split life that Carr talks about. Partly this is because, as
seen in the last section, the role is relatively indeterminate. But it is also
because there are traditions of business throughout the world that make
the business role mesh with private life through the role of family
member. Family businesses are not only typical examples of business;
they are disproportionately represented among socially responsible

business. In the UK, for example, the Clarks, the Lewises, the Moores, the Cadburys and the Pilkingtons are all families whose large manufacturing and retailing businesses are or have been the vehicles for the moral values of prominent family members. In the case of the Clarks and the Cadburys the values have been associated with Quakerism. And there are similar examples from America. Malden Mills, run by the Feuerstein family of Brookline, Massachusetts, kept its employees on its payroll during a recent period in which the business came to a standstill as a result of a huge fire in its factory. The case made a local hero of Aaron Feuerstein, the head of the firm, whose family had always seen the business both as a means of securing independence to practice a devout Judaism, and as a means of expressing the ethics of Judaism. Although not every family business is high-minded, the very category of family business gives the lie to the idea that home and office have to belong to separate spheres, and that the ethics of the home has to be out of place in the business. There can easily be a continuity of sleaze, and there can sometimes be a continuity of its opposite. Both business practice and moral theory, then, are able to challenge Carr's separate spheres thesis.

A virtue theory or utilitarianism that is able to disagree with Carr can at the same time be pro-business. But it need not be a fawning or supine moral theory. On the contrary, both utilitarianism and virtue theory are easily able to avoid both the alienation problem *and* the overrationalisation problem. This is not to say that utilitarianism is incapable of generating a moral conclusion that will strike mainstream business as outrageous. For example, it is readily adapted to showing that the sum total of welfare is most effectively increased by radical reforms of our treatment of animals, which might raise the costs of farming and the prices of agricultural products far above what is currently regarded as reasonable in the food production and retailing industries. The point is that utilitarianism does not necessarily have an anti-business thrust, even though as a formal moral theory it is a philosopher's invention. The same is true of virtue theory. Whether or not the same is true of every standard moral theory that philosophers recognise is less clear. Although it has its defenders as a vehicle for business ethics in the real world,[12] Kantianism, with its tradition of requiring that genuinely moral motivation be untainted by self-interest, may or may not be the exception that proves Stark's conclusion about the moral myopia and irrelevance of moral philosophy in relation to business. But even if he is right about Kantianism,[13] Stark is wrong about moral philosophy in general. Moral philosophy is no more incapable of articulating a real-world business ethics than it is of articulating the at-first-sight much more difficult justification for mass killing in war. The unworldliness of moral philosophy, in short, has been much exaggerated by critics like Stark.

It might turn out in any case that the unreality Stark complains of in some business ethics writing is in fact a clumsy attempt at upholding the distinction between 'ought' and 'is'. Unless everything is morally all right in the business world, one *expects* to find business as usual falling short of what is morally required. Taking this view is not a matter of occupying a moral high ground, or a particularly rarefied moral perspective, but of occupying any moral perspective. This perspective is available in life as usual just as much as business as usual, and it is expressed by the background thought of participants in life and in business that 'we're no angels'. This background thought is not usually associated with the question of why anybody should bother to be an angel: usually people accept that they can and should aspire to better behaviour than they display. Now there is no reason to think that this background thought from life – that we're no angels – is inaccessible in business, and it is one of the things that gives business ethics its point within the context of business. Of course it may be a strategic mistake to engage the background thought with an absolutist or purist moral theory, one that maximises the distance between the ideal and the actual, one that takes the angel's rather than the decent person's point of view of business; but *some* distance is required for even a moderate and sympathetic moral message. The perspective that gives moral distance from business life is not the special preserve of theorists or academics: it is latent in life, and therefore in business. In calling for realism there is always the danger that one is trying to get rid of this perspective, rather than exaggerations of the moral distance that the perspective makes available. If so, then in calling for realism one may be calling not only for the end of moral haughtiness, or preachiness, but for the end of moralising, and this is not a legitimate cost of making business ethics user-friendly.

Near-realistic Business Ethics

So far I have been pointing out the compatibility of very standard moral theories in philosophy with moral views prevalent among business people themselves. I now turn to a piece of mainstream business ethics and indicate how it avoids the twin pitfalls of alienation and overrationalisation in a different but, once again, perfectly acceptable way. The standard piece of business ethics I have in mind is stakeholder theory, the approach to business ethics that has grown out of contesting the

Friedmanite maxim that business ethics begins and ends with the responsibilities of managers to owners of a business, including stock-holders.[14] Stakeholders are people at whose expense or for whose benefit a business may be run. Or, what I take to amount to the same thing, they are people whose welfare is importantly affected by the manage-ment of a business. Such people may be managers, employees, cus-tomers, suppliers, creditors, residents in the vicinity of the relevant firm's premises, *as well as* shareholders (if the company is public) or as well as outright owners. Less standardly included among stakeholders are a firm's competitors, one or more governments, even non-persons like local plants or landscapes affected by the firm's activities.

Perhaps the most sophisticated recent version of the theory is due to R. Edward Freeman.[15] Freeman is out to sketch a theory that challenges 'the basic idea of managerial capitalism': namely, that 'in return for con-trolling the firm, management vigorously pursues the interests of stock-holders', where the 'vigorously' is a euphemism for 'single-mindedly' or 'ruthlessly'. Stakeholder theory conflicts with the thinking behind man-agerial capitalism because it identifies interests – those of stakeholders other than stockholders – that constrain the pursuit of stockholder inter-ests. It also challenges the managerial capitalist definition of the purpose of the firm, which as Freeman understands it, is to maximise stockholder welfare as the best means of promoting the general welfare or as the best means of promoting property rights. Freeman's preferred version of stakeholder theory is more pluralistic than managerial capitalism not just about whose welfare is to be promoted but also the grounds for welfare promotion. Freeman envisages a cluster of stakeholder theories with dif-ferent and in principle compatible grounds for core precepts about how a company should be governed and what managers should do. Thus there might be a 'fair contracts' stakeholder theory, a 'feminist stand-point' stakeholder theory or an 'ecological' stakeholder theory, among others.[16]

Freeman himself elaborates a 'fair contracts' approach to stakehold-ing, intended to reflect the assumptions and methodology of the modern liberal theory of justice and property rights. This faces fewer risks of internal incoherence than its feminist and ecological counterparts, and uses principles readily intelligible to those who are familiar with market economics. For example, it is a ground rule of the approach that the conditions for entering, dissolving, and renegotiating contracts should be clear to all parties; it is another ground rule that someone not party to a contract who is adversely affected by it should be able to become party to the contract, and so on. The guiding idea is that principles of corporate governance and management in a given firm ought to be acceptable if they could be agreed to by all stakeholders in ignorance of their actual stakes.[17] Not only does this theory appear to escape entirely the objection that it is purist or otherworldly; it is supported by two lines of argument that I believe are particularly effective in converting business people to it. One of these lines of argument is legal,[18] the other economic.[19] Both kinds of argument are potentially very fruitful in discharging the rhetorical task that from the beginning I have been claiming is central to business ethics. The legal argument consists of a review of US court decisions whose joint effect is to make it a legal requirement for companies to consider the interests of the groups identified by stakeholder theory. The economic argument says that unless the behaviour of people in the market is regulated, it will tend to be monopolistic, free-riding, and externality-creating. The legal constraints that outlaw these phenomena are in effect acknowledgements of the infringement of the corresponding interests: those of consumers, competitors, and fellow occupants of the market. The upshot of the legal and economic arguments in a rhetoric directed at firms is that the shape of the business environment is changing in such a way that business activity has to accommodate itself to the very interests stakeholder theory talks about. This is no rhetoric based on the first principles of moral philosophy. On the other hand, moral philosophy, in particular contractualist arguments from moral philosophy, support the legal and economic arguments. These supporting arguments do not need to be given, however, for the economic and legal arguments to be persuasive. Business people do not need to be roused from their dogmatic slumbers to register the legal or economic message. It is the sort of message they are constantly attuned to. The point here is that it is a message that moral philosophy harmonises with.

Moral Reasons Again

The last three sections can be summarised by saying that a worldly *and* critical academic business ethics is possible, and that some of the materials for it are already available. In short, the rhetorical task of business ethics is soluble.[20] The rhetorical task of business ethics is not its sole task, however. Nothing has yet been done to address the problem of why the rightness of a thing is not always (even in business) a non-overridable reason for doing it. Stark's complaint that this problem is overemphasised in the business ethics literature may be justified; but that is not to concede that there is no problem. The most that Stark shows (though it is important enough to show this) is that the eager or even willing audience for a discussion of this problem is unlikely to come from mainstream business, and it will alienate the business audience for business ethics if the status of moral reasons is discussed to the exclusion of other things that are more down to earth. The willing audience is likely to be made up not of business people but moral philosophers, and these people are not the main or the most important audience for business ethics. All of that may be agreed and yet it still be necessary for business ethics to face the problem that Stark thinks is the height of purism.

To face the problem is at the very least to explain how business reasons for or against a certain action can *seem* to outweigh moral reasons. Moral reasons are sometimes naturally outweighed, as when the actions that they promote fall into the category of the supererogatory: they are right but not obligatory. Perhaps the most straightforward examples are actions that benefit people other than the agent only if the agent goes to the extremes of self-sacrifice or generosity. How are these actions related to actions or policies approved of in business ethics? Business ethicists tend to praise firms that give high rewards to their workforces, and that minimise hierarchy in firms for the sake of good industrial relations. One UK retailing firm, John Lewis, attracts particular praise from ethicists. It has been organised into a partnership of all employees, with a share of profits going to everyone from van drivers to top managers. The idea of a partnership addresses the hierarchy and rewards issues simultaneously. John Lewis also has a no-fuss refunds policy even in cases where refunds are requested for purchases that the customer has made recklessly or on a whim. These policies are enshrined in a constitution for the company arrived at by its idealistic owner in the early part of this century. The motivation for these policies was not the enlightened self-interest of the corporate social responsibility theorists, but something more elevated. The owner had a certain vision of how a fair working and shopping environment could be engineered, and he was in a position to realise this vision as a sort of elaborate social and business experiment. He did not need to find business reasons for his vision: the business was his to develop as he liked. Few firms that might follow the example of John Lewis are led by people as unanswerable to others as the founder of the Partnership. So one would not necessarily condemn these companies for refusing to go as far as John Lewis did, even if they agreed that the policies just outlined were admirable. The idea that the John Lewis policies are supererogatory is intelligible, then, however much they are held up as an example in business ethics. The John Lewis Constitution calls for a sort of treatment of employees and consumers that is right in the way that generous actions are, but other firms may reasonably refuse to follow this example on the grounds that for them John Lewis policies would be too costly: major shareholders might object; top management might feel hemmed in by a fixed use for at least some of the firm's profit, and so on.

Business ethics does not just present examples of enlightened business practice that *might* be followed by firms willing to do so. It also represents certain things as obligatory for all business, such as the protection of employee safety, or the fair representation of a firm's financial position to shareholders. These obligatory things are often required by law. Yet mainstream business sometimes lobbies against such legal constraints in the name of cutting red tape. Thus, it is sometimes said to create too much red tape to fix a legal minimum wage, or to introduce tribunals to hear claims of unfair dismissal. Can the moral reasons there are for setting a minimum wage and for having legal remedies against unfair dismissal *also* be claimed to promote policies that go beyond the call of duty? In other words, can even things regarded by business ethics as obligatory turn out to be supererogatory? There are facts of business life which make it *look* that way. Perhaps the most weighty one in the eyes of business people is competition, which, if effective, is supposed to push into bankruptcy firms that fail to innovate, fail to make best use of resources, or fail to accommodate customers. The law of the market may make business life seem to participants to be like a continual fight to the death, and in fights to the death the cost of observing even the routine requirements of morality may be death. If agents really have reason to believe that they risk corporate death – bankruptcy – if they meet even legal requirements, can they be blamed for trying to avoid or break these requirements? Don't the rules of war apply, along with their excuses for breaching conventional morality?

I believe that this way of thinking does indeed operate in business, and that it seems to business people to justify not only omitting the supererogatory but getting the supererogatory to absorb more and more of the obligatory. Is the way of thinking sound? Two questions arise about it. First, *does* business life ever really resemble a fight to the death closely enough to excuse what seem to be obligations? Second, does war itself sustain those excuses, or does it only seem to?

A reason for thinking that business competition is not a fight to the death is that corporate death does not necessarily involve loss of life. A firm's going out of business is normally a bad thing for people close to the business, but in a developed commercial legal system there are limits to *how* bad things can be. Limited liability protects many business people from ruin when the debts of the business are unsupportable; and for individuals there are ways of rising from the ashes more than once in a business life. Business people may have fewer than the nine lives, but they have more lives than one, at least in principle. This means that the excusing power of doing something to protect one's commercial survival is limited, as is the significance of a threat to that survival.

Small business probably has the most potent argument for being excused from normal obligations, because the distinction between the business identity and the identity of the people who run or are employed by the business can be vanishingly small. The closer it comes to the truth to say that the individual is the business, the bigger the personal losses of business failure. And what is true of business death is also true of business life: that, too, is typically harder when a business *is* a person than when it is a collective enterprise. So even if the failure of a one-person business or a family business does not mean the death of anyone, it can involve very great loss, not just of money but of invested time and effort (usually a very great deal of time and effort in these days of 24-hour convenience shops). The relatively hard life of small business, however, is often reflected in tax advantages, legal protections and exemptions from the red tape that the business community as a whole lobbies against. As in the case of limited liability, there are often institutional means of keeping at manageable levels the pressure to depart from a moral minimum.

In the absence of the relevant institutions, things are not so clear. The emerging capitalist countries of Eastern Europe so far offer a very insecure environment for business, and even the basic legal obligations of companies to the state – such as the obligation to pay taxes – often fail to be honoured. Business people are vulnerable to extortion from organised crime, and officials with authority over business are often corrupt. Conditions like these are far worse than, and often are present alongside, the extreme competitive pressures that operate in western economies. Are they so bad that they excuse businesses from paying taxes or presenting accurate accounts or resorting to legal means of protection from crime? Before we jump to the conclusion that in these circumstances anything goes, we need to ask why it isn't just as plausible, or more plausible, to claim that in these circumstances it is urgent for the missing institutions to be put in place. Joining the lawlessness seems no more justifiable than introducing mechanisms to control it.

The conclusion to which we are heading is that competition and the risk of bankruptcy do not by themselves provide excusing conditions from moral obligations of business normally reflected in law. A corollary is that lobbying to eliminate the relevant legal constraints may be wrong. It is wrong if institutions already make allowance for what makes business life hard. Another way of putting the conclusion is by saying that business competition is not enough like war to provide the sort of exemption from moral requirements that war may seem to provide. The local lawlessness of some business environments is more like war, but it is disputable that even then what businesses should do is join the fray and abandon morality.

What about genuine wars and undoubted threats to survival? Do these really let people off the hook morally? Hobbes's understanding of the relation between threats to survival and moral obligation makes it incoherent to suppose that one is ever obliged by morality – or anything else – to give up one's life.[21] So Hobbes's theory lends itself to an anti-Utopian business ethics, one that denies that morality can reasonably ask a business to do something that will make it go under. But Hobbes's theory may be too extreme to serve as a plausible basis even for an anti-Utopian business ethics. One does not have to be Utopian to think that there are some kinds of life so intolerable that it would be better or necessary to end one's life, or fight to the death, to avoid them. And here 'better' can mean 'morally better' and 'necessary' can mean 'morally necessary'. Hobbes's theory excludes the possibility of moral compulsion for suicide, for war, even for a life-risking pregnancy, and it excludes the possibility of moral rules for doing life-risking things. Above all, it excludes the possibility of rules for conducting a just war. War is altogether outside the scope of morality, according to Hobbes, and takes away the conditions for an effective morality. But this exclusion is highly questionable. Just wars are intelligible, and not just as theoretical possibilities. There are examples of them in history, even recent history. Their hallmarks are their being waged against aggressive, unjust regimes and the repudiation of excessive force by those who fight against those aggressive regimes.

The Deep Problem in Business Ethics

No ground for the thought that business reasons can override moral reasons has yet emerged. We have seen a basis for the *impression* that business reasons can override moral reasons, namely, an analogy between a fact of business life – intense competition – and a supposed condition for exemptions from moral requirements: war. But the analogy has proved questionable, as has the supposition that even war supplies an exemption from moral requirements. Is there no support in theory, then, for the resistance of business to moralisation? Perhaps there is.

What is difficult about business is that its goals do not have obvious moral content, and so cannot straightforwardly excuse or counterbalance some of the things done to realise those goals. People are in business typically to maximise profits for themselves or shareholders, not to benefit as many people as possible. Though it is a social and (usually) public activity, business is not conducted for the *sake* of the public or for the *sake* of society, and there are influential writers who think that it is a perversion of business to heed any call to social responsibility. Even if these writers are wrong and it is not a perversion of business to be socially responsible, it is at least plausible to claim that the goals of business are independent of those of social duty, independent rather than incompatible. In other words, trying to maximise profits is neither sufficient nor necessary for the public good; it is not sufficient, since it can lead to socially divisive disparities of income. It is not necessary either, since it is at least conceivable that everyone would be better off consuming less and manufacturing less and marketing less and borrowing less, which would be incompatible with trying to maximise the profits of retailers, manufacturers, advertisers and banks. The logical independence of the goals of business from the public good does not mean that the public good cannot be significantly increased as a by-product of business activity. The point is rather that this effect is not aimed at by business people, and is often produced without being willed at all, let alone being willed because of the public good.

The dualism of practical reason

The logical independence of the goals of business people from the public good is naturally described as a special case of the tension between self-interest and morality. But this is too gross a description. Like the Friedmanite attack on corporate social responsibility and the Marxist thesis of the intrinsic immorality of capitalism, it represents the relation between morality and business as fundamentally one of antagonism, and so makes it mysterious that the public good is ever promoted even as a by-product of business activity. A better model for the relation of business to the public good can be found in one philosophical treatment – Sidgwick's – of the relation between self-interest and social duty or, in his terminology, the relation between two methods of ethics: egoistic hedonism on the one hand and universal hedonism on the other.[22] Sidgwick speaks of a dualism of practical reason, according to which action aims both at personal happiness and at the general happiness, without one aim being able to be subsumed by the other.[23] It can contribute to one's personal happiness to promote the general happiness, as it can promote profit-making to go in for corporate social responsibility. But it is not necessary for promoting one's own happiness that one always do what will promote the general happiness, and it will sometimes be in one's interest to ignore the demands of universal hedonism to satisfy egoistic hedonism. In the same way, it is implausible to say that corporate social responsibility and profit-making always harmonise as goals. It will sometimes be profitable to do what would be socially irresponsible.

Sidgwick thought that it was impossible to *demonstrate* that universal hedonism was rationally superior to egoistic hedonism; but he believed that *intuition* favoured the course of universal hedonism where there was a conflict with that of egoistic hedonism, and he believed that adjudicating between the demands of the two hedonisms was a legitimate application of an otherwise suspect intuitionist method of ethics. For our purposes Sidgwick's way of reconciling the methods of ethics is less important than his recognition of the dualism of practical reason. It may be that when the authority of moral reasons is resisted in business we have just a special case of the resistance of egoism to universalism, without this implying in the least a wholesale incompatibility. Business reasons do not *have* to point in a different direction from considerations of the public good, which is why utilitarianism is the natural framework for business ethics. But, and here we echo Sidgwick, to say that there does not have to be a conflict is not to say there can't be one or that there isn't often one or that there isn't usually one. 'Business ethics' is not an oxymoron, but it does label a dualism, and a deep one.

Identifying the anomaly

Does the dualism described in the last section constitute an anomaly? Does it prevent moral theory from applying to business? Given the dualism, there is a permanent possibility of business always pursuing private good and never pursuing public good. There is a possibility, in other words, of business always being self-interested, and of its contributing to the public good only unintentionally. This possibility is a reason for thinking that business in general – trading or manufacturing for profit – is morally inferior as an activity to activities that by definition aim at the public good, such as law, medicine, political office-holding, and law enforcement. The moral inferiority of at any rate some familiar kinds of business may even be implied by utilitarianism, if it turns out that aiming at the public good has a lot of utility the more widely it is practised and the more any one activity is dedicated to it. Moral inferiority is not of course the same as moral badness. Business may turn out merely to be low on the totem pole of utility-promoters rather than to have a lot of *disutility*. But there is a sense in which business, because of the deep dualism, is specially open to what we might call the *moral condescension* of moral theory. Even utilitarianism, which is well equipped otherwise to endow business with moral worth, requires people to produce the greatest good for the greatest number. If it is unbusinesslike to aim at this, then so much the worse for business, even if by aiming at something else it actually contributes more to the public good than activities dedicated to the public good.

In a clear sense theory has to apply to business in order to condescend to it, in order to pass the judgement on it that it is morally inferior. If that is so, and if what is necessary for anomaly is for a theory to be left speechless by a question addressed to it, then the question of whether business can be ethical is not anomalous. Perhaps business is not even anomalous in the sense that it is strange for so established and widely practised (and currently, so admired) an activity to be considered morally worse by theory than other things that are conventionally put on a par with business and connected to business, like corporate law, or management in the public sector. Perhaps it is not strange that business is regarded as inferior to these related things: after all, moral theory is not constrained to bear out *every* conventional pre-theoretical value judgement. And if it has to choose *which* pre-theoretical ideas to bear out, the idea that moral value depends on aiming at the public good seems a likely one, even if bearing it out involves condescension towards business in the sense outlined. The idea behind the moral condescension implies that it is morally better for people to occupy their time playing a role in which they do aim at the public good; and so long as there is no implication that it is morally bad or morally prohibited to do business, what is wrong with the implication?

Perhaps what is wrong with it is not that it raises its eyebrows at the moral worth of business, but that it seems to desert the people who are upright (or better) and in business at the same time. There are people (perhaps not many) who are scrupulous employers or suppliers, who would be scrupulous even if it cost them their profits or made them suffer short-term losses, and yet who are, and think of themselves as, engaged primarily in business. They do not manufacture textiles in Lawrence, Massachusetts or make shoes in Street, Somerset, in order to keep people in work or meet the expectations of retailers or other manufacturers. Rather they behave as scrupulous employers and suppliers in the course of manufacturing textiles or shoes. And they might think it perverse to go on manufacturing anything if there were no demand for it (regardless of their scruples as employers). These people are not typical business people. But they do not desert the role of business people in being scrupulous. Rather they show in practice that it is possible to make a seamless connection between being ethical in a clear sense – subordinating profit to the good of people within the business – and being in business. Ethical business along these lines is not business turned over to the public good – the scruples are primarily reserved for those with a connection to the business – but it is a form of activity that is surely more creditable morally than, for example, routine real estate conveyancing, however much public good the practice of law and the legal institution of property normally promotes.

There is a moral reason, then, for moral theory to temper a condescension towards business with sensitivity to the variety of practice that the role makes room for. Aaron Feuerstein, the textile manufacturer who heroically kept the whole staff of Malden Mills on the payroll while trying to restart the business after a devastating factory fire, did what he did for the business as much as for people who were long-serving employees. In his way of doing business those things did not come apart. And although what he did looked extremely generous to the employees who benefited, as well as to senior management in his firm; although it was motivated partly by his strongly devout Judaism, the effect of it all was widely regarded as an unusual business turnaround, rather than something that had been transformed by morals into a piece of unadulterated altruism. The category of business is roomy enough to accommodate even the morally admirable turnaround as a case of successful business. The dualism of practical reason – the distinction between pursuing the good of the firm and pursuing the general good – does not rule out this fusion of business and ethics in practice, and a condescension of moral theory based upon the dualism should not rule it out either. Although the Feuerstein case does not square the circle and show that business is sometimes wholly altruistic, that is, although it does nothing to diminish the dualism, it shows that there is business that is not always morally inferior to, say, law, just because law aims at the public good. On the contrary, the conduct of business can outshine the routine practice of law, as it does whenever an example like that of Malden Mills is set.

We are now in a position to say what form the anomaly for standard moral theories may take in relation to business. It may take the form of Aaron Feuerstein, the morally admirable owner of Malden Mills, who, despite the dualism of practical reason, manages to effect a fusion in his business practice between what a generous person would do and what serves the cause of business survival. Somehow it is hard for moral theory to give this fusion its due at the same time as it is morally condescending to business. Since I have argued that the moral condescension is morally in order, I do not see how theory, in the form of Kantianism or utilitarianism, can be got off the hook. Kantianism may be unable to grant moral worth to an action that is done even partly for business reasons. And utilitarianism, as we saw above, seems to imply that any performer of a business role starts off at a disadvantage in the order of moral merit, because other roles, unlike the business role, do aim at the public good. This means that the average performer of those other roles – the average lawyer or doctor – is more likely to do better morally than the average business person. Although Feuerstein's actions will no doubt get greater moral credit than those of an average lawyer or doctor, even from utlitarianism, they may still not get enough credit, for Feuerstein will always be dragged down more than he should be by the fact that he is a businessman and that the business does not aim at the general good.

It does not solve this problem to say that Aaron Feuerstein's actions are supererogatory and therefore raise the moral value of his business practice to a level at which moral condescension is out of order. For it is not as if Aaron Feuerstein comes by his business practice to be merely on a par with the moderately scrupulous politician or policeman. His practice makes him *more* admirable than those scrupulous occupants of morally superior roles. He does more good than they do in a setting in which it is more difficult to do that much good. In other words, he shows that there is a way of filling the business role that turns on its head the usual valuations of acting in a business role relative to acting in other roles. He turns justified moral condescension into justified moral admiration. The crucial point is that he does this not by rising above the role of business, but by making that role rise with him. If it were merely rising above the role – doing more than the role required morally – despite being in business, there would be no anomaly.

So it may not be the very idea of business ethics that is anomalous, but getting over the dualism of practical reason while remaining in a business role. Feuerstein shows that the business role allows for overcoming the dualism – the gap between what serves the firm's interest and what helps people in general – but because Feuerstein's way of playing the business role is unlikely to be widely imitated, utilitarianism may not be able to revalue upwards the moral potential of the business role. It may give Feuerstein credit, but not *qua* businessman. So it fails to distinguish the value of of rising above the role from the value of making the role rise with one. Virtue theory could conceivably do better, but probably it would supply reasons, as utilitarianism does, for not going into business at all. That is, it might supply reasons for entering a profession in which one were much less likely than in business to be torn between what it requires and what ethics requires. In short, there might be better reasons in theory for not going into business than for imitating Feuerstein's example within business.

Although the Feuersteins of the business world strike me as exotic and theoretically interesting, the niche in which they operate is reasonably humdrum. It is the niche where personal morality is able to determine the character of role morality because of the convergence of the role of business person with family member or the convergence of a firm with a person. If the moral possibilities of personal or family business are easily missed, that may be because in life, as in the academic literature, people who think of business think of big business. This is the cinematic end of commercial activity, but not, perhaps, its moral frontier.

4

Politics, Power and Partisanship

Wielding political power is another activity that is often claimed to be out of the reach of ordinary morality. Like businessmen, politicians sometimes regard moralising about what they do as naïve and Utopian; while the public, looking at the standards of MPs or Congressmen from the outside, no more expect upright behaviour from members of legislatures than from members of stock exchanges. There is an important disanalogy, however. We have agreed that business, though it is conducted in public and though it often benefits the public, is not carried on for the sake of the public. Politics, on the other hand, democratic politics most conspicuously, *is* supposed to do the rest of us good, and not merely incidentally. Politicians are supposed to *aim* at the public good, with their own personal interests being served, if at all, only as a by-product of serving the public interest. This means, at least in theory, that when things go wrong in politics, or when wrong is done by politicians, it can be in a good cause. A related point can be made about the *role* of politician. Carrying out this role can provide moral opportunities and reflect well on a person who is something of a moral failure in his private life. The careerist Cabinet Minister who never finds time for his wife and family and who is economical with the truth in his dealings with the tax authorities can for all that be an excellent representative, exerting influence skilfully on behalf of needy and helpless constituents. Or the politician can introduce legislation that helps a much wider public: not only all of the people of East Finchley or a certain congressional district in California, but all of the blind people in Britain, or all of the widows of military men in the United States.

The scope for benefiting a wide public is probably greatest in national legislatures. But national legislatures are places where narrower interests are guaranteed representation and where responsibilities to different constituencies can conflict. They are also places where legislators who are members of the government have to reckon with the weight of reasons of state in addition to the weight of other considerations about the public interest. These facts of political life raise at least two moral questions that are hard for moral theory to answer. First, how can it be morally right to represent the interests of a relatively small constituency or one's party when these are known to be narrower and sometimes in conflict with the national interest or the interest of humanity? If politics is supposed to represent the public interest, doesn't the wider public interest always take precedence over the narrower? This is like asking how a genuine business *ethics* can permit a business interest to trump the public interest. I broach this question at the end of the chapter. Second, how far can reasons of state justify actions such as murder, torture, deception, misinformation and the use of force that, in private life, would be prohibited by morality? Is there a special morality that governs the use of government power, so that the politician or the prince does something wrong if he allows reasons of ordinary morality to outweigh reasons of state; or is there only a single morality which political power gives the illusion of immunity from? This question is broadly analogous to asking whether in business, as opposed to private life, a ruthless gambler's morality can take the place of ordinary morality.

The two questions before us can be interpreted as claims that ordinary morality, and a moral theory incorporating that morality, do not apply. Moral theory no more easily justifies action in the service of a narrow interest group, when more would benefit if a wider interest group were helped, than it easily justifies acting in one's self-interest when wider interests are at stake. Again, moral theory does not easily justify the double standards that the segregation of political from ordinary morality suggests. It does not easily justify this, any more than it easily justifies the segregation of morality in business practice from ordinary morality. As will emerge, the treatment of these questions about politics is prey to the same tensions as the treatment of questions in business. There is a strong temptation to reduce the gap between 'ought' and 'is' and abandon the normativity of morals, as when one attempts to use theory to rationalise well-intentioned political behaviour that would normally be wrong; there is a strong and contrary temptation to insist that wrong is wrong, so that even wrong that is done exceptionally and reluctantly and to protect the public shouldn't have been done. Despite the parallels, I shall suggest that the tensions of applying moral theory to politics are actually less strong than the tensions of applying theory to business.

Political Morality: the Moral Risks of Power for the Public Good

The idea that politics operates by different rules from those of ordinary morality is not just put about by cynics, but by moralists impressed by the harshness of life at the top, and by the central place of power in political life. It has long been held that politicians in general and heads of state in particular need to be tough, and need to be able to use their power to the full when necessary: it may be too much to expect people to be tough *and* morally painstaking. In difficult times scrupulousness can look like indecision and generosity like weakness, and these unwanted appearances can reduce a political leader's authority and so his effectiveness in carrying out any policy, even one that is morally admirable. In order to exercise without undercutting their power rulers are advised by writers such as Hobbes and Machiavelli to show that they are willing to resort to force. Even democratic politicians are regularly urged by the newspapers to impose their will in the interest of demonstrating leadership. The common theme of these suggestions is that political power cannot quietly lie in reserve, but must be shown and exercised if it is not to ebb away. The need to keep using power, the moral risks of unleashing it at all and of using it ineffectively – these things already stake out a distinctive territory for political morality.

Not that power is peculiar to politics. Private life can involve the exercise of power or resistance to the exercise of power, but a power structure is not essential, and if a marriage or a family only stays together because one person is weaker than another, who exploits that advantage, something has gone badly wrong: positive sentiment and ties of common interest should do most of the work of keeping these associations intact. By contrast, there is nothing necessarily wrong with a country or state that would break up in the absence of all its coercive mechanisms. That sort of power structure, which makes the few disproportionately strong, even if only for a short term of office, does not necessarily taint nations or large associations of other kinds. Of course, there are conditions that have to be met for the submission and the authority or power it sustains to be legitimate; but the submission of the many to the few is not illegitimate in itself, and if what brings it about is fair elections, and if it is constrained by just constitutional arrangements, the submission is not illegitimate at all.

The fact that the powers of those who govern are inflated far beyond their individual powers by the submission or compliance of the many, and the fact that these powers carry distinctive risks – these facts by themselves suggest that the problems of political morality will differ from those of, for instance, personal morality. Indeed, isn't political morality *so* distinctive that it comes apart entirely from personal morality? Might not political morality even involve a sort of inversion of the values of personal life, as Machiavelli claimed, so that in order to function effectively in public office the honourable private citizen has to *unlearn* his morality?

The moral demands of public emergencies

The idea that the norms of personal morality go into abeyance in politics has some justification. Whatever the form of government, the effects of public policy are often unpredictable, hard to reverse, and likely to occasion dispute even when they are benign. This means that in matters of collective life things can very easily go badly. Again, they can quickly go from bad to worse. These facts register institutionally in more than one way. Legislative or spending decisions are often exposed to formal review by oversight bodies and criticism and questioning by an established political opposition. These institutions may be used to embarrass a government but they can also save it from wasting money or passing unworkable laws, thereby preventing one sort of misfortune public policy is prey to. The relevant institutions work by putting heads together and producing second thoughts about government proposals. When all goes well, the main pitfalls of proposed policies are anticipated, and avoided by appropriate recasting. In this way fallible governments become more equal to the complexity of the problems they face.

Other institutions exist to cope with types of public emergency that collective experience has shown to be severe and not entirely preventable. Thus there are established, politically controlled bodies to deal with military invasion, with disease, with threats from the extremes of weather to food production and shelter, and with the breakdown of the financial system. Some of these calamities result from acts of God, others from large-scale imprudence or aggression. In the case of those that are humanly produced, institutions like armies and banking authorities often know where the threats are likely to come from, and take steps to discourage the relevant agents. But to deal with the actions of dangerous people across the board, other measures and institutions, perhaps less public and more questionable, may also have to be contemplated. Thus, if it is a moral requirement on governments that they be ready for terrorism or that they act to contain aggressive regimes abroad, it may also be a moral requirement that governments be ready to carry out assassinations or acts of sabotage, if there is reason to believe that the danger can be met in no other way. Action that might seem unthinkable to individual agents in danger may have to be considered seriously by the authorities if thousands are at risk.

The need in ordinary political life to prepare for or prevent emergency, or to respond to it when it has already occurred, seems to require those in government to be *ready* at all times to put scruples aside, even if circumstances never force them to act. But isn't this readiness itself a kind of unscrupulousness? If things do not go badly, for example there is no terrorist bombing to prevent by drastic means, isn't the general moral character of a government that is prepared to use those means already that of an agent who is ruthless and hard? And isn't such a government morally worse than a government that is unprepared just *because* it has scruples, which it has to use precious time to put aside? After all, an armed robber who is never disturbed and never has to draw his weapon but who would not have hesitated to do so is, intuitively, worse than the robber who hates violence, who avoids going out armed for that reason, but who is more vulnerable when he is detected and needs to escape. Isn't the ruthless, undisturbed robber like the tough government that never has to act and the government with scruples like the vulnerable, non-violent robber who reluctantly beats up a householder to get away before the police come? Although the analogy has some intuitive appeal, it leaves out too much context. If what faces a government is an emergency, and if pre-emptive violence (for example, killing terrorists before they plant a powerful bomb in a city centre), is for protecting the public rather than getting away with a robbery, surely what we have in the ready government is not ruthlessness in carrying out evil, but determination in preventing a worse evil by the only means that will be effective. It is unclear how readiness to carry out such action points to a defect of character. To say this is not to deny that when the policy is implemented people are killed, that it is better to prevent terrorism without loss of life than to do so by killing, and that the policy of taking pre-emptive action against terrorists is morally very risky, depending as it does on very accurate information about the identities and intentions of people who may not even have a criminal record.[1]

If there is evil at all in acting pre-emptively to protect the public good, it may be a lesser evil than doing nothing, and it need not reflect badly on the character of the authorities who are responsible. In this respect the excusing power of the public emergency in politics is far greater than the excusing power of hostile competition in business. Emergencies and competition each make life difficult for the relevant corporate agent – a government or a business – but only the emergency fully excuses taking action that is normally wrong, because the public good and probably many lives are at stake. And the fact that emergencies are exceptional events also matters. When competition is urged as an excusing background condition for wrongdoing or as a condition that exempts business from the normal requirements of morality in the first place, one of the factors that makes the position hard to accept is that it affords such a sweeping exemption or excuse. If severe competition always allows corners to be cut morally, then it may license cutting corners all the time, since severe competition is intelligible as a pervasive background condition of business. In the case of politics the only thing that is permissible all the time, according to the account so far sketched, is a readiness to do whatever is necessary to deal with emergency. This is hardly a permissive permission. On the contrary, it is compatible with glossing 'doing whatever is necessary' as 'doing the least evil that can reasonably be believed to be effective'.

Dirty Hands

I have spoken of public emergencies as 'excusing conditions' in politics. Does this terminology fit? Only wrongdoing can be excused, and perhaps killing-to-meet-a-public-emergency is not wrong, even if killing normally is. Similarly for other things that are normally wrong and that might be done by governments in the belief that they are ways out of a public emergency. Part of what is in question here is whether the feeling of having 'dirty hands' in politics is well grounded when the dirty deed is done in a good cause and careful deliberation fails to disclose a more acceptable alternative. When a political leader looks back and feels tainted by an act of public deception, or by a decision to have a terrorist assassinated, or by a campaign to put down an insurrection at the cost of many lives, does the fact that deception, assassination and bloodletting are normally to be avoided show that the leader is *right* to feel tainted?

Different moral theories answer this question in different ways. Utilitarianism denies that that there are any types of action that are intrinsically wrong, that is, wrong regardless of their consequences; and so it leaves open the possibility that the consequences can make it right to break a moral rule. When this possibility is realised utilitarianism says that no wrong is done and no real dirt is on any one's hands. The hands may *feel* dirty – guilt may be experienced by those who break any moral rule, even one that there is utilitarian justification for breaking – but the guilt is baseless, according to utilitarianism. Again according to utilitarianism, it may be useful for guilt to be felt, for if it never were it would be psychologically easy to break moral rules, which would be a source of disutility. It may also be understandable for guilt to be felt: the loyalty to the rule one has broken may die hard. But there is not necessarily any moral ground for feeling it, and nothing wrong with someone who realises as much and casts off the guilt.

At first sight, utilitarianism looks cavalier in its treatment of dirty hands,[2] even when what has dirtied them is an action with the best consequences in the circumstances. Utilitarianism seems to deal counterintuitively with the associated feelings of guilt, denying that feelings of guilt are necessary for a good character, and denying that guilt should attend the violation of mere rules of thumb. Intuitively, to feel one has dirty hands *is* evidence of good character – a character that shrinks from wrongdoing – and, again intuitively, moral rules are more than rules of thumb. Intuitively, moral rules prohibit what they prohibit categorically and feelings of guilt are in order when the rules are broken because of their categorical content, not because of the good effects of feeling guilty. Moral character depends on the feelings one has about one's actions, and utilitarianism says that the consequences determine what feelings are appropriate, not the content of the rules. But someone who feels guilt only on finding out the consequences of an act of torture or assassination – who does not react to the very idea of an act of his being an act of torture or assassination, is, again intuitively, either drained of moral character altogether or has a character inferior to that of the agent with automatic guilt feelings.

Non-utilitarian moral theories are able to accommodate intuitions about character, but they may do less well at accommodating intuitions about what is permissible in times of emergency. This is because they tend to represent moral requirements as exceptionless, and wrong or evil as unquantifiable. The idea of one evil being bigger than another, which utilitarianism captures by reference to the relative preferability of different states of affairs in the view of different numbers of rational choosers, is at best reflected in arguments about certain prohibitions or precepts being able to be ranked in order of priority. These rankings are sometimes implausible or controversial – as when truth-telling is supposed to trump life-saving – and they may imply that the more high-order the prohibition that appears to be threatened in an emergency, the more urgent it is to abide by the prohibition and take the consequences, even if the consequences are disastrous.

Here as elsewhere in moral philosophy utilitarianism seems to capture part of the truth, and its competition seems to capture another part.

Utilitarianism captures the truth that dirty hands are sometimes morally necessary, but falters in dealing with the truth that the associated guilt feelings always have a ground, even if acting in accordance with the guilt feelings is not justified overall. Non-utilitarian theories capture the truth that the feelings associated with dirty hands are often well grounded, while denying the truth that the actions that occasion those feelings are sometimes morally necessary. What is common ground between the two theories, however, is the recognition that (1) feelings of dirty hands exist; (2) the feelings are explicable; (3) they are associated with people who take the prohibitions and prescriptions of morality seriously; and (4) everyone *ought* to take the prohibitions and prescriptions of morality seriously. I am not sure that more than this common ground, more even than a suitable treatment of (2), is required to make moral sense of the feeling of dirty hands. Dirty hands need not be a theoretical blindspot, even for utilitarianism.

To see this, it is important to notice that utilitarian and non-utilitarian theories alike can make sense of the feeling of dirty hands as a by-product of practical deliberation that involves moral conflict. The conflict is between the dictates of welfare in the face of emergency and the dictates of morality in normal times. Welfare considerations in the face of emergency often require actions that moral rules normally prohibit or prohibit full stop. A Kantian theory does not deny that welfare considerations can make an unsavoury action *appear* necessary. Kant's own theory has elaborate claims about moral motivation to explain why happiness or welfare seems to determine what is right, namely that desire and inclination, not just self-regarding desire and inclination, but also sympathy and philanthropy, are important motivating factors in human action in general, and ineradicable even when one has limited their influence enough to let the messages of pure practical reason get through. When an agent decides on the basis of considerations about happiness that something prohibited by a categorical imperative must be done, that decision is not, then, inexplicable according to Kant. It is not even unusual, since it is part of what is radically wrong with human beings that they often subordinate what morality requires to other things. But it is also not right. So if the agent acts on welfare considerations in preference to a categorical imperative, he *has* dirty hands, whether or not he feels he has.

Utilitarianism, for its part, can also make sense of a dirty or dirty-seeming action as the result of a moral conflict in the course of practical deliberation. But, and now contrary to Walzer, the utilitarian treatment can justify the feelings associated with dirty hands. It is open to utilitarianism to say that the following happens in the course of deliberation, for example over whether by torturing or killing a couple of terrorists ten thousand lives can be saved. The consequences of killing or torturing are considered and found frightful; the consequences of letting an emergency take its course when it could be prevented by killing or torturing are found worse still; so the torture and killing are carried out. What justifies feelings of dirty hands after the unsavoury action has been carried out is exactly what justified keeping the rule against killing or torturing while deliberation was taking place. In short, feelings of dirty hands are justified by whatever justified keeping one's hands clean in the first place: the rule against killing, the rule against torturing, and the consequentialist justification for those rules in turn. So long as the action that occasions the feeling of dirty hands issues from moral conflict of this kind, there is always a ground for the feeling even if it is concluded that there is more utility in doing the dirty thing. A utilitarianism along these lines is not cavalier with feelings of dirty hands. It says that there is a piece of reasoning that counts against what was done, not just a baseless feeling that makes the action unpleasant in retrospect. But it also says that the force of that piece of reasoning can be outweighed.

Now it may be true that moral conflict is not registered in the conclusion of a piece of utilitarian practical deliberation. The conclusion may not be qualified by an 'all things considered' or 'one is reluctantly forced to concede that' or 'unfortunately'. But that does not mean that it is arrived at in the same way as the conclusion of a piece of practical reasoning in which reasons against doing what is decided upon all along seem weak or far-fetched. An agent's conclusion may be unqualified and yet issue from heartsearching. Thus it may issue from a long period of deliberation by a single agent, who feels torn, or it may come from a committee divided down the middle that reaches a judgement by a tie-break or the narrowest of majorities. The fact that the division is not alluded to in the conclusion reached by the committee does not mean that division does not affect the decision. Utilitarianism can reach the unqualified conclusion and yet do so with scruples. It is not clear to me that more than this is required to take the sting out of dirty hands.

Public Morality, Private Morality and Moral Schizophrenia

I have said that dirty hands need not constitute a theoretical blind spot, since the feeling of dirty hands can stand to reason, even in utilitarianism. The feeling can be justified *and* the justification be outweighed by the justification for killing or torturing or deceiving in the face of an emergency. But even if there is no theoretical problem with giving weight in practical reasoning to the grounds for feelings of dirty hands, perhaps there is a theoretical problem elsewhere, namely in making sense of how a public person can be justified in killing a terrorist and a private person not be justified, when private and public person are one and the same. Let us change the example we are considering and imagine that a policeman has collected legally inadmissible evidence showing beyond doubt that a certain suspect is planning a terrorist outrage, and that if the policeman arrested the terrorist then and there the case against the terrorist would fail in court, and the terrorist would walk free not only to make more bombs but also make some credible and (to the police) damaging claims of wrongful detention or harassment. The policeman decides to take matters into his own hands when off duty, ambushes the terrorist and kills him, as it happens at the very moment the terrorist was equipped with a bomb he was about to plant. It is wrong for policemen to take the law into their own hands, but presumably permissible for them to take drastic action against a terrorist about to commit a terrorist atrocity. If the terrorist's intentions were known at the time of the ambush, the vigilante policeman could have put on his policeman's hat and have been morally justified; but he guns down the terrorist not knowing his intentions and so falls foul of the excellent reasons for not tolerating vigilantes.

There is a sort of tragic irony about the killing in our example, but no real paradox. It is true that the same person is both vigilante and policeman, and that what the vigilante does is wrong while the same act done by a policeman with the relevant knowledge would probably have been permissible. But given the construction of the case, the killing was not done with the right knowledge or the right intentions to be permissible. The vigilante-policeman's justification for taking the drastic action *then* was not the excusing one that otherwise the terrorist would have successfully planted a bomb, but rather that the public good would be served by anyone's putting the terrorist out of action at the earliest opportunity. This is the justification that, outside the context of the emergency of the terrorist's going out to plant the bomb, is outweighed by considerations about the wrongness of vigilante behaviour – behaviour in which, from a certain point of view, the terrorist himself indulges.

A more likely source of paradox is the following. As a ruler or member of a government, an individual must always be ready to authorise killing or torture if the threat to public safety is big enough; but in private life the very same person should be very averse to doing anything of the kind and should probably show reluctance to take up public office if there is any likelihood of its involving dirty deeds. Yet public office should not – morally should not – be shirked by good people who are competent to carry it out: the reason is that the good that public office is supposed to promote or protect is bigger than the individual good. So the good private individual who is competent to manage public affairs should both avoid and not avoid political office. Here, too, the paradox is more apparent than real, because it is part of politics not only to carry out the duties of office, but to arrange things so that, in carrying them out, it is hard or harder to dirty one's hands. This may mean arranging for more and more political action to be done in public; or it may mean working for the adoption throughout public life of the rules of procedural justice, so that fewer of the people who become public dangers and against whom dirty-handed action is taken, need to resort to clandestine or criminal or vigilante action themselves. In short, someone who has a horror of dirty hands in politics may have more of an obligation to adopt political means to eradicate underhand practice than to avoid politics.

Even if the demands of private and public morality do not have to pull against one another to the point of making the individual politician disintegrate, aren't the two spheres – that of private and public morality – uncomfortably separate, so that the agent disappears into his role and becomes subject to its morality when carrying out the duties of office, and becomes himself and takes on the different constraints of personal morality at other times? Yes and no. Occupying political office does require an individual agent to identify with the public interest, or at least the interest of a section of a public, but it can be a decision in private life to try to acquire political office with its responsibilities, and obtaining that office may depend on the further personal decisions of other people, often thousands of other people, when the way one obtains office is through election. If one acquires office after standing for it, it is a personal obligation to shoulder its obligations, and to face the tensions with other personal obligations that the duties of office may bring with them. The decisions of private individuals that result in an office being held, as well as the purposes of the office itself, create the split moral personality of politicians, but just because the acts that result in office often derive from the decisions of a private individual made *as* private citizen, the appearance of split personality is all it is. Becoming subject to political morality is not a matter of dropping one's status as an individual or one's personality; it is more a matter of choosing to invest one's personality in a certain activity. So the responsibility of being a politician is often clearly personal. The exception to this rule may be the ruler-politician who has the role thrust upon him by heredity.

The problem of specifying a basis for political morality: Machiavelli and Hobbes

Even if an individual's political responsibilities are traceable to a decision governed by his personal morality, so that public and private morality do not entirely come apart, it is a non-trivial task of moral theory to rationalise the permissibility of dirty deeds done in political office beyond saying that they promote the public good. Machiavelli appears to hold that the rationale for these acts may lie in defining features of effective political office itself. Effective political office, by definition, requires power, including power in the form of popular support and submission. So the greatest misuse of office must be that which reduces power or threatens to eliminate power, as the political acts of the scrupulous can do. This is political office self-defeatingly co-operating in making itself redundant. On the other hand, ruthless deeds tend to preserve or increase power; so they are appropriate to political office. The problem with this position is that it does not offer a moral basis for the concentration of power in holders of political office. If the reason political office-holders ought to have power is that political power makes it easier to maximise the public happiness, then, since the costs of ruthlessness in human misery and fear may also be very high, perhaps power should be privatised and diffused, that is, limited to the resources an individual can freely acquire and defend by individual effort.

Hobbes has an argument for this last possibility being the worst option of all. According to him, the state of affairs in which each person is free to acquire what he will and keep what he can is a war in which no one can be blamed for being personally bloodthirsty or ruthlessly acquisitive if they sincerely think that otherwise they will risk death or loss of the means of secure life. For Hobbes the concentration of power in a sovereign authority is a better means of obtaining security and well-being than the pursuit by each of safety and well-being in conditions of perfect freedom. Just as the institution of a sovereign authority with unlimited power is a better bet for individuals than individual freedom, so the exercise of that power – even in a dirty-handed way – is a lesser evil than epidemic ruthlessness on the part of individuals.

Like Machiavelli, Hobbes believes that the sovereign authority can properly act very roughly both domestically and with respect to other governments in the interest of maintaining security and promoting well-being. The basis for this proper ruthlessness is the fact that with respect to both subjects and other governments the sovereign is a free agent, and must remain so in order to do his job. His outward behaviour is for his own judgement to determine. It is different for inward acts of will, which are bound by morality. The basis for being able to adjust one's will but not necessarily one's actions to moral requirements is the retention of what Hobbes calls the 'right of nature': the right of judging when an action conduces to one's safety and when it doesn't. Every private individual has this right; every *citizen*, on the other hand, can be understood to have transferred it to the government that is entrusted with the citizen's security. The sovereign is not a citizen. He *represents* citizens, according to Hobbes, and is *authorized* by citizens in whatever way will secure the peace; he *personifies* the union of citizens; but he does not contract with citizens to do this. On the contrary, he is an external beneficiary of a contract citizens made among themselves in a pre-political state. He benefits by the agreement of the many to obey him, and in return for this gift of submission he is expected to keep the peace among them through legal and other institutions.[3]

The sovereign may be a single human being; or the sovereign may be a body of human beings, a council or a parliament. The sovereign is an agent for the parties to the social contract, but not one who is told how to act by those he is agent for. He makes laws but is not subject to them. If he is a single human being with the irregular passions of a human being, the sovereign may be tempted to use his unlimited power for his own enrichment and aggrandisement. There is nothing strictly wrong with his doing so, if he reasonably believes that these are means of making him a better keeper of the general peace. But, Hobbes says,[4] it is imprudent to do so. The sovereign who impoverishes his subjects, or takes away so much of their means as to make them dependent, also disempowers himself in the person of the state. Since it is only by being able to channel the actions of obedient citizens in the direction required by his goal of peace that he has power at all, the sovereign does better to organise the state so that his subjects are robust and able to produce for themselves. If he fails to do so, and the citizens become so insecure that they would have as good chances of survival submitting to the sovereign as not submitting, then the sovereign has failed to secure peace, the citizens are *de facto* free and no longer subjects, and the sovereign's powers reduce to that of a single human being – only one that is likely to be a target of the disappointed rabble.

To survive not only in office but even bodily once the submission of the many has been given, the sovereign must identify in a particularly thoroughgoing way with the union of the many. He must do what will keep the union intact, and ignore the passions of the person he is biologically. To carry out this mission the individual person of the sovereign must become self-effacing, and act instead as a disinterested evaluator of the best means of keeping each subject permanently out of the state of war. The sovereign will be less successful in this task if it is a group than if it is an individual, for when many members of a council have the right to judge about the collective welfare, the result is a version of the war of all against all albeit in miniature. The more that power is concentrated the better, then. Not that a sovereign should ignore advice: he should listen to it, especially when it comes out of the vellum-covered text of *Leviathan*; what he cannot afford to do is give executive power to the many who aid in deliberation. Executive power must rest with him alone.

Hobbes's account of the relation between political morality and private morality is very rich, since it has the resources to connect political morality with far more than the idea of power. It connects political morality not just with ordinary personal moral requirements – what Hobbes calls 'the laws of nature' – but also with collective and public acts of authorisation, and relations of representation and personification between the individual sovereign and the many or the sovereign council and the many. According to Hobbes, as according to any account that can cover the basis of political morality in a democracy, the prerogatives of political office that lead to dirty hands are justified partly by the responsibilities of office-holders to those they represent. And the standpoint from which people who hold office or have authority are supposed to act is from some sort of identification with the public, so that the one holding office identifies his or her interest from the point of view of the many or the union of the many, rather than from the self-interest of the private person. Unfortunately, Hobbes's own distinctive variations on themes of authorisation and personification, and his distinctive organisation of the requirements of morality under a supreme requirement of seeking security, are all pretty disputable. Hobbesian representation is mainly a device for diverting responsibility for the sovereign's actions to the parties to the contract, so that they cannot complain of iniquity at another's hands. The idea of personification, though it captures the imagination, is none too clear. As for organising the laws of nature, including the requirement of being just, under a supreme requirement of seeking peace, which justice serves only as a means, rather than being a free-standing moral goal – it has the effect of legislating away the question of whether there is any moral necessity to keeping a peace, when the peace looks unjust in a pre-theoretical, non-Hobbesian sense.

Hampshire's Anti-theory of Political Morality

A general account of political morality which, unlike Hobbes's, is initially attractive *and* faces up to the problem of dirty hands has been sketched by Stuart Hampshire.[5] Hampshire's account concedes quite a lot to Machiavelli, for it agrees that innocence and a dedication to innocence[6] can be a liability in a political role.[7] Hampshire's account also allows for the possibility that in some conflicts in political deliberation, a sufficiently great gain in welfare may sometimes justify an injustice,[8] if the injustice is not very big. On the other hand, Hampshire argues for the indispensability of what he calls 'procedural justice': the justice of hearing and adjudicating fairly between conflicting claims. He even identifies disrespect for procedural justice or a willingness to respond violently or by conquest to its judgements as evil.[9] So the account both supports the idea that justice is the supreme virtue and concedes that in politics it is not always possible to do the virtuous thing.

Hampshire is able to steer a middle course between absolutism and utilitarianism by putting at the centre of his account two theses: that the primary good can consist of the prevention of great evil[10] and that political choice can sometimes best be described, and in dirty-hands cases is naturally described, as choosing the lesser evil.[11] These theses are made central in the (in my view correct) belief that it is easier to be definite and uncontroversial about evil than about the good.[12] Thus, as Hampshire points out, the aim of destroying life or pursuing a policy of domination is widely agreed to be evil; so is praise for violence and contempt for argument and persuasion; so is a ready tolerance for, or a willingness to glorify, misery and pain. People differ far more over the good. There are also, Hampshire says, clear examples of great evils from the twentieth century that are particularly important to moral thought, and that illustrate the indispensable guidance given to moral thought by history: the examples of Nazi tyranny and conquest in the 1930s and 1940s, and the Russian Revolution.[13]

The thesis about preventing great evils and choosing lesser ones is combined with certain theses about the claims that can fairly be made on those in political power:

> What can reasonably be demanded of those who incur the responsibility of political power? The first demand is that they should recognise the weight of their particular responsibility in disposing of the lives of others. The second is that they should be clear-headed, and not divided in mind, about their obligations to protect the reasonable interests of their

innocent fellow citizens; this is the Machiavellian thesis. The third demand is that they should at all times be prepared for the occurrence of an uncontrolled conflict in duties in situations which seem to preclude the possibility of a decent outcome, and in which all lines of action seem dishonourable and blameworthy. This is the point at which the contrast between innocence and experience becomes indispensable in ethics. . . . A person of experience has come to expect that his usual choice will be the lesser of two or more evils.[14]

These demands are similar in effect to a requirement that the politically powerful identify with the interests of the public, and make best use of their experience in trying to serve the public. According to the passage, the fact that someone is powerful, so that others are vulnerable to the effects of that power, by itself carries the obligation to be careful in exercising power. Further conditions do not have to be met. So, for example, people are obliged to be careful in using their power even when not elected by those who are vulnerable to uses of it, or even when not their chosen representative. Again, experience alone ought to make powerful people expect that some of the choices they will face will be choices between evils. They fail in their duty in a political role if the fact that they are going to be faced by such choices catches them by surprise.

Hampshire's position has something, perhaps a lot, in common with utilitarianism, because choosing the lesser of two evils often means doing what will produce less misery or take away less from the welfare of those whom the politician represents. Again, some of the hallmarks of evil that Hampshire recognises – loss of life, misery etc. – have kinds of disvalue utilitarianism easily accommodates. But the account is *non-utilitarian* in at least three ways. First, it recognises that justice is distinct from welfare, and it refuses a subsumption of welfare by justice. Second, it insists on the moral importance of facts, such as facts in the personal history or cultural history of agents that utilitarianism requires be disregarded. Thus customs that there might be utilitarian objections to, because they involve the infliction of pain, appear from the perspective of Hampshire's account to be legitimate, because ways of life preserve identity and have a worth conferred by history,[15] however irrational they may seem. Hampshire's third departure from utilitarianism consists of denying that rationality is the main intellectual tool or the only respectable intellectual tool in the resolution of particular conflicts. Sometimes a practical option is decided against, not for reasons that can be articulated, but because it registers through a non-rational perceptual faculty.[16]

Although it is an attractive account that differs from more standard theories, it passes over some natural questions in silence. First, how stable is the distinction between questions of substantive justice and questions of procedural justice? Aren't some people's claims to procedural justice compromised by their repudiation of its standards, or by the heinousness of their crimes? Do the demands on holders of political power themselves have a basis that constrains their actions when faced with unpalatable courses of action? Are the inarticulate, the extremely unpopular and the unreasonable as well served by the likely embodiments of procedural justice as the articulate, the reasonable and the moderate, who are less likely to need procedural justice? Finally, how can Hampshire acknowledge the separate claims of justice and utilitarianism without facing up to the conflicts those claims famously generate?

He has both a normative ethical and a metaethical answer. The normative ethical answer, as already seen, is that preventing great evils is one of the principal goods, and presumably is the special preserve of politics. The idea of a great evil is probably neutral between injustice and a great reduction of welfare, and is perhaps able to adjudicate between the demands of justice or the demands of utility where they conflict; but if so, there is still a legitimate theoretical task in making clear how evils are to be compared when they fall on either side of the divide between justice and utility. For example, is a small injustice always a worse evil than a small reduction in welfare? If, as it seems to be, the answer is 'Yes', when doesn't justice always trump welfare? Another approach that might fairly be expected to be developed by Hampshire is that of connecting the prevention of great evil with the vulnerability of those without political power. If politicians are always a danger to those with little power or those with less than the politicians, perhaps the avoiding-injury requirement of justice we have already encountered in O'Neill both particularly constrains political agents and partly justifies welfare-protecting dirty-handed acts.

These speculations about the directions in which Hampshire's theory might be developed sit uneasily, however, with his metaethical answer to the problem of adjudicating conflicts between justice and utility. His answer is that one has to live with this conflict, and that living with this and other conflicts is characteristic of morality:

[T]here is a large difference, and a logical independence, between two moral philosophies, often confused. First, there is a moral philosophy that prescribes rational evaluation of moral claims and institutions and that in normal circumstances prescribes the rejection of moral claims and institutions which damage human welfare or are unjust in their operation; but there sometimes are overriding considerations when the damage caused is not too great and the injustice too extreme and when the opposing values are far from trivial. This moral philosophy, defended here, asserts that there always will be, and always ought to be, conflicts arising from the universal requirements of utility and justice, and moral requirements that are based on specific loyalties and on conventions and customs of love and friendship and family loyalty, historically explicable conventions. The second moral philosophy asserts that any moral claim is finally valid if and only if it either contributes to human welfare or promotes justice; there is a double criterion which should solve conflicts by entirely rational arguments, except when justice and utility conflict. . . . The first moral theory asserts that moral conflicts are of their nature ineliminable and that there is no morally acceptable and overriding criterion, simple or double, to be appealed to, and no constant method of resolving conflicts. The worth and value of a person's life and character, and also of a social structure, are always underdetermined by purely rational considerations.[17]

I call the theory that Hampshire endorses an 'anti-theory' because once one believes that there is no small number of definite goods to guide deliberation and resolve conflict, it is hard to see what distinguishes theoretical from pre-theoretical resources for resolving conflicts. Theory in the sphere of practical deliberation works by referring choices to criteria of rightness or principles or precepts that are general. There may be more than one sort of principle, and conflict between different principles, but this need not exclude very great agreement over what is right and wrong. Principles of utility and justice agree in many of the types of act they call right and wrong, but disagree over why they are right and wrong. The agreement may be more important than the disagreement if theory is conceived primarily as identifying the impermissible and indicating the permissible: when utilitarianism and Kantianism from their different starting points come to the conclusion that something is all right to do, or conclude that something is wrong, the fact they do so from the different points of view *adds* to the authority of the conclusion. It does not take anything away. It certainly does not call attention to the limitations of reason in morality. This is not to deny that the two theories also disagree, and in morally important cases. Even when this happens however, it does not seem to flow from an internal connection between the concept of morality, or of a historically evolved social practice, and the possibility of rational conflict, as Hampshire claims. The conflict may rather be a by-product of two theories getting hold of different aspects of the same practical questions. On this interpretation the fact of conflict does not rub our noses in a limitation of reason, but in the *variety* of reasons, which some conflict between theories recapitulates.

Hampshire's anti-theory expresses a much deeper scepticism about moral theory than the willingness to live with conflict, given pluralism about reasons for action. Sometimes this scepticism is more or less explicit in Hampshire's writings as a set of claims about the limits of rationality in morals.[18] At any rate, the scepticism seems to be founded on the existence of three, partly overlapping, dichotomies that importantly affect the range and content of moral questions and make answers to these questions elusive. There is the distinction between the natural and the conventional in human behaviour; the distinction between the private and the public; and the distinction between the abnormal and the normal in circumstances of choice. The distinction between the natural and the conventional is presupposed by the existence of the many different ways of life adopted by human beings. The customs and histories that help to make up the ways of life are not biologically inevitable, nor are they without competition from other customs and histories; but they can make sense and even catch on outside their starting place. Though they can make sense, they are not open to rational justification as a whole; but that does not mean that their disappearance or reduction would not matter, or that ways of life ought to be revised or encroached upon by practices that *are* rational. Ways of life have a certain integrity, and their importance to the people involved with them creates a presumption in favour of their continuing. Across these ways of life cut facts of human life that are pretty pervasive through the species: love, friendship, sexual relations, child-rearing, ageing, sickness, life in families, and so on. Some customs in different ways of life are a response to these common phenomena, and often they are conflicting responses. Although some of these customs and practices are open to rational and moral criticism, many are not, and there is no reducing the acceptable customs or ways of life to one. There are irreducibly many acceptable ways of life, not all mutually compatible. This is one of the conflicts that morality and moral theory have to live with. Another is presented by choice in particularly adverse and abnormal circumstance; and then there is the conflict between the public and private, as when loyalty to someone with whom one is personally involved conflicts with treatment that is unobjectionable from the point of view of procedural justice.

The existence of these different kinds of conflict is not, in Hampshire's view, a problem for moral theory to deal with but a deep fact of life to which moral theory needs to reconcile itself. If it does not, it may be guilty of trying to model practical knowledge on scientific, and trying futilely to find a reality beyond the conflicts, such as an abstract human nature, to deduce its prescriptions from, rather as physics tries to deduce the behavior of medium-sized physical objects from the behaviour of particles of matter.[19] Although I think the aspiration to a unitary moral theory is likely to founder on the fact that reasons for action are diverse, I do not believe that the aspiration to a unitary moral theory has to be associated with failing to recognise an unscientific subject-matter of ethics, and many writers who are working on the statement of such a theory are alive to the dangers of the scientific model. Among the great theorists in the history of moral philosophy, Aristotle and Kant were both perfectly confident that ethics was not natural science in its form of reasoning. Hampshire seems to think that rationalistic approaches to subject-matters must be scientistic, and so is more hospitable to the unreasonable and the arational than he ought to be. Thus Hampshire's account may invite the overrationalisation of ways of life that, from the supposedly wrongheaded rationalistic perspective of moral theory, are open to moral criticism. If we take to heart the idea that some practices are so embedded in a way of life that to attack the practice is to attack a way of life, to which, according to Hampshire, people can be unreasoningly but still legitimately attached, then perhaps criticism of the practice has to be foregone on pain of moralising overreaching itself. This line of thought is not unfamiliar in discussions of the ethics of female circumcision, where its implications are also particularly worrying.

A more acceptable position, in view of the fact that Hampshire thinks that ways of life are not in principle closed off from moral criticism, is to say that all practices are *open* to moral criticism. This is compatible with the criticism being clumsy or insensitive, or turning out to be unjustified. But it is also compatible with the possibility that the critics of female circumcision are right. Still, for a practice to be *open* to criticism is for it to be within the scope of a rationalist technique and not part of its background. So it is a big concession for someone as convinced as Hampshire of the unwelcomeness of reason in morals to make. I do not see, however, why the concession, combined with agnosticism about philosophers' abilities to find the relevant techniques, is not as reasonable as Hampshire's scepticism. If that is right, then Hampshire's account of political morality seems undermotivated as an anti-theory, while as a positive theory, that is, in its preventing-greater-evil mode, it seems underspecified.

The Difference Democracy Makes

Since one can get dirt on one's hands even from choosing the lesser of two evils as an honourable politician, it may look as if it is a kind of moral bad luck to end up with political power. The chances of seeing out one's term of office with nothing to regret or of having an unblemished reign are probably small, and yet *someone* has to go into public life, and the more honourable the people are who do so, the better. If people repudiate public life, as they can sometimes repudiate certain types of private life, because they are too pure for it, that can be as morally suspect as what they are avoiding. Although no one seems to think it is a form of dirty hands in turn, dropping out politically or keeping out of politics in a democracy can also justify criticism, and perhaps more criticism than passive obedience under an unjust undemocratic regime.

That democracy makes a difference to dirty hands has been noticed before now. As Thompson has pointed out,[20] democracy spreads responsibility: not only politicians but also their electors are implicated. On the other hand, the justification for democracy also rubs off on dirty-handed acts committed under its auspices, especially when institutional measures have been taken to reduce the area in which dirty handed acts can go undetected, unquestioned and unpunished. At least in theory, democracy introduces controls on political activity and costs for political wrongdoing. The controls may not allow for the immediate control of ineffective or morally wrong policies, but it ensures at least the possibility of a decision to change course in relatively short order. Since democracy can also impose big standing obstacles to certain kinds of action against citizens or in the name of its citizens, it can act constitutionally against at least certain kinds of dirty hands. On the other hand, when democratically elected politicians do go in for dirty-handed acts, the moral arguments for democracy being better than other frameworks for taking political decisions may lend legitimacy to those decisions, since, on one accepted understanding of democratic office-holding, people are supposed to have the latitude to use their judgement for the best within the law. It would be incredible if the allowable latitude were so limited that dirty-handed acts became unthinkable or unchoosable. Even so, democracy does seem to provide a cleaner environment for political decisions than other forms of government. If politicians get their hands dirty in a democracy that is not due to the dirty atmosphere they inhabit.

Theoretically, too, democracy makes a difference: the prospects of clearing up what is paradoxical about dirty hands seem to improve when democracy is brought in. If a politician is in power quite independently of the choices of those ruled over, it does look as if there is something distinctively unfortunate about being a politician who acts for the public good by doing the least wrong thing. For however justified by welfare a dirty-handed act is, the dirt in it can always be a reason for moral condemnation by a people who, even though they benefit by it, do not consent to it, and therefore stand more as spectators to it than as co-authors or authorisers of it. The more democratic the regime is, the less justified the condemnation of citizens is, because their moral distance from the act shrinks. Democracy can even expose everyone – all citizens – to the same moral risks. Thus some forms of democratic organisation require office to rotate among all those involved. It is sheer luck if one's term is up just as circumstances go sour, so that one's successor is left with dirty hands – and that can be generally acknowledged. Dirty hands in this setting can intelligibly prompt empathy rather than condemnation.

Thompson thinks that the biggest obstacle to reducing the politician's moral burden through democracy is secrecy: the government's need for secrecy in carrying out some of its legitimate functions, on the one hand, and, on the other hand, the politician's temptation to cover up or keep things secret where publicity would be personally or party-politically costly. Ordinary citizens, Thompson says, cannot be blamed for what they couldn't have known about, and yet it is out of the question for them to know everything, since this would render self-defeating some otherwise effective and legitimate measures for, for example, detecting and controlling crime and preventing and waging war. Where relevant knowledge is withheld from the voting public by politicians, on the other hand, something wrong is always done, and this wrong can compound the wrong in dirty hands.

I doubt that secrecy has the general moral significance that Thompson's account claims for it. For one thing, it is not always true that ignorance due to secrecy excuses. If a young child secretly commits arson but is known by his parents to be fascinated by matches, then more than ignorance of the act of arson due to the child's secrecy is required to absolve the parents of all responsibility: they need to have done their best to have dispelled the child's fascination with fire. In a democracy in which it is common knowledge that some political decisions are made in secret, and in which it is known that there is political advantage in keeping things secret, ignorance under conditions of vigilance rather than simple ignorance may be the minimum fully exculpating condition. If people co-operate in being kept in the dark by not wanting to know, or by not caring about politics, if that is also the reason why they would run a mile from taking on even local political office, then that, as much as official or unofficial secrecy, can increase the moral burdens on those who do fill the political vacuum. Another and different reason why ignorance due to secrecy need not excuse people from responsibility for secret dirty-handed acts is that citizens can be consulted about the scope of secrecy and vote that it remain wider than even Thompson would recommend. If we agree that in democracy partially blank cheques of this kind can legitimately even if wrongheadedly be written, then secrecy is not in the permanent tension with democracy that Thompson seems to think it is in.

Democracy and Partisanship

So far democracy has appeared as a framework that makes it harder to do wrong than other forms of political constitution, and that lightens the burden of responsibility when wrong is done by office-holders for the sake of the public. This morally improving character of democracy, however, may be counterbalanced by something else: the identification of different political agents with interests far narrower than the public interest. When a parliamentary representative of an extremely wealthy constituency argues for tax cuts that would make publicly funded schools worse or extend waiting times for publicly funded hospitals, he can be held to be arguing legitimately both for the interests of those he represents and the party he belongs to. Yet the tax cuts may be wrong from the standpoint of justice as well as utility. If they are wrong, is it really legitimate to argue for them? And since the already well off can command the resources to promote their case outside of legislatures, is it really as legitimate to give them access to legislators and influence over them as it is to open special channels of access and influence to those who find it hardest to make their reasonable interests visible or audible to politicians?

The difficult questions do not stop there. Since the least well off in some democracies are very well off by world standards, there is a parallel argument, at the level of international democratic institutions, for giving the least well off more access to and influence over decision-making and resource allocation, so that the narrow interests of the already well off do not always end up prevailing over the interests of those whose needs are greater. This can mean, as it sometimes *has* meant, in recent world trade negotiations, that tariff barriers that protect the jobs of relatively poor workers in the rich countries have to be lifted – morally have to be lifted – to allow growth in the manufacturing sector of much poorer countries. In other words, for the same general reason that the least well off in the rich countries need to be supported by taxes, the poor of the poorest countries may need the support of *all* the people of the rich countries, including the neediest in the rich countries.

Adopting this perspective does not come naturally, and perhaps the right of each person to have and lead their own life limits the authority this perspective can have,[21] a point I will return to. As things are, the democratic voters in the world do not expect their representatives to speak for other people's interests, even the interests of the much poorer. They vote for people who they believe will defend their own interests, whatever they are, morally good or morally bad, against the competing claims of other people.[22] Thus it is perfectly intelligible that the representative of one constitutency should oppose the building of an indisputably necessary transportation link or prison or home for the mentally ill in his locality;[23] it may even be said that it is his moral duty to do so, though justice and utility both favour siting the link or the prison or home at exactly the place he refuses to countenance. A constituency of unselfish electors might elect a representative who had the freedom to vote, for once, from the point of view of the whole public and not just a section of it. But unselfishness is not a qualifying condition for being an elector, and the tiny impact of one's personal vote makes moral agonising over how it should be cast slightly ridiculous. Changing all of this would be a big task. But the upshot of these considerations is that it may be *necessary* to change it: democracy at the grass-roots level, the level of the many, the level which for Thompson helps to moralise dirty-handedness, includes elements of sectarianism that themselves need to be moralised. This presents a challenge both to the powers of moral theory, and the powers of democratic theory, understood as a theory of the democratic institutions and practices that would be required to balance interests in practice.

It may be that the moralisation of the democratic grass roots can partly be brought about by institutions that enshrine procedural fairness, where these include the sorts of checks and balances that mean that narrow interests always meet or can meet opposition that more general interests do not meet. It may be a testimony to the effectiveness of some of the institutions that actually exist in some places in the West that the perception of fairness matters to people in some areas of collective life even more than self-interest.[24] The point is that some elements of democracy may have to be acted against by morality, and that sometimes justice and self-interest are independent and conflicting motivations in democratic life.

When the moral limits imposed on democracy by self-interest, sectional interest and partisanship (in the broad sense of giving particular weight to the interests of those closest to one) are brought into the picture, do they reintroduce for political ethics a version of the dualism of practical reason that operates in business ethics? I am not sure. This is because cosmopolitanism, thought and action in which one identifies one's own interests with those of the the widest possible community in which one is included, is intelligibly an ideal in politics – an ideal even in non-democratic politics – in a way nothing similar is in business. Again, one does not need to desert politics – change the subject or the activity – for the competing demands of morals and politics to be dealt with. It takes political means to curtail the excesses of collective self-interest in business; but one does not need extra-political means of curtailing the excesses of self-interest in politics. Politics is in that sense the more inclusive activity. And the ethical resources needed to think about how to regulate it never appear, as in business, to call in question the internal goals of the activity itself.

Nagel's legitimation problem

Still, a *version* of the dualism of practical reason – a version of the dualism of the reasons pursuing the narrower good and the reasons for pursuing the wider good – seems to pervade political life, and perhaps to give rise to anomaly. In *Equality and Partiality* Thomas Nagel has charted the depth of the problem I have been clumsily describing. He argues that in order for a system of political arrangements to be legitimate, it has to strive for the possibility of unanimous endorsement by all participants, which it can probably only ever achieve to a very limited extent. The general form of a system which would achieve legitimacy for Nagel is one that realises the ideal of egalitarian impartiality by a certain kind of moral division of labour. It entrenches impartiality by means of public institutions and roles, while allowing occupants of those roles also to pursue a life in which what matters personally, and what matters locally and communally, is also respected. In this latter connection the system of politics tries to be consistent with the principle that what matters in life to each person matters full stop, so that people's lives cannot simply be subordinated to those that might be chosen by an agent who was all-knowing, impartial and benevolent.

> A workable system must define a set of overlapping roles such as citizen, voter, and taxpayer, as well as particular roles in the the economy, the professions, the military, the educational system, the governmental bureaucracy, and the judicial system. Any given individual's identity will involve more than one of these, as well as his personal position in a family, a religion, or a cultural, racial, or ethnic subcommunity. The competition for each individual's motivational allegiance is inevitably severe. But if in addition we require that the political and economic structures in which these roles are embedded should meet a high standard of impartiality in its

effects on the equally valuable lives of all participants, the potential conflicts are even greater.[25]

Nagel thinks that some of these conflicts are likely to be rationally unresolvable.

Nagel's view recognises, what has already emerged, that public life is not *all* about the exercise of political power. It is also about the participation of individuals in civic life. Even small roles in education and the military – even a role at the level of the small cog in the machine – can carry with it significant demands of impartiality that can conflict with personal life. And even low-level public office can carry significant demands of impartiality that conflict with a constituency interest. There is no avoiding the makings of the conflicts, according to Nagel, if a political system is non-authoritarian and realistic about human motivation while aiming to be egalitarian. At the same time, according to Nagel, it is morally undesirable to let the elements of the conflict – impartial benevolence and reasonable partiality to one's own life – fight it out in each person's choices. It is better if people are able to detach themselves to some degree from their personal interests through involvement in roles and institutions that are geared to both impartiality and promoting welfare, starting with those in most need.[26] Here is where utilitarianism seems to enter Nagel's conditions for legitimacy of a political system. Utilitarianism cannot be all there is to it, Nagel says, because the general form of practical problem in politics is not the utilitarian one of giving advice to an impartial benevolent, and powerful outsider about what *he* should do for those inside a political order. The general form of practical problem is that of agreeing to do something oneself. More explicitly, it is a matter of agreeing with everyone else to do things and create institutions that will meet others' needs, where the individuals being asked to do things and create institutions have their own lives to lead. The participants cannot reasonably be asked to take up the vantage point of the impartial outsider, as if their lives did not matter, but that leaves them with the problem of drawing the line between the reasonable demands of their own lives and the reasonable demands of impartial egalitarianism. Within considerable limits there are many rational ways of drawing the line, Nagel shows.

It is possible to describe this line-drawing problem in Nagel's way, as the Kantian problem of integrating the personal and impersonal perspectives. And it is possible to describe it as the problem of trying personally and through the roles one occupies to do what the powerful and benevolent outsider would approve of. Either way we have a deep problem. It may be that by identifying more strongly with the role of citizen and less strongly with other roles one will be able to moralise public life at the level of the individual. But theory may not supply a good enough reason for developing this form of identification. There may be no reason not to be partisan and partial within quite broad limits. That seems to be Nagel's conclusion, working within a Kantian theory, and it is a possible conclusion about utilitarianism as well. This standoff over the acceptable limits of partiality may be the source of anomaly.

5

Feminism and Moral Theory

There is not just one feminist critique of moral theory, and feminism is not primarily an attack on theory at all. It is an attack on institutions and practices world-wide that, over millennia, have been developed and controlled by men and have benefited men often at the expense of women. Historically, women have been excluded from the most prestigious male institutions, and when they have been allowed to participate at all, they have usually done so in inferior positions. Even as outsiders, however, women have often supported men, or taken their place in the home, making it possible for them to have a place in public affairs. While shouldering most of the burdens of home life, women have rarely been regarded as possible heads of households; on the contrary, they have often been reckoned a part of a man's household property. Traditional moral theory has been criticised by feminists for rationalising this state of affairs, or for not questioning it, or for ignoring it; and the criticism is compelling. When they have not been outright misogynists, the male creators of the most influential moral theories in the tradition have often displayed a thoughtlessness about women that would be unacceptable in any restatement of their theories produced today.

Theorists are one thing, however, and theories are another. Aristotle assumed that women were inferior by nature to men and he was an apologist for slavery, but his theory contains an account of human nature and an account of justice that probably can be turned against Aristotle's own applications of it. In our own day, Rawls's lapses in relation to justice and the family have been held not to be in the spirit of Rawls's theory of justice anyway.[1] And liberalism generally may have resources for bolstering the case of feminists, even radical feminists.[2] That liberal theorists and politicians have not recognised these possibilities, or not wanted to put their resources to these uses, no more impugns liberalism than Aristotle's support for slavery impugns Aristotelian moral theory.

One way of considering the relation between moral theory and feminism is by asking whether conventional theories can be amended so as to give feminists what they say they want. Certain feminists say that they can't be. They insist that a distinctively feminist theory is needed if everything that is at stake morally in, for example, reproductive ethics or in the ethics of child-rearing or even in the prevention of war is to be given due weight by moral theory. After looking into claims of this kind, I shall suggest that they give rise to a dilemma. Either the distinctively feminist theory proposed revolves around notions like connectedness and caring that seem compatible with, or at least not likely to dislodge, male domination; or else a theory geared more uncompromisingly to equality is in question, in which case it is not distinctively feminist.

Claims about the way conventional moral theories fail to answer moral questions are one thing. There is also a strand of feminist criticism that says that theory itself – systematic understanding that tries to get particulars subsumed by either general moral concepts (justice, equality, welfare, rational choice) or general principles using these concepts – is an inauthentic and distorting form of moral understanding, or at least a distorting form for the purposes of feminist moral understanding. Theory altogether is supposed to be a bad vehicle for bearing out feminism because it is a too confining or too alien a way of articulating values that are distinctively feminine, or values that, to a feminist or feminine perspective, are the central ethical ones. According to some feminists, what matters morally is irremediably particular, rather than universal, situational rather than world-historical; intimate rather than public and impersonal. And that is not all. An appetite for principle, and for generality and system may be a product and a contaminating medium of patriarchal domination. At least in any familiar form, moral theory may turn out to be a kind of Trojan horse: more likely to invade and disable feminism than to take it forward.

In a way, the feminist challenge to theory in general recapitulates the general scepticism about theory that I tried to counter at the beginning of this book; and the resistance continues in this chapter. I point out the compatibility of a feminist ethic of caring with orthodox moral philosophy, noting at the same time criticisms that the caring ethic prompts from some radical feminists. I then point out the extent to which even radical feminism appears to involve itself with generality, system, and principles, in particular, egalitarian principles that are the height of orthodoxy in moral theory.

If radical feminism consisted only of feminist ethical theory and a feminist critique of traditional theory, the challenge to theory from feminism might be met pretty straightforwardly. But there is also the challenge of radical feminist *practice*, and questions this raises may lead after all to anomaly. Certain all-female communities whose value to members seems to be moral, operate forms of exclusion that, from the angle of traditional theory, seem to be immoral. People who stand outside these communities sometimes seem, from the standpoint of orthodox theory, to deserve solidarity if insiders do, but in practice only insiders are supported. Again, insiders in such communities appear to be exempt from criticism for behaviour that would be condemned by the community if it were practised by outsiders. These ways of treating insiders and outsiders are not incidental to the female communities in question, nor, paradoxically, to what makes them morally valuable, despite the demand in moral theory for treatment that is blind to distinctions between genders, and blind to the distinction between insiders and outsiders. The double standards can be morally justified if they are responses to oppression. And they are. But the oppression is hard for orthodox theory to recognise as being essentially male: whatever makes male oppression wrong is something that makes other forms of oppression wrong as well. According to orthodox theory, it is the 'oppression' rather than the 'male' in 'male oppression' that justifies the defensive reactions of women, and the fact that it is women on the defensive may not engage the theory either; instead their humanity does. Yet there is something odd about the thought that gender makes no essential difference to what makes forms of male domination wrong or to what might make forms of female solidarity right.

How Conventional Theories Let Women Down

I begin with feminist criticisms of the traditional moral theories, as opposed to moral theory in general. Bioethics is a focal point of much of this criticism, partly because of the inclusion of reproductive ethics in bioethics. Thus, the morality of abortion has been taken to confront women more directly than men, and the arguments for and against abortion have made the ethics of the prevention of pregnancy a feminist issue as well. Not only has it been claimed that women with unwanted pregnancies should have a decisive say in whether abortion takes place; the whole question of the unequal burdens that result from pregnancy has added to the sense that women have not experienced the benefits of the liberalisation of sexual practice that men have. Then there is the consideration that men have dominated the medical profession, and that doctors have often been insensitive to the effects on women both of undergoing abortions and of being prevented from having them.

The development of new reproductive technologies has widened the ethical debate. *In vitro* fertilization and surrogate mothering have both raised questions about the place of women in the process leading to having children, and often the answers to these questions have added to the sense that women suffer certain injustices just because they are women. The claim that conventional moral theories do not register or diagnose these injustices very well has been put by many feminist writers.[3] I shall focus on a representative contribution to this literature, Susan Sherwin's 'Feminist ethics and in vitro fertilization'.[4]

Sherwin considers what can be said by utilitarian, consequentialist and theologically inspired philosophers about the many issues raised by *in vitro* fertilization (IVF). Although she admits that it is hard to be conclusive about what can be said, because the main theoretical approaches admit of a number of versions,[5] she thinks that even the deontological approach, which gives weight to many values that feminist theory emphasises, falls short of providing the required treatment. Both deontologists and consequentialists, she says, often make the permissibility of IVF hang on the status of the embryo that develops if IVF is successful. They also take into account the money costs of the procedure, and raise questions about why it should be so important for couples to have their 'own' child rather than adopt a child not biologically related to them. It is in their depth of treatment of this last issue – why it should matter so much – that Sherwin thinks feminist and orthodox moral theories part company.

Feminist theories alone, she thinks, face up to the full complexity of the fact that 'the capitalism, racism, sexism and elitism of our culture have combined to create a set of attitudes which views children as commodities whose value is derived from their possession of parental chromosomes'.[6] For example, feminist theory is able to explain why it matters so much by reference to the hypothesis that women get their sense of self-worth from giving birth to and raising children, rather than from their jobs, close friendships or romantic attachments. Feminist theory is also likely to register as morally important the eligibility criteria for IVF treatment in some western countries, which include being married and in a stable relationship with a man, and being solvent. Then there are the psychological and physical costs to women of undergoing IVF procedures; these are more likely to be noticed by feminist theories than by orthodox theories. Not that orthodox theories *cannot* give weight to these costs. But the genderlessness of their perspective makes this unlikely.

Again, feminist theory might imply that it is more urgent to combat the conditions that interfere with female fertility than to carry out IVF: orthodox theories might be neutral about whether reproduction took place within a fertile woman or *in vitro*, if other things were equal.

By a 'feminist ethics' Sherwin means 'a moral theory that focuses on relations among persons as well as on individuals.

> It has as a model an inter-connected social fabric, rather than the famil- iar one of isolated, independent atoms; and it gives primacy to bonds among people rather than independence. It is a theory that focuses on concrete situations and persons and not on free-floating abstract actions.[7]

Sherwin goes on to say that a feminist ethics would contain elements of the 'caring' ethic of Noddings and Gilligan, as well as the 'trust' ethics of Annette Baier (to be discussed in the next section). But can't a theory with these elements be an extension of either a deontological or utili- tarian theory, or perhaps some sort of political theory that provides for the value of sub-communities while providing an explanation of what is unjust about racism, and about mistreatment based on social class? Some kinds of psychological and social costs fall differentially on some groups, and some people's autonomy is interfered with by the sub- servient social roles which are open to them. Both of these facts can be taken into account by theories which, like utilitarianism and Kantian- ism, are able to use a levelling or equalising unit of moral importance – the person or human being. These theories both produce arguments against treating people worse on the basis of gender, race or class, and Kantianism at least has resources for not commodifying young persons and for taking away obstacles to autonomy. If a feminist theory is to make a break from these theories, we should expect its ideas to be some- thing entirely different. As will emerge in later sections, it is not so clear that the caring ethic really does break new ground.

A case similar to Sherwin's has been made by several writers in rela- tion to the ability of orthodox theories and institutions to deal with ques- tions of justice within the family. Martha Minow and Mary Shanley have claimed that the dominant theoretical understandings of justice within the family – contractarian, communitarian and rights-based – are each inadequate. An acceptable regime of family law must

> take account of two paradoxical aspects of family life and the family's rela- tion to the state. First, the individual must be seen simultaneously as an individual and as a person fundamentally involved in relationships of dependence, care, and responsibility. . . . Second, family law and political

theory must take account of the additional paradox that family relationships are simultaneously outside of and yet shaped by the political order.[8]

In practice, a family law that gave weight to the first paradoxical aspect
might give a surrogate mother some leeway to break her contract, in view
of her connection to the child through pregnancy and childbirth. The
second aspect might be given weight by a family law that recognised that
some prevalent views of the family enforce questionable stereotypes of
potential parents and of the resources that are ideally required for child-
rearing. Like Sherwin, Minow and Shanley believe that to the extent that
these aspects need to be catered for by a non-liberal theory, they are
likely to bring into play an ethic of care.[9]

Moral Theory after Gilligan

It is time, then, to see what material for a distinctively female *and* feminist approach to moral theory might be found in an ethic of care. One
source of this ethic is the writings of the psychologist, Carol Gilligan.
Gilligan's *In a Different Voice* has inspired the claim that there can be an
'ethic of care' that stands apart from, and in a sense competes with, an
ethic centred on justice. The ethic of care is supposed to be prefigured
in contrasts between boys' and girls' moral reactions, as revealed in
psychological testing carried out by Lawrence Kohlberg with the use
of descriptions of moral dilemmas. Boys' reactions are supposed to
conform to a model of human moral maturity that associates advanced
moral development with the application of more or less explicit principles. Girls' reactions in Kohlberg's model belong to earlier stages of
development: specifically, stages organised round an ideal of maintaining good relations with others. Gilligan sought girls' reactions to
Kohlberg-type moral dilemmas, but she also asked questions designed
to elicit their conception of the moral and of moral progress. Her
findings suggest that while girls' reactions do conform to what Kohlberg
calls the 'conventional' rather than the 'post-conventional', the implicit
valuation of the latter over the former in Kohlberg's model is questionable. The emphasis in girls' responses on 'connection' and 'relation' was
no more a sign of moral underdevelopment than the greater abstractness of boys' reactions was a sign of moral maturity. Rather, the two
types of reactions can be interpreted as evidence of distinct, but
complementary, forms of moral development in human beings. These
differences may be associated in turn with the tendency to encourage
boys but not girls to separate themselves from their mothers. In any

case, under Gilligan's approach, the stages of moral development do not coincide with sex differences but cover both sexes.

Gilligan's research is supposed to show the need for a new approach to modelling moral development as well as the need to revalue upwards the stage of moral development normally reached by girls; this much seems to be uncontroversial. Feminists who think that a distinctive moral theory is latent in the authentic 'different voice' of girls[10] can agree with it; and so can feminists who think that the voice is inauthentic, and suggestive of something contemptibly submissive.[11] The fact that the feminist reception for Gilligan's work has been mixed, however, is itself important, and perhaps damaging to the suggestion that it has in it the makings of feminism's anti-theory. Why has Gilligan been thought to be the basis for such a theory? And how strong are the objections to that way of interpreting it?

One reason why Gilligan has been seen to be the basis for an alternative theory is that she takes very seriously the possibility that female thinking about moral questions is itself systematically different from male thinking. Some of the evidence she assembles concerns women's thinking about abortion. Gilligan discusses the reactions of Claire, a counsellor in an abortion clinic, to applying the clinic's policy of telling women who asked to see what was evacuated from the uterus, 'You can't see anything now. It just looks like jelly at this point.' Claire felt uncomfortable with what she was told to say and decided to look at a foetus evacuated in a late abortion. Here is how she described the effect of this decision.

> I just couldn't kid myself anymore and say that there was nothing in the uterus, just a tiny speck. This is not true, and I knew it wasn't true, but I sort of had to see it. And yet at the same time I knew that's what was going on. I also believed that it was right; it should have happened. But I couldn't say, 'Well, this is right and this is wrong. I was just constantly torn.'[12]

Eventually Claire was able to go beyond being constantly torn.

> Finally, I just had to reconcile myself – I really do believe this, but it is not an easy thing that you can say without emotions and maybe regret – that yes, life is sacred but the quality of life is also important, and it has to be the determining thing in this particular case. The quality of that mother's life, the quality of an unborn child's life – I have seen too many pictures of babies in trash cans and that sort of thing, and it's so easy to say, 'Well, either/or,' and it just isn't like that. And I had to be able to say, 'Yes, this is killing, there is no way around it, but I am willing to accept that, but I am willing to go ahead with it, and it's hard.' I don't think I can explain it. I don't think I can really verbalise the justification.[13]

Carol Gilligan comments:

> Claire's inability to articulate her moral position stems in part from the fact that hers is a contextual judgement, bound to the particulars of time and place, contingent always on 'that mother' and that 'unborn child', and thus resisting a categorical formulation. To her, the possibilities of imagination outstrip the capacity for generalisation.[14]

But Gilligan's commentary seems to give more weight to Claire's feeling of being unable to state her position than to the position that she actually succeeds in stating. What Claire says, as I understand her, is that though abortion is killing, it can be justified on balance, because the bad quality of life that killing can prevent can count for more in a particular case than the bad in killing. The conclusion is one about what is best on balance, rather than about what it is definitely best to do, because there are costs whatever one does. In that respect the decision is not clear-cut, not an either/or matter. That is Claire's position, and though it is reached with the case of 'that' mother in mind, there is no suggestion as I read it that it is only a position about one mother or one unborn baby. On the contrary, it is a pro-abortion position, but one that recognises that there is a lot to be said on the other side. It is not, as far as I can see, specially geared to particulars, and Claire's overall statement seems to me to warrant no conclusion whatever about the relative possibilities in her view of generalisation and imagination. What is more, I do not see that a devotee of theory need disagree very much with Claire. I do not see that a theorist needs to hold that there are no hard cases, no cases where the best conclusion is one about what is best on balance, and where the best available course of action is one which will turn out to be in some respects regrettable.

Although I believe her treatment of Claire's case is tendentious, Gilligan does go on to identify one thing which is both recognisably at work in Claire's thought about abortion, and repeatedly encountered in her reports of other women's thoughts about 'relationships'. This is the importance of a connection or attachment being sustained. If attachment between mother and child cannot be sustained or cannot be created in the first place, if the baby is likely to end up in the trash-can or be kept by a mother who wishes it were dead, then perhaps abortion is better than carrying the pregnancy to term. A moral theory without the resources to give weight to attachment in general, or perhaps without the resources to connect the formation of attachments with certain stages of pregnancy, may miss something that is intuitively or pre-philosophically of moral importance to abortion. Similarly, a moral theory that gives no particular weight in its reasoning about quality of life to the burdens that fall differentially on women in different cultures, is in no position to see what impact on the quality of life abortion may have. Gilligan's case study of women's moral thought about abortion revealed two other things that theory needs to recognise: first, that some very young women who became pregnant simply disbelieved that this was possible; and second, that some pregnancies 'coincided with efforts on the part of the women to end a relationship', efforts that could be 'seen as a manifestation of ambivalence or as a way of putting a relationship to the ultimate test of commitment . . . making the baby an ally in the search for male support and protection, or, that failing, a companion victim of male rejection.'[15]

In trying to accommodate everything that on reflection seems relevant to deciding whether abortion is right or wrong on balance, theory may be constrained to take into account sources of relevant considerations that are distinctively female or distinctively feminist. Must the effort of accommodating these sources prove too much for standard theories? I do not see why it must. But even if it does, that is not a reason for thinking that the effort will be too much for a non-standard theory. It is not as if to do justice to the experience of women or to promote the values of women, women feel they must abandon theory.[16]

There is more than one appropriation of Gilligan for theory. I shall concentrate on two examples of the tendency, each of which attempts to show that Gilligan's findings have radical implications, and that her approach is new and necessary for moral understanding. Perhaps the largest claims made for Gilligan come from Susan Hekman,[17] who credits her with nothing less than a paradigm shift in moral theory,[18] one that ruptures the development of moral thought from the Enlightenment. Then there is the case made in a number of essays by Annette Baier.[19] I start with Hekman, whose book outlines what she takes to be Gilligan's methodological innovations, as well as what is supposed to be groundbreaking in her moral theory.

According to Hekman, Gilligan's principal innovation, and the one that can be considered the focal point of her contribution to psychology as well as to moral thought, is her use of narrative. To hear the different voice Gilligan needs a special medium, and this is the words used by her subjects themselves, sometimes evoked through dialogue and not just through passive reception of subjects' own answers to questionnaires. Since about the mid-1980s, Hekman points out, Gilligan and her collaborators met with silence when they tried to get adolescent females to give narrative answers to questions. The subjects had to be able to ask questions of their own and get answers from the researchers. Far from contaminating the data, this approach made available what would otherwise have been held back. 'We would stay in relationship with the girls and move where they seemed to be taking us, change our design and rewrite our questions so that we could explore the changes we were hearing in the girls voices . . . We would follow the associative logic of girls' psyches, we would move where the girls led us.'[20] This incorporates into the treatment of subjects for investigative purposes the very ethic of relation that the subjects were bringing to the researchers' notice. Hekman congratulates Gilligan and her collaborator for adopting a methodology that at a stroke deconstructs the researcher/subject dichotomy, and, more than that, turns the ethic of relating into an investigative procedure.

Overall, Hekman sees in Gilligan's work after *In a Different Voice* a gradual emancipation from 'empiricism' and the aspiration to truth and objectivity that Gilligan is supposed to have inherited from her teacher, Kohlberg, and from purveyors of other orthodoxies in psychology. In fact, according to Hekman, there are two interpretations that fit *In a Different Voice* – one objectivist, the other anti-objectivist[21] – while later work moves further and further away from objectivism. This methodological change, or rather a consistent adherence by Gilligan in her later work to an approach that was discernible from early on, creates

a clear alternative to the empiricist tradition of psychological research. Taken in conjunction with Gilligan's other work, the methodology employed [in *Meeting at the Crossroads*] constitutes a paradigm shift: a move from an objectivist method to a relational one, from the search for factual data to the collection of stories, from a detached 'scientific' approach to a committed, political one. It is her use of this method that allows Gilligan to 'hear' silenced moral voices. Her method constitutes her data just as, in Kohlberg's researches, his method constitutes the parameters of the moral domain.[22]

Hekman claims that Gilligan's methodological turn underlies the paradigm shift that she is responsible for in moral theory.

[F]or the purposes of my interpretation of Gilligan, the question of method is central. It is my contention that particular moral theories are inextricably linked to particular epistemologies . . . the epistemology that informs modernist moral theory necessary assumes a disembodied knower that constitutes abstract, universal truth. The individual who occupies Kohlberg's Stage 6 is such a knower. The moral truth that this knower constitutes is singular, universal and absolute; it is a truth that is disembodied, removed from the relationships and connectedness of everyday life that, on this view distort moral judgements.

Gilligan has effectively deconstructed this moral knower and his abstract moral knowledge. The epistemology implicit in her work replaces the disembodied knower with the relational self. The knowledge constituted by this relational self is a very different kind of knowledge. The relational self produces knowledge that is connected, a product of discourses that constitute forms of life; it is plural rather than singular. Gilligan hears moral voices speaking from the lives of connected, situated selves, not the single truth of disembodied moral principle. She hears these voices because she defines moral knowledge as plural and heterogenous.[23]

These claims about what Gilligan has accomplished are large and striking. Are they well grounded?

It is hard to say, because it is hard to know what Hekman means by 'moral theory'. Sometimes, as in the passage just quoted, it seems to be a psychologist's theory of moral development; in other places[24] it is moral philosophy: normative ethics, metaethics, or both. The unclarity matters: it is not obvious that methodological innovation in the empirical theory of moral development would do anything to induce a paradigm shift in moral philosophy, unless philosophical moral theories all incorporated theories of moral development, which they don't.[25] Again, Hekman repeatedly acknowledges strong *continuity* between some of what Gilligan is saying and Aristotelian and Humean elements of traditional moral philosophy.[26] Even if she is right to say that these elements are not representative of the dominant approach to moral philosophy as we now have it, talk of a paradigm shift sounds like overstatement if there is any continuity at all.

Some of these problems in interpreting Hekman's claims are not of her own making. The borderline between the philosophy of morals and the empirical psychology of morals is bound to blur when, as she points out,[27] figures such as Rawls and Kohlberg endorse one another's claims. Again, disagreements over the adequacy of Kohlberg's model are likely to be philosophical as well as empirical. Still, since the Kantian and utilitarian emphasis on explicit principle has faced criticism in philosophy long before Gilligan, and in our own day quite independently of her work (for example by Bernard Williams), there is quite a burden of proof to discharge if anyone is going to sustain the claim of a paradigm shift, let alone one due to Gilligan. Hekman tries to discharge the burden but fails, partly because she irrelevantly criticises philosophical claims as if they were part of a methodology of psychological field-work. She quotes Martha Nussbaum to the effect that Anglo-American moral philosophy is moving away from Enlightenment ideals and towards a moral philosophy geared to ideas about the virtues. Hekman agrees that this is a movement in Gilligan's direction, but insists that it is still burdened with the intellectual baggage of pre-Gilligan moral thought, principally a distinction between moral relativism and absolutism and a fear of relativism. Hekman also thinks that the neo-Aristotelianism of Nussbaum and others ignores issues of 'power and hegemony' in the formation of moral discourses and ignores the role of subjectivity.[28] Similar oversights and an insufficiently relaxed attitude towards relativism are attributed to other would-be 'care-theorists' among twentieth-century moral philosophers and their predecessors.[29] Finally, Hekman claims that otherwise attractive elements in the communitarian critique of liberalism is compromised by patriarchal assumptions.[30]

Even Anglo-American moral philosophers who she thinks are enlightened are criticised by Hekman for being overintimidated by relativism, overintimidated by it because she takes Gilligan to have taken the sting out of relativism. Gilligan does this, in Hekman's view, by getting unconventional and non-objectivist materials to do explanatory work. The materials she has in mind include an investigative technique that allows subjects and not just researchers to ask questions, the revaluation upwards of the explanatory power of stories, as well as Gilligan's belief in a certain harmony between girls' and boys' moral views notwithstanding the differences. But a defence of this sort of relativism does not begin to address the question of the relativism that moral philosophers worry about: i.e. the relativism that threatens to eliminate any literal meaning for terms like 'right', 'wrong' and 'just'. This confusion over relativism is a by-product of the equivocation on 'moral theory'. As for the supposed failure of even the enlightened moral philosophers to take account of the relation of power, hegemony and subjectivity to moral discourse, this is to complain of moral philosophers staying within discipline boundaries rather than doing the sociology of morals.

Annette Baier's case for Gilligan's importance raises fewer objections than Hekman's.[31] Baier recognises that many non-feminist and male writers have identified limitations in a Kantian framework for moral theory, and she thinks Gilligan is best interpreted as a critic of Kant as well. On the other hand, Baier does not think that Gilligan simply repeats claims made by other critics of Kant, and when Gilligan's claims converge with those of the non-feminist anti-Kantians, they converge, according to Baier, from a different direction. What is supposed to be distinctive of Gilligan's approach, or a Gilligan-inspired approach, to moral theory, is that it acknowledges that many personal relationships with moral importance are not chosen, obtain between agents who are unequal in power, and properly make demands on passion before reason.[32] Relationships between parents and young children have all three of these aspects, and they are much more widely discussed in feminist ethics than in traditional ethics. Perhaps they are not the outlying cases of moral relations that conventional theory makes them seem. Perhaps the aspects they display set the pattern for other moral relations.

Relative powerlessness, after all, is not confined to the parent/child relation. It runs through relations between professionals and their clients, particularly doctors and patients,[33] between governments and governed, between rich and poor, between racial groups in different countries, and between men and women in childless relationships. The powerless or relatively powerless need more than justice, and an ethic of care caters to the more that is needed. The fact that morally important relations are not, and, according to Baier, *should* not, be chosen also has a place outside the context of parenting. It has a place in questions about how many resources we should consume now, given how much less our successors may have as a result. It has a place in considerations about the obligation we would have to a stranger in great distress, if that stranger happened to be in the next seat on the train or collapsed on one's own doorstep, or tried to flag us down on a motorway.

On the other hand, the parenting relation that is often discussed by feminist moralists is not just any old relation among the relations that one enters without making a choice, and in which one can turn out to be relatively powerless. It is a particularly crucial such relation, because it is so important to shaping all one's other moral reactions. As Baier puts it,

> Contract soon ceases to seem the paradigm source of moral obligation, once we attend to parental responsibility, and justice as a virtue of social institutions will come to seem at best only first equal with the virtue, whatever its name, that ensures that members of each new generation are made appropriately welcome and prepared for their adult lives.
>
> This all constitutes a belated reminder to Western moral theorists of a fact they have always known, that . . . we are born into families, and the first society we belong to, one that fits or misfits us for later ones, is the small society of parents. . . . This . . . is at the same time a reminder of the role of human emotions as much as human reason and will in moral development as it actually comes about.[34]

These points are well taken, but in Baier's hands they are not part of a case for an ethic of care that stands apart from an ethic of justice. They support a view according to which *both* justice and care are important.

A hybrid ethic of care *and* justice seems inevitable once unchosen relations and relative powerlessness are in play in moral theory. For of course both affect relations that are large scale and impersonal and for which care within the family may not prepare us. For example, the rich and poor of the world often find themselves in their respective categories irrespective of choice, and so in relation to one another independent of choice as well. But being in the one position or the other is morally significant, especially for members closest to the two extremes of wealth and poverty. The latter require help urgently, and the former are in the best position to give it. On the other hand, the former may feel no connection with the latter partly *because* the latter are not family, not tribe, not 'us' at all. Justice may need to take up the slack here. The care ethic, which seems so powerful for bringing out the distinctive sources of family obligation, may leave entirely indeterminate the source of our obligations to strangers.[35]

The fact that Baier inclines towards a hybrid ethic with a place for the orthodox theoretical concept of justice does not make her overall approach to moral theory orthodox. On the contrary, her position is *un*orthodox both because it is hybrid, and because care is one of the components of the preferred ethic. Still, unorthodox though it is as a position in moral philosophy, Baier is not anti-theoretical. She does not think that systematic thought is unsuited to morals. She does not even think that the right sort of systematic thought can only be found in women writers. She finds much of value, and much that is consonant with a Gilligan-type approach to morals, in the dead white male philosopher David Hume. I infer that Baier's work is not the right place to look for a radical challenge to moral theory, rooted though it is in Gilligan.[36]

Beyond Care? Sarah Hoagland's *Lesbian Ethics*

It may be that Gilligan's approach itself is less challenging than it has been thought to be. Both feminists who are friendly to the concept of care,[37] and those who are not, find the concept of 'caring' compatible with mainstream moral theory. Feminists who think that there are pro-women applications of mainstream moral theory do not mind the compatibility, while their more radical colleagues are worried by it. They think that the ethic of caring is too slight and faltering a move away from mainstream theory to keep feminism at a safe distance from it. For example, feminists sympathetic to an ethic of care, such as Nel Noddings, are sometimes held to react in the wrong way to a patriarchal ethics that stresses the independence and autonomy of the (male) agent. When feminists – not only Noddings, but Baier and others as well – give weight to the countervailing notion of dependence in ethics, they come uncomfortably close to the patriarchal, or, as it is sometimes put, the 'heterosexualist', understanding of the feminine, especially when mothering is the concept used to revalue upwards relations of dependence. A more emancipated feminism, the criticism goes on, would transcend the heterosexualist understanding of the feminine as well as the heterosexualist favouritism of the masculine. This is Sarah Hoagland's complaint against Noddings.[38]

What Hoagland calls 'lesbian ethics' is much more thoroughgoing in its break from the 'masculinist' model of the feminine.[39] For example, it allows for disenchantment about mothering in a way that Baier, Noddings and Ruddick cannot, and in setting 'amazons' above 'mothers' in its mythic pecking order,[40] it seems to gesture at ideas about exemplary relations between people that are quite foreign to conventional moral theory, even conventional moral theory with a clear feminist thrust, as in Baier and Friedman. Hoagland's remarkable book on lesbian ethics[41] seems to me to be a much more likely starting point than Gilligan for the sort of break from male moral theory that radical feminists say is required. For one thing, Hoagland does not only believe that male domination has *often* been accompanied by injustice. She thinks it is a wholly pervasive and detestable fact of life, at least outside lesbian communities, that it characteristically takes a violent form, and that radical feminism needs to be heeded when it insists that 'there is a declared war against women from rape to poverty to child sexual abuse to sexual harassment'.[42]

One artifact of male domination is a concept and ideal of the feminine which is disabling to those wishing to resist and escape male domination, and yet widely accepted by those who suffer from this domination. Femininity in the relevant sense puts men at the centre of life, either as attackers or protectors. Bonds with other women appear from the vantage point of femity to be secondary or peripheral, and to be less urgent to form than relations with men. Challenging femininity is one of the negative aims of Hoagland's book. The complementary positive aim is to make intelligible and attractive a way of life in which the central relations are those between members of a female resistance to the declared war upon them, or perhaps between members of a separatist community living as far as possible separately from men. The virtues required for this separatist life are unusual, and up to a point in conflict with the kinds of behaviour that are necessary if this life is to be a possibility at all. Survival skills, including the skills of manipulation, and the willingness to be awkward, even aggressive, although they are invaluable in resisting male domination, may have to be unlearned in dealings with other women. New kinds of behaviour need to be conceived and chosen and practised, some of which were foreign even to lesbian communities that existed around the time *Lesbian Ethics* was published. But these practices can be described and chosen. This is the way Hoagland thinks genuinely 'new' value is constructed.

A first step is separation. Hoagland acknowledges the influence on her work of lesbian separatism, but she does not understand by separation some sort of living apart or in seclusion from men or heterosexual life. Some of her examples suggest that she has in mind a way of living that self-consciously goes against the grain of heterosexual behaviour while located in its midst, even while appearing to mimic it. Commenting on the lesbian practice of appearing in public as a couple made up of a 'butch' and a 'femme', she quotes approvingly a lesbian called Judy Grahn, making the point that, in her experience, the 'butch' partner is not an imitation man:

> We always kept something back: a high-pitched voice, a slant of the head, or a limpness of hand, something that was clearly labeled female. I believe our statement was 'here is another way of being a woman,' not 'Here is a woman trying to be taken for a man.'[43]

At other times separation seems to consist of joint anti-heterosexualist political pursuits with other lesbians, as in the case of a lesbian collective that grew up in Chicago in the 1970s around the newspaper *Lavender Woman*. Hoagland promotes the value of separation in opposition to those who think that ethics divorced from participation is meaningless. For her, participation, even in the form of rebellion or reform can be compromising, since she thinks that there is a kind of deference to a thing even in the act of criticising it or rebelling against it. This is clearest, she thinks, in feminism which aims merely at moral reform of heterosexualist life, and not at dismantling its ethos of domination.

Separation presupposes what Hoagland calls self-understanding rather than self-sacrifice, or any form – including mothering, the care-theorist's preferred form – of handing over one's identity to someone or something else. By self-understanding she seems to mean something like candid self-appraisal in the service of intimacy, which strikes a balance between making oneself so open to others as to be vulnerable to them, and never opening up at all.[44] The cultivation of vulnerability is a particular target of Hoagland's ethics, even when it is a cultivation of vulnerability approved of by some lesbians. Intimacy, on the other hand – forming bonds over a long time with only a few – is one of the aims of a lesbian ethic. Hoagland distinguishes it from forced closeness,[45] and from the grumpy solidarity of the ghetto-ised group bound together by distrust of outsiders.[46] Intimacy is the prerogative of lesbians only if they integrate reasoning and the emotions. This means, among other things, not seeing emotions as things that essentially need control, or that have no cognitive content. It means seeing emotions as sources of strength or energy, and as forces that are the opposite of anti-social.[47]

Power has a place in a lesbian ethic, but it does not take the form of control, even protective control for the sake of some fellow lesbian. It consists instead (as I understand it) of sympathetic attention ('attending')[48] which is effective when the misfortune of the one being 'attended' is known by that person to be shared and understood, rather than taken over, or used to make the attender indispensable to the helped. Attending in this sense comes close to enablement or empowerment of some kind, but Hoagland is wary of either terminology. She notes that the rhetoric of power as enablement can cover unwanted forms of enablement, including, as in the case of those who support alcoholics, manipulative support geared to prolonging the pleasure of playing the supporter's role rather than enabling the alcoholic to break a dependence on alcohol. The wholesome power that Hoagland tries to point to is supposed to be cut off from the ethic of dominance one finds in heterosexualism. Two other goals of a lesbian ethics concern group life, and means of keeping the individual lesbian from being engulfed by, or overly detached from, the community. One is 'autkoenony'; another is intelligibility. Autokoenony is making one's own contribution to community life. It is taking part, as well as belonging. Intelligibility is Hoagland's answer to conventional practices for regulating conflict, practises centring on punishment. The value of making intelligible is preferred to blaming, and the value of understanding oneself as one among others is preferred to independence or autonomy in the form of control. Throughout, the guiding idea is to choose ways of living that undo domination.

Not all of the elements of Hoagland's account have been welcomed by those who identify with lesbianism, and three criticisms of her treatment from insiders rather than from anti-feminists strike me as particularly important, from the angle of concerns being pursued in the present chapter. At least one of Hoagland's readers has questioned her ban on blame;[49] some others have queried her separatism;[50] and another, Marylin Frye, has asked whether 'ethics' is really what Hoagland has in mind or ought to have in mind at all.[51] I begin with Frye, and with her suspicion that women who passionately desire to be good are most often women who suppose that by being good they can achieve vicarious citizenship, that is vicarious participation in the privileges and privileged status of the dominating races and classes. Women with no such hope would not be likely to manifest their ambition for dignity, soundness of character and judgement, and effectiveness in the world as a desire to be good.

If this is so, it seems that it would behoove women who claim to abhor race and class privilege to give up the habit of pursuing them by being and trying to be good. The discovery that one is not good, or doesn't know how to be good, might be welcomed as releasing one from the game of good and evil and thus from the will-bindings that keep us bonded to our oppressors. . . . Thinking on this leads me to wonder if instead of seeking to create a lesbian ethics, many of us who are attracted by a book with the title *Lesbian Ethics* might consider learning to do without ethics entirely.[52]

Since Hoagland realises that certain would-be virtues of subservience and caring can extend heterosexualism, she, too, is in a position to see the uselessness of one kind of expression of a desire to be good. Whether any similar desire to be good or any desire to be good at all motivates adherence to her own positive ethic, however, is very far from being clear, at least to me. In a way Hoagland's book is guidance in how *not* to be good, and it acknowledges the worth of even behaviours she *criticises* in lesbians, when they are directed against heterosexualism. What Hoagland seems to me to address is not a new version of the aspiring woman's appetite for ethics, but the problem of showing that there is a place to go *at all* when one tries to separate from the rule *and* the ethics of the father. In other words, her question is that of how it is possible for there to be *new* value. She is asking whether one must recur to the father's ethics to identify the sins of the father, and she is wondering whether one is tied to the father's ethics in working out remedies.

Apparently the answer is 'No', for it is hard to see orthodox ethics in Hoagland's prescriptions for waging the war of resistance against heterosexualism. The theory is too separatist and partisan for that. For example, male vulnerability or pain or resistance to domination is not devalued or undervalued but wholly and utterly ignored. The section on 'social justice' in the closing chapter of *Lesbian Ethics* is about how ill-advised it is for small-scale lesbian groupings to resort to ostracism or punishment. It is not about how lesbian values could transform a society also including men. Hoagland's is an ethics for a community apart, and a small-scale community at that. On the other hand, it is an ethics which gives *reasons* for the community to stay apart. So it is not a theory with universalist pretensions that turns out to have embarrassing gaps or exclusions, but an anti-universalist theory which intends its application to be for the few who choose to separate. This may mean that objections to its separatism are wide of the mark, and perhaps something similar is true of doubts concerning Hoagland's treatment of blame. Blame belongs to a tradition of punishment that Hoagland sees as carrying on the patterns of domination that run through patriarchal society. She wants a break from this pattern in lesbian communities, but not a break that disallows all criticism of bad behaviour, still less a break that consists of a denial of bad behaviour. On the contrary, Hoagland herself is openly critical of punishment in the form of ostracism, which she thinks commonly operates in lesbian communities,[53] and we have seen that she identifies suspect forms of enablement, though enablement is sometimes praised in lesbian communities. Perhaps this is enough to clear her of the charge of excusing or condoning wrongdoing by writing against blame.[54]

Theory without Patriarchy?

Hoagland's is not an orthodox moral theory. But it is plainly a *theory:* it is systematic and applies to whole classes of action and omission. It prescribes some things and says that other things are wrong. It produces arguments for its choice of apparatus, and for some of its normative ethical judgements. Doesn't this show that it is indebted to, or even a specimen of, academic applied philosophy (albeit an unusual specimen)? If the answer is 'Yes', doesn't the theory suffer from an unwanted involvement with some sector of patriarchal thought? Surely it would be improbable to claim that philosophy and its methods, including applied philosophy and its methods, are gender neutral, still less in solidarity with lesbianism? Yet Hoagland repeatedly identifies herself as a philosopher,[55] where this appears to mean, in part, having been formally trained in and belonging to the profession as conventionally recognised, and although she claims (surely correctly) that hers is not a traditional ethics, it may not depart from tradition in all of the ways she supposes it does.

To begin with, her theory is supposed to dispense with moral principles, or at least to approach principles sceptically,[56] even though she thinks principles are taken seriously in lesbian communities. She thinks that principles appeal to people who want to be certain about what to do, and yet this is a false attraction, because principles are as open to challenge as unprincipled choices. On the other hand, when principles do give determinate practical guidance, this is morally harmful, according to Hoagland, since reliance on principles can spare people the necessary trouble of thinking in detail about whether principles apply, or whether people should be blamed for violating them when they are capable of changing. People who are best able to use principles are good at making judgements, but the ability to make judgements makes redundant the appeal to principles. Hoagland adds that principles are a staple of traditional ethics, whose social function has been to enforce subservience to those higher up in the hierarchy than the agent. Whatever its avowed purpose is, the ethics of principle has not in fact promoted integrity or agency: it has prolonged domination, according to Hoagland.

This line of thought is questionable at almost every point. Principles can appeal to people independently of their supposed power of producing practical certainty in advance of acting; they can appeal, for example, because it is important even after the fact to be able to justify actions when they are challenged. It may be true that the reasons produced are particular and applied to only one action that is under discussion, but reasons that justify are, or depend upon, general reasons, reasons that apply to this case *and* others – and all principles are, are general reasons. Again, principles give people the equipment to challenge what others do, including things done to further oppression. Principles can even inform one's opposition to an ethic of principles. For example, one can understand as a principle Hoagland's view that ethics *shouldn't* support all existing hierarchies. And not only is this intelligible as a principle; it is a readily recognised special case of widely accepted liberal principles. Again, principles may be implicit in what Hoagland calls 'judgements': they are not an optional and perhaps useless extra. Many of Hoagland's own prescriptions for lesbian communities are indeed reformulable as explicit principles, for example 'It's wrong to ostracise', 'It's wrong to avoid risk.' And some of the principles that she is apparently committed to have long had a place in conventional theories. Like many other feminists, Hoagland is sensitive to issues of race and class within communities of women. Doesn't this mean that her theory implicitly takes on board the judgements that racism and class disadvantage are wrong? If it does, doesn't it also take on board some egalitarian principles violated by racism and class disadvantage: namely that people should not have restricted access to goods everyone wants because of their skin colour or their poverty; or in other words, that other things being equal, there should be equal access to these goods?

Traditional ethics is as hard to dismiss wholesale as it is to escape; and of course Hoagland does not escape traditional ethics if what she objects to in it or in heterosexualism is its obsession with power and violent domination. Objections to that are readily formulated in traditional ethics, even if the connections between violent domination and hetero-sexuality or masculinity are untraditional. Ironically enough, what Hoagland calls the ethics of the fathers – with its concepts of duty, obliga-tion, and the moral agent as isolated individual – readily makes sense of some of the wrong in violent domination. It can certainly make sense of the wrong of rape, sexual abuse and battering, though, admittedly, it does not regard these types of action as characteristic of male behaviour. Again, it can and does acknowledge the value of some kinds of agency and com-munity – the foci, according to Hoagland, of an alternative ethics. The communitarian strands of traditional ethics may have many objection-able, patriarchal elements, as Hekman notes; but the fact that traditional ethics makes room for communtarianism and a rich concept of agency – as in Hegel or, in our own day, Charles Taylor – makes it a question whether the supposed dichotomies of duty and agency or individual and community are the key to the opposition between the ethics of the fathers and the ethics of amazons. The preferred elements of these dichotomies have attracted plenty of fatherly endorsement.

Indeed, Hoagland's separatism makes it harder for her to appropri-ate communitarian ideas than for a non-separatist feminist ethicist to do so. On the one hand, she wishes to gear her ethics to a specifically female-suffered oppression; on the other hand, she cannot ignore the multiple oppressions that some women face, where some of this oppression is shared with their male counterparts. If race and class oppression make the oppression of women worse, then race and class oppression are bad in themselves, regardless of gender. That being so, isn't it a question, even in her theory, whether lesbians do not owe support or solidarity to members of other oppressed groups? Perhaps male homosexuals are hard for the theory to ignore, particularly when they suffer from het-erosexualism themselves or eschew its values. Yet male homosexuals are presumably not members of the lesbian community. Similarly for bisex-uals. And this is to say nothing of male members of groups that suffer racism while also engaged in what Hoagland regards as a war against women.

The conclusion towards which the present line of thought is headed is not that Hoagland's moral theory is traditional moral theory in dis-guise, but rather that it breaks less from traditional theory than she claims, if the break is measured in a supposed sharp contrast between the concepts of traditional theory and the concepts of her theory. It is not the concepts of the theory that are convincingly untraditional or anti-traditional. Instead, and ironically enough, it is the principles of her theory that set it apart. What is distinctive is the principles of separatism and partisanship, and the application of her principles to lesbian ways of life that are not separate or partisan enough.

The Challenge of Practice: Two True Stories

The value of Hoagland's work may lie not in her critique of traditional theories or her alternative to them, but in her willingness to take seriously the *practice* of lesbians, the ways of life that they have adopted in response to heterosexualism. Hoagland seeks to articulate principles which endorse some of this practice, and answer some moral questions that arise within it. Traditional theories may also be asked these questions, and may be unable to do much with them. Hoagland's theory works particularly well in justifying aspects of lesbian ways of life that conventional theories cannot easily justify , but arguably *ought* to be able to justify. Perhaps the clearest case of such an area of justification is one in which conventional theory would say that a double standard was being observed.

(1)   In this connection it is possible to make use of the personal story of Rosie B as told to the readers of the periodical, *Lesbian Ethics*.[57] Writing about the existence of cruelty in lesbian communities,[58] Rosie B admits that this is in some ways a taboo subject: to write about it is in a way to show disloyalty to the lesbian community, as well as to invite reprisals from those in the community at whose hands this cruelty has been suffered. On the other hand, not to write about it would be a kind of denial of a kind of behaviour that needs to be resisted. Rosie B tried to steer a course between these two dangers. First, she wrote just about the cruelty she herself had experienced, taking care not to represent it as typical; second, she distinguished the cruelty she experienced from the cruelty that she felt was meted out in the wider heterosexual community. By comparison with that wider community, the lesbian community was in a certain sense not cruel at all, and the abuse that the writer had personally suffered at the hands of men, and that she turned to a lesbian community to escape, was not to be compared with the much milder cruelty of other lesbians.

Rosie B tells of having been raped and tortured as a child at the hands of a member or members of her family. She describes herself as 'a survivor of repeated life-threatening violence as a girl', which was associated with a habit of blaming herself for what she suffered. Her experience of abuse was one of the things that drew her to lesbianism. Yet a form of abuse also manifested itself among lesbians. Within a community of politically active lesbians she 'was victimized by a gang-up of my ex-lover and her friends, all political Lesbians'.[59] What she says she was victimised *for* was a certain kind of 'bad behaviour':

> My 'bad behavior' towards my ex-lover was that I doggedly, often loudly, resisted her attempts to control and bully me, while she pressured me to change my name, my appearance, my clothes, my beliefs and feelings, and ultimately, my very self-image. My rebellion earned me the accusation of being her 'abuser'. When I began to feel stronger and move away from her, she threatened to 'expose me to the Dykes we knew as her abuser'. Knowing that I had bought her accusation, this was a powerful threat, which she in fact carried out.[60]

Rosie B accepted the description of herself as an abuser, which made the treatment she received from her ex-lover's friends particularly painful. Mostly it consisted of being 'badmouthed' and ostracised by other lesbians who sided with her ex-lover against her. Within her relationship with her ex-lover she was not only under strong psychological pressure to change; she was battered. The lesbians who sided with her ex-lover mostly did not ask for Rosie B's side of the story; and those who did were often disbelieving. This treatment reawakened memories of the treatment she had received within her family as a child; and apart from the pain of this 'triggering',

> it can be plain dangerous to resist Lesbians who are behaving abusively – if they tend to be violent, we risk being physically attacked. There's the risk of ostracism in taking unpopular stances, especially if the abusive one has a lot of privilege or high community status. One friend who supported me got nasty letters from my abusive ex-lover. My new partner was ostracized and badmouthed along with me; she was exposed to the abuse I received in the form of harassing phone calls to our home, and the stress of supporting me when my ex-lover and her friends continued to bully and threaten me. *It's usually the abusive Lesbian who gets community support, not her victim, and until that changes, it'll continue to be extremely difficult to confront and end violence and abuse in our communities.*[61] (emphasis in original)

Abuse does not always have to take the form of battering or harassing telephone calls. A range of treatment, some of it apparently milder than that, qualifies:

> Lesbians who are being abused may experience some of the following: their lover blames them for all their relationship problems; they do more than their fair share of work, including household work (this partly

depends on physical ability) and money work (which also partly depends on class, ability, education, and other privilege); their lover's friends ostracize them; they are portrayed as 'having problems,' including being 'crazy'; they are very unassuming and take the blame in all conflicts they experience; they frequently put themselves down; they always defend their lover, even when she's clearly in the wrong. They perceive their lover as all-powerful and are grateful to her – they won't listen to any version of reality except their lover's.[62]

One question that arises about the abuse lesbians suffer – in these forms or in the form of outright battering – is whether it reproduces a pattern of abuse met with in the heterosexual world. If the answer is 'Yes', then it would seem that a lesbian ethics must condemn the abuse in the same terms it uses to condemn what is seen in the heterosexual world. If the answer is 'No', then some account is needed of why the abuse is different, and how, if at all, it should be differently condemned.

Rosie B's claim about 'triggering' (to the effect that patterns of abuse she encountered in the lesbian community called to mind the heterosexualist abuse of her girlhood), certainly suggests that the pattern is similar in some important respect, if not the same. When Rosie B criticises her ex-lover's behaviour, she paints a picture of attempts to dominate and control, and dominance is what Hoagland is turning her back on in sketching a lesbian ethics. When Rosie B *defines* abuse, she connects it with dominance in a way that Hoagland's ethics apparently would in discussing male behaviour. Abuse is 'a consistent pattern of behaviour in which one (or more than one) Lesbian has gained power over another by being verbally cruel or oppressive, being emotionally abusive, and/or being physically abusive'. Yet Rosie B apparently denies that lesbian communities reproduce the abuse that heterosexuals practice. In a section of her paper entitled 'Dykes may not be perfect, but we're still fantastic', she writes,

Our communities are still much safer, more egalitarian, and kinder than the mainstream male/heterosexual world. I believe we're less likely to be cruel or violent than men and heterosexual women. When Dykes talk about abuse among Lesbians, a comparison is often made between us and violent men; and it's not only inappropriate, it's Lesbian-hating. Lesbians are nothing like men; Lesbians who behave violently do so for very different reasons than men. The power dynamics are just not the same . . .

Over the last few years I've often heard heterosexual feminists routinely including Lesbian (and Gay male) 'domestic violence' along with male violence against women. I guess they think they're being liberal and inclusive, but I always feel offended and invaded. I want Lesbians to get support, but that doesn't feel like support, because no one but Lesbians really understands what abuse in our communities is about. When one of the most powerful Lesbian-hating stereotypes in the patriarchal world is that we're 'violent' and 'masculine', only Lesbians have the awareness (and the right) to honestly and effectively discuss violence among Lesbians. Lesbians aren't the only group to act out our oppression as violence against each other – it's fairly typical behavior among oppressed groups. We have no need to feel ashamed about it.[63]

Is Rosie B simply being inconsistent, condemning Lesbian abuse in one breath and excusing it in another? It is hard to be sure. Passages already quoted appear to condemn it. Yet the last passage can also be interpreted to excuse it by suggesting that when lesbian abuse occurs, it is patriarchy acting through its lesbian perpetrators. On the one hand, lesbians are maimed by patriarchy; on the other hand their violence cannot be compared to the violence of the main agents in patriarchy – men, or violent men.

What appears to be inconsistency may actually be the coherent expression of loyal opposition. Rosie B is loyal to lesbians, but opposed to the practices of some lesbians. She is loyal to lesbians in the face of criticism of lesbians that sustains the caricature of them as masculine. Instead of seeing their abusive behaviour as a sign of masculinity, as even the heterosexual feminists insinuate, Rosie B thinks of it as a perversion of the relatively safe, egalitarian and kind way of life that lesbian communities can sustain at their best. Her quarrel is with lesbians who deny that there is ever any falling away from this ideal; but this quarrel does not put her in the camp of the lesbian haters. Now this loyal opposition to lesbian abuse seems to be in the spirit of Hoagland's theory. It tries for understanding rather than blame; but it is critical. It says that lesbian abuse is bad, and that those who suffer it need support, not ostracism. As for those who practice it, they need to be the target of politics rather than abuse in turn, according to Rosie B.[64]

Staunch solidarity with lesbians who are in the separatist community is the other side of the coin of separatism. If choosing to give up a certain pattern of life is sufficient for separatism, and if it is at the same time a choice to enter a special sort of community rather than no community, then one has obligations to others who have opted out to be fellow members of that community, obligations that one does not have to other women or even other lesbians who are not separatists. The fellow opters-out are those who want to put in practice a repudiation of dominance, and even when the departure from the rejected way of life seems not to be thoroughgoing enough to everyone involved, as it does not to those who think that there is cruelty in lesbian communities, it can still make sense for even those disappointed fellow members of the community to say that the cruelty they experience in lesbian communities is much milder than the one they leave behind in the male-dominated world, and even that it is different in kind from the cruelty of heterosexuals, women as well as men. Though lesbian cruelty is wrong, it can be wrong in a lesbian ethic to criticise it as if it were no different from other kinds of cruelty.

Can orthodox theory bear out the idea that male-initiated cruelty in the heterosexual world is one thing morally and lesbian-initiated cruelty in a lesbian community is something else? A final passage from Rosie B helps to focus the issue in this connection:

> Lesbians who abuse are very unlikely to admit it, while their victims may be coerced into taking responsibility. Lesbians who abuse can be very sneaky and manipulative; they will often do all of their abuse behind closed doors while looking perfectly sweet, even vulnerable and powerless, in public. Some of the Lesbians who hit me are very charming, popular, and well thought of in the community.[65]

A Kantian theory cannot fail to condemn the behaviour Rosie B is describing, if the description she gives is taken literally. Coercion and violence and manipulation are simply wrong if the perpetrators are responsible agents. Special reasons would need to be given for utilitarianism not to reach a similar conclusion, and it is hard to get this description to engage with virtue theory and not get the conclusion that lesbian abusers are variously unjust – just as male abusers similarly described would be.

It is possible that the appropriate weight could be given to loyalty by orthodox theory if it were to take seriously the radical feminist idea that most conspicuous forms of male domination of women amount to a standing declaration of war against women. Then loyalty to one's own side in the face of the enemy might itself be a requirement of justice. But whether all male behaviour implicates all males in this war is not so clear. There are also questions about who belongs to each side in this war. Heterosexual women are not all feminists, and heterosexual feminists sometimes go in for a rhetoric that may put them on the enemy side.

(2)   The difficulties for theory in distinguishing between cruelties has a counterpart in the difficulties for theory of distinguishing between kindnesses. Here a second story will help to sharpen the issues. Linda Strega writes about the support she received from other lesbians when she discovered that she had cancer in addition to other debilitating

medical disorders.[66] At the time she discovered her illness she was a member of a separatist lesbian community. Her story does not make clear how big this community was, but six women from it were particularly active in helping her from day to day. These six helped with everything from getting advice about doctors and treatments and raising money, to cooking, shopping, collecting medical records, accompanying Strega to medical appointments, and obtaining necessary supplies for Strega's hospital stay when the time for surgery came. Four of the six kept Strega company in hospital and took turns to attend her day and night, and the same people helped her at short notice to leave hospital and come home. Finally, this core group kept other lesbians informed about Stega's condition, including many, both in the US and abroad, who hardly knew her, some of whom, what is more, did not share her lesbian separatist politics:

> It was heartening to get help from friends and acquaintances who didn't socialise with me any more but who said they sill care about me. I even received some cards and donations from Separatists I've had painful conflicts with in the past. It was a profoundly emotional and aware time in my life, and I felt these messages and gifts came from Lesbians who have a sense of us belonging with each other as Lesbians and as Separatists in ways that go beyond personal differences or discomforts with one another.[67]

Strega, admittedly, was not just any old member of the lesbian community. She was the co-author of an influential book that meant a lot to other lesbians, but that, by the same token, put her closer to the cutting edge of political life, with all its animosities, in the lesbian community. Her story is that of someone who had both friends *and* opponents in different sectors of the lesbian community, and so reasons not to expect support from quarters it actually came from. What accounts for the help that Strega received, in her opinion, was a policy on the part of some lesbians of putting lesbians first.

Strega does not talk about any kindness she received from heterosexuals working in the San Francisco hospital where she was treated; and though she says in passing that some of her medical expenses were covered by state health insurance, and though she appears to have got help from some non-lesbian health institutions, not least the hospital, these sources of support don't inspire any warmth from her at all. Does help not count as help when it comes from the community that Strega has separated from? Perhaps the question makes an issue of something where none exists: help from friends naturally matters to people in ways that anonymous or impersonal help does not. On the other hand, it can make sense also to be grateful for impersonal or anonymous help, without in any way being committed to holding that it must count for the same as the help, especially the very sustained help, of friends. For a lesbian separatist, on the other hand, gratitude for state help is presumably out of order, since it is at best a paternalistic mitigation of a hostile, violent and oppressive patriarchy. When a few effects of patriarchy turn out to be benign, why should that be given much or even any weight? Even ogres can decide capriciously to spare their victims pain or have unaggressive moments. But that does not mean that on those occasions the victims of ogres should be grateful. Gratitude is in order against a background of neutral treatment, not whenever there is a break in a pattern of appalling treatment. And perhaps the patriarchal state is like the ogre. If so, it makes sense for a lesbian separatist victim of patriarchy to be selective in recognising forms of treatment that have helped.

To put it another way, there are limits to the acknowledgment of help from the powerful in an ethic of resistance to the powerful, even though the powerful are in a sense in the best position to help. For better or worse, Hoagland's lesbian ethic is able to bear out this thought. It resists a way of life in which men are at the centre of things either as attackers *or* protectors. And just as there is no tension in the repudiation of protection when it is paternalist, and a high value is put on autonomy, so there is no great tension when paternalist help is repudiated, if the most that patriarchal help can be is paternalistic. Perhaps conventional theory is able to see how paternalism taints its products, and perhaps Hoagland is only making clear how theory needs to accommodate resistance to paternalism as the other side of the coin of resistance to violent and life-threatening patriarchy. Each form of resistance involves double standards; but there are moral reasons why some forms of help and some forms of criticism are held to be appropriate, while some forms of help and some forms of criticism are not.[68]

Conclusion

Radical feminism seems to give reasons why it is not only desirable but right for women to put women first. Solidarity of this kind seems to be a morally justified response to oppression directed in some ways differentially against women. Why shouldn't women want to experiment with possibilities of community that those fiercely loyal to women have described or that they may conjure up in the future? And why can't these experiments, when they seem to work, be morally valuable, even if their benefits are not for everyone? Why can't they be morally valuable even if they are inspired by criticism of men that does not fit every man, and that is even unfair to some men? These questions, which seem perfectly natural when asked against the background of the personal histories that make some women embrace lesbian separatism, are not easy for traditional moral theories to answer, as I have tried to show. Still, even if they point to an anomaly of some kind, it is not on the scale contemplated by those who call for women-only moral theory or women-only anti-theory. On the contrary. The preceding discussion does not imply that the problems of male domination have nothing in common with other forms of domination, or that orthodox theories are unequal to talking about many, maybe even *most*, of the rights and wrongs of domination. The claim was, rather, that what the forms of domination have in common is not all that matters morally. There are distinctive moral problems that arise from male domination, and distinctive moral problems that arise from racial oppression, which is why those who suffer from multiple forms of oppression are morally justified in thinking twice about which alliances to form. But the failure on the part of some theories to discern the variety is not tantamount to a wholesale failure of the theories to apply. It is even compatible with reasonable comprehensiveness of coverage.

6

Environmentalism and Moral Theory

For anomaly on a significant scale it may be necessary to look at moral theory in application to matters well beyond the human world. I say '*well* beyond the human world', because non-humans do register with moral theory when they are involved with people, particularly when they suffer ill effects from that involvement. For example, many non-human animals experience pain, and some experience it in the course of being reared or experimented upon for the purpose of various forms of human consumption. Many animals end up as human food or clothing; and some suffer along the way, because the production processes in which they are caught up deny them the space, light, food, water, and shelter that they need in order to be healthy. The pain, distress and loss of health of animals involved in food production or in experiments that may not even indirectly relieve the suffering of any other creatures – these things are accessible to some orthodox moral theories. Utilitarianism is well able to count costs in pain and suffering, even when the subjects of the pain and suffering are not human; and virtue theory, which talks about traits of character that promote human flourishing, can be adapted to the case of other animals and even plants that are capable of flourishing.[1] Kantian theories extend less well, because the features that make respect appropriate – rationality, autonomy, self-control – are not even very well distributed among humans of all ages and conditions, let alone spread throughout the biological world. It would be a mistake to call Kant's theory speciesist, as if it maintained that it was our *biological* humanity that merited respect; it is not. An extra-terrestrial would do as well as a human as a Kantian moral subject if it could legislate for itself; but it is true that Kant's moral theory is not easily extended to animals and plants.[2]

Some orthodox theories do better than others, then, in confronting questions of the treatment of other species. When it comes to inanimate nature and *its* value, on the other hand, all three standard moral theories are apparently reduced to something like silence. Either they ground the supposed wrong of damaging the environment in the bad side effects for the sentient (utilitarianism); or perhaps in the reduced chances of flourishing for plants and animals (virtue theory); or they deny that the damage is a case of wrongdoing at all, while conceding it is bad in some respect e.g. aesthetically. If this denial is in order, there is no anomaly; what there is instead is a case where moral theory *shouldn't* apply. But a considerable literature has been written in the belief that wilful damage to the environment *is* morally wrong, and that the ground for this wrong eludes orthodox theory. This is the literature associated with 'deep ecology' or 'deep environmentalism'. I believe that the negative claim made by deep ecology against the orthodox theories is sound, but that its positive claims are often hard to understand, and when intelligible, are hard to agree with. In this chapter I consider critically some of the tenets of deep ecology as they emerge in representative samples of the literature. I then extract from a piece of analytic environmental ethics the basis of a promising way of grounding obligations to the environment. Although this account is unorthodox enough to support the claim of anomaly, it is not altogether disconnected from orthodox theory, still less from some traditional, pre-philosophical understandings of justice. At the end, I turn to some of the *practice* of the deep ecologists, and see whether this gives rise to anomaly. Some of this practice *seems* morally valuable, and yet difficult for orthodox moral theories to bear out as morally valuable. So practical deep ecology may also turn out to be a source of anomaly, even if not a large one.

The Land Ethic and its Competitors

A good starting point for a discussion of deep environmentalism, given my preoccupations in this book, is J. Baird Callicott's widely anthologised article, 'Animal liberation: a triangular affair'.[3] The paper exposes some of the tensions between three approaches to the treatment of animals in ethical theory: what he calls a 'Benthamite' or 'humane moralist' approach; what he calls 'humanism'; and what he calls, following Aldo Leopold, the 'land ethic'. Callicott endorses the third of these approaches, which appears to depart markedly not only from the other two theories in its treatment of non-human animals, but also from moral common sense in its treatment of humans and from some otherwise attractive ethical egalitarianism in its choice of the highest good. The land ethic is certainly abnormal moral theory; it is certainly a version of deep environmentalism; and a first question for this chapter is whether its abnormality is a reflection of anomaly.

The 'land ethic' can be formulated in a preliminary way by reference to its criterion of right: 'A thing is right when it tends to preserve the integrity, stability, and beauty of the biotic community. It is wrong when it tends otherwise.'[4] The distinctive feature of this criterion, and what suits it to the purposes of deep environmentalism, is its being articulated from a particularly inclusive point of view. The land ethic has room not only for all biological species, but also for soils, rocks and waters. The land ethic includes everything, and it is a levelling ethic. Its point of view does not accord any special value or authority to the human species. It is as if the criterion were being expressed from the point of view *of* the natural world, rather than from a point of view *in* the natural world. But the same feature that suits it for articulating an environmental ethic also makes it unacceptable, or appears to make it unacceptable, to animal liberationists on the one hand, and humanists on the other. The criterion of right of the land ethic stands up for a nature red in tooth and claw; for it implies that killing that does not disturb the stability of nature is permissible, and that killing that restores the stability is flatly obligatory. This has some unwelcome consequences for human beings. On some plausible assumptions about the effect of the burgeoning human population on the environment, and about the effect of the heavy consuming populations of the western world in particular, one can quickly reach the conclusion that the world would be better off with far fewer humans. The land ethic justifies action in keeping with this conclusion. Suppose that the action were more extreme than to lobby for birth control. Suppose someone went about eliminating a lot of human beings for the sake of the rest of the biotic community. That person might be doing something right, according to the criterion of right of the land ethic. Hence the tension between the land ethic and an ethic centred on the value of human life.

So far we have the land ethic and a humanistic ethic at odds with one another. What involves the land ethic in a three-cornered dispute is the utilitarian moral theory of some of the leading animal liberationists. This gives great weight morally to the avoidance and elimination of pain and the promotion of welfare, and where this can only be accomplished at the expense of degrading a watercourse or removing a forest, utilitarianism says that one should not hesitate to degrade the watercourse or remove the forest, since the damage to those inanimate things by itself does not weigh in the balance with the pain and pleasure of the sentient. The sentient creatures who depend for their welfare on the forest or watercourse are of course to be taken into account in moral deliberation; but apart from the effects on them, the value of acting on the watercourse or forest is not moral. Now the land ethic recoils as much from a broad bias in favour of the sentient as it does from a narrow bias in favour of the human. And to underline its even handedness, it has as little objection to feeding some of the sentient animals to human beings, as it does to feeding some of the humans to the sharks. So long as the biotic community is not unbalanced by the feeding, it is all right. Hunting deer and rabbit, even on quite a large scale, may be a service to the biotic community, on this view. So might cannibalism be. And sparing one of the relatively few bears, even when it goes about savaging and killing campers, might be right according to the land ethic. On the other hand, degrading the watercourse and damaging the forest would not be right in all circumstances where the interests of the sentient were at stake.

The land ethic, then, unsettles both conventional morality, which limits the morally relevant community to adult human beings or beings like them, and the less conventional morality that extends the community to include the sentient at large. Believers in the land ethic are not committed by their criterion of right to vegetarianism, nor even to the most humane forms of hunting. They are committed at best to eating organically grown food, whether it is meat *or* plants; and they object to vegetarianism if the plants consumed are factory-farmed, or if vegetarianism results in devoting yet more land to farming.[5] The land ethic regards domesticated animals as unfortunate human artifacts not to be compared in value to wild animals.[6] It also revalues upwards pain,[7] calling attention to its place in the vigorous lives of wild animals and those of pre-domesticated humans. So it disagrees more than it agrees with animal liberationists who make the avoidance of pain primary in ethics. There is some irony in all of this, as Callicott points out; for the pro-animal ethicists would naturally expect to make common cause with environmentalists; and yet if environmentalists take the form of Aldo Leopold, who hunted and ate meat without apology, this expectation is disappointed. With friends like this, the animal liberationists might ask, who needs enemies?

Callicott's answer, as far as I can see, is in two parts. First, whatever the reaction of animal liberationists might be, *animals* are better served by the land ethic than by Benthamite humaneness. This is because the land ethic has a more inclusive view of the mistreatment of animals than the Benthamites do, and a more penetrating diagnosis of what makes it wrong. In the land ethic, domestication is a great evil, and denaturing animals for the purposes of farming is part of this process. Domestication is wrong not because of the pain it produces, for there is nothing necessarily intrinsically wrong with pain, but because it denatures the animals it transforms. Factory farming is also denaturing: it ruins land, reduces the amount of wilderness, and interferes with the lives of plants and animals that are displaced or destroyed for its sake. Even the humane philosophy of the Benthamites is denaturing; for it gives ground for shunning danger and trying to avoid death at any cost, and also for pursuing pleasures at the expense of nature, all things that a less domesticated (and, for the land ethic, less denatured) human being would have repudiated through living vigorously. On the one hand, then, the land ethic revalues some of the things claimed to be evil by its closest rival as an ethic, and, on the other hand – this is the second part of its answer to utilitarianism – it has a place for more than its humanist or pro-animal competition. It is, as Callicott repeatedly says, holist, whereas its competition is atomist.[8] And by holist, Callicott seems to mean something more than inclusive, that is, something more than managing to embrace within a single framework plants, humans, non-human animals, waters and soils. He seems to mean also an ethic in which the morally proper treatment of parts of a whole is derived from truths about the good of the whole.

Is the Land Ethic a Moral Theory?

Because the land ethic is holist and more robustly opposed than its competition to anything that denatures human beings, non-human animals, plants, soils and waters, it ought to prevail in the tug-of-war between theories. Or so I take to Callicott to argue. But this defence, if it is one, of the land ethic, does not do the first thing to show that the land ethic is even a moral theory, since it does not show that there is any ethical content in contributing to the good of nature overall, or in acting to preserve the stability, integrity and beauty of the biotic community, *alias* the system of nature. In one section of his paper Callicott seems to claim that he *has* established the status of the land ethic as a moral theory, and this on the strength of its resemblance to an undoubted, though unmodern, moral theory, namely, Plato's.

Plato's moral theory, like the land ethic, has implications that seem counterintuitive. In particular, Callicott says, Plato 'seems to regard individual human life and suffering with complete indifference'.[9] What matters is the good of the community, which in Plato, as Callicott reads him, can justify infanticide, a (to modern eyes) grudging and skimpy form of medicine, eugenics, and the abolition of the nuclear family. Although these are apparent costs to inhabitants of Plato's Republic, they are justified by the good that life in that Republic makes available. Similarly, what matters in the land ethic is the good of the biotic community, however much pursuing that good exacts from individual humans and domestic animals. In insisting that the good of the biotic community can call for the death of human beings, and big reductions in the populations of other species, or other restrictions on them, and a big reduction in their welfare, the land ethic is not asking its audience to accept anything Plato has not already asked them to accept: it is merely following Plato in demanding that the good of the whole should override the good of the parts where the two appear to conflict. And yet no one questions the claim of Plato's theory to count as a moral theory. The claims of the land ethic to a similar status should not be regarded as any more tenuous:

> Given these formal similarities to Plato's moral philosophy, we may con-
> clude that the land ethic – with its holistic good and its assignment of dif-
> ferential values to the several parts of the environment irrespective of their
> intelligence, sensibility, degree of complexity, or any other characteristic
> discernible in the parts considered separately – is somewhat foreign to
> modern systems of ethical philosophy, but perfectly familiar in the context
> of classical Western philosophy. If, therefore, Plato's system of public and
> private justice is properly an 'ethical' system, then so is the land ethic in
> relation to environmental virtue and excellence.[10]

This is a shaky argument, since merely *formal* similarities to an ethical system seem irrelevant to whether its content is moral. The fact that a moral theory refers the rightness and wrongness of a host of actions to a small number of principles is formally similar to the subsumption of many observations by a small number of natural laws; but this does not show that the system of natural laws plus observations is an ethical system.

For something to count as an ethical system it has to guide action, and systematically. This it typically does by setting out precepts which are unified and justified by some criterion of right or good. We have already seen the criterion of right or good favoured by Leopold. We have already seen some of the distinctive prescriptions it would justify in regard to farming, hunting and so on. This is enough to make it into a system of practical guidance. But whether the system of practical guidance is ethical is not so clear, since certain things customarily prescribed or prohibited, or at any rate discussed, by proponents of moral systems are apparently ignored. Lying, keeping promises, participating as a citizen in political life, stealing – the bearing of a land ethic on these things, if there is one, is wholly obscure. Perhaps that is because a land ethic is not supposed to be a complete system of practical guidance. This much is implied by Callicott where he says that just as Plato's is an ethical system with respect to its chosen subject-matter, 'public and private justice', so the land ethic ought to count as an ethical theory 'in relation to environmental virtue and excellence'. Unfortunately, this leaves an important obscurity over the kinds of subject-matter the two theories have. Does 'environmental virtue' include a virtue of justice or is it *sui generis*? If it is *sui generis*, then the idea that the land ethic does more of the *same* thing as Plato's theory appears to be undercut, and the question of whether the land ethic is an ethical theory because Plato's is immediately reopens. On the other hand, if the right way of behaving in and towards the biotic community *is* justice, how is that sort of justice related to the justice of not stealing, not lying, or (to go very Platonic) the justice of never pretending to know what one doesn't know?

The more the latter question is pressed, the more the abnormal character of the land ethic is brought home. For either the land ethic does have something to say about the rightness of telling the truth, keeping one's promises and so on; or it is silent about them. It seems to be silent about them, perhaps for the (by its lights) very good reason that these things are life-denying, that they do not have a bearing on the human being *qua* member of the biotic community. Contracts, truth-telling, respect for property – all may belong for Callicott with the trappings of 'civilisation' that take human beings away from their vital roots, and that come between human beings and their vigorous encounters with other beasts, waters, soils and mountains in the wilderness. The same implicit theory of the badness of denatured things and the importance of affirming life may (and in the hands of Nietzsche certainly did) turn the associated precepts into an anti-theory of morality, rather than as, Callicott seems to hope, a merely unusual specimen of a moral theory. There is no straightforward way simply of conjoining one's duties to the biotic community with one's duties more conventionally regarded; for the basis of conventional duties is the 'bad old' foundations of humanism – the value of human reason or perhaps rationality, the disvalue of pain – which the land ethic calls in question.

How Thoroughgoing is the Land Ethic?

Either the land ethic is as subversive as Callicott wants it to be, in which case its status as a moral theory is open to doubt; or else it *is* a moral theory, but one that ignores, or argues controversially for the irrelevance of, whole tracts of orthodox moral territory. The problems with the land ethic do not end there. For, ironically, although it goes quite far enough when it comes to distancing itself from humanism and Benthamite morality, it does not seem to be nearly thoroughgoing enough in taking the point of view of nature. The reason is that while it has some claim to take up the perspective of the whole of *this* natural world in deriving its prescriptions and prohibitions, the perspective of *this* world – earth – falls far short of the perspective of nature. If it is nature that is being said to be good and not merely nature here, in this backwater of the universe, then surely what we do matters vanishingly little to the good of nature, since we are infinitesimal and, by cosmic standards, infinitesimally short-lived in comparison to nature, and therefore unable to affect it much for good or evil.

To put it slightly differently: suppose, as Callicott and others say with great plausibility, that it is a global catastrophe that we human beings reproduce ourselves relentlessly and turn more and more of the earth's resources to our consumption.[11] Why should what is catastrophic for the earth be a bad thing cosmically speaking, that is, within the grand scheme of nature as a whole? Just as it is only a calamity from a certain point of view that a few thousand human beings are wiped out in a plague, why should it be any more than locally calamitous that human beings consuming and reproducing themselves ceaselessly drive out other species from the planet? Why is this any worse, cosmically speaking, than, from a perspective closer to our own size, the painful deaths of a couple of gazelle in a death struggle with lions? If it is only sentimental to feel for the gazelles; if the right thing to worry about is whether the two species of lions and gazelles survive, or whether the life of the African plains does, then similarly, why should the destruction of the earth matter, if so much of the rest of the cosmos, presumably with lots of life in it, survives? After all, there will be a *lot* more of the universe left when the earth has been consumed. And if nature can survive without the earth, why does it matter, from the point of view of nature, if the species on earth are depleted by human beings? There may be enormously many species left in the universe as a whole. Even if there are not, why should extinction matter so much? Why should continuing to exist from *now* matter with respect to species? It is not as if those species have never been. Why isn't the important thing *to have been* on the cosmic record rather than to be there permanently or for a cosmically long time, or even for as long as possible?[12] It is no answer to say that the earth here and now has to be our frame of reference because the earth is practically the only place we can act upon; for what is at issue is whether anything we do in the place we are efficacious is worth doing for the good of nature. On incontrovertible assumptions about our smallness relative to the whole of nature, and the ease of survival of the rest of the universe without us, the answer must be 'No'.

Perhaps for earth-bound, relatively ineffectual, agents like ourselves, promoting the good of nature is *faute de mieux* trying to protect local nature. Still, there is a problem with interpreting the requirement of protecting nature, and the problem is aggravated by talk of a biotic community. The problem is that the 'whole' emphasised by the land ethic may be regarded as a system of *tensions* between animals, plants, soils and waters, and not a series of harmonies of parts, as talk of a 'community' implies. Perhaps protecting nature is protecting the tensions, rather than what they are tensions between. One tension, or one set of tensions, is created by human encroachments on wilderness, the human consumption of non-renewable forms of energy, and human population growth. But if these encroachments, and the modifications to ourselves and our environment that drive consumption, are 'natural' for our species,[13] then to persist in these tendencies is to protect nature, even if, paradoxically, what is being preserved has its destructive and antisocial or anti-community side. Perhaps the point is being laboured: it is that the naturalism of environmental ethics threatens to count as good everything that has a biological explanation; and biology may explain, and so, on the environmentalist view, may also excuse, what under other descriptions seem to be human excesses. Talk of nature or nature on earth as a biotic community may then seem question-begging. It would have looked that way in any case, since, as the previous paragraph reminds us, nature is simply too big and too varied and too long-lived for any implicit assertion of a common interest among the parts – surely implied by talk of community – to be credible without argument.

The Problem of Grounding Reconsidered

The criterion of right proposed in the land ethic has proved to be objectionable on four counts. It does not seem to speak to the rightness and wrongness of enough actions and practices; its judgements of right and wrong within its chosen sphere are controversial, and yet not grounded in anything less controversial; its talk of the biotic seems parochial: an ethic for earth rather than the whole of nature; and it helps itself to the doubtfully coherent notion of a biotic community. Could a different environmental ethics avoid these problems and yet claim to get away from the narrow point of view of the humanists and Benthamites? Before we cast about for better formulations of the good or the right from nature's point of view, we had better ask whether anything narrower *must* be unacceptable. There is a line of thought familiar from the environmental ethics literature that stigmatises as anthropocentric any attempt to include ecosystems or species or rocks or soils in a list of morally considerable entities that starts with rational adult humans. This 'extensionist' strategy[14] is just another way, so it is alleged, of making the environment a moral add-on, something that has a strong a claim to moral standing by analogy with a central case rather than in its own right. One of the reasons that the land ethic looks attractive to environmentalists, or looks a *heroic* failure, rather than a failure plain and simple, is that it is so strongly anti-extensionist.

There are philosophers who hold that a deep environmental ethic must do more than avoid extensionism and anthropocentrism in its explanation of what we owe to nature. According to them, an acceptable environmental ethic must do nothing less than enable us to reconceptualise our relation to nature. It is an anti-nature *conceptual scheme* as much as self-indulgence and weakness of will that supports the continuing human onslaught against nature; and much of what stands in the way of our behaving better could be swept aside if we overcame our alienation from nature and *identified* with nature in a more thoroughgoing way. A much-quoted remark of Warwick Fox sets the tone: 'We can make no firm ontological divide in the field of existence . . . there is no bifurcation in reality between the human and the non-human realms . . . to the extent that we perceive boundaries, we fall short of deep ecological consciousness.'[15] One-ness in nature is Fox's theme, and he is not alone in putting it at the centre of the thinking behind deep ecology.[16] Like other critics of deep environmentalism,[17] I find many of the treatments of the idea deeply obscure. What is more, they seem unnecessary for giving deep ecology the conceptual apparatus it needs in its own right, and in order to count as a distinctive part of normative ethics. It is true that an ethic geared to identifying with nature avoids extensionism, but if this is a virtue at all in an account of obligations to ecosystems, it must not prevent the account from taking its place alongside or as part of an account of other moral obligations we have, including obligations to adult human beings. The problem with the land ethic and with Fox's alternative to it is that they are silent about those other obligations. Either that, or they base obligations to nature on a criterion that revises our obligations to other human beings or that simply conflicts with criteria of right for the treatment of human beings.

An account which overcomes this problem need not be extensionist. Instead of finding analogies between the human and non-human that allows obligations to the one to transfer to the other, it can try to locate a common source for all those obligations, including our obligations to adult human beings. We have already come across a plausible principle that would justify at a stroke some of our obligations to other people *and* to some ecosystems: this is Onora O'Neill's institutional policy of rejecting injury, where injury can be understood not only as a harm to an agent or agency, but as debilitation more generally.[18] Even a policy of rejecting damage would do the trick if damage were to be seen as the genus of which injury or interference with agency or loss of capacity for survival were species. Something less fancy still may work, if certain illusions about the basis for moral theory are dispelled. For example, Mary Midgley has argued that the concept of justice itself grounds duties to islands, such as the duty not to destroy them,[19] and that the main obstacle in the way of seeing this is the prevalence of theories of justice founded on the social contract. She is also critical of a metaethical position, according to which strongly counterintuitive consequences of a theory can be overlooked if the alternative is to have no theory at all. Midgley particularly presses two points: that, pre-theoretically, injustice and wrongness are concepts with similar scope; so that some reason needs to be given why, for example, cruelty is insufficient for injustice. The fact that cruelty can involve parties and non-parties to a social contract is not a good reason, since that begs the question of whether justice is a matter of contracting. She sums it up by saying that justice is a *pervading* virtue:[20] justice that depended on contracting would be less than a pervading virtue. Second, Midgley notes that the weak and inarticulate, far from lying outside the scope of justice, are foremost among those whom justice makes it a duty to care for, both in traditional moral philosophy and in pre-philosophical thought.[21] So the fact that islands cannot talk or reason no more shows that they are incapable of suffering injustice than the muteness and pre-rationality of a new-born baby shows that it is. What matters is whether islands, or redwood forests, or other things are capable of damage or destruction by human activity. If they are, then the onus is on humans to justify the damage or destruction. Other things being equal, Midgley seems to be saying, it is wrong or unjust to damage or destroy things; which is why we can have duties that extend far beyond the set of adult rational humans.

This is a simple but apt basis for more of ethics than environmental ethics, but it will do as a starting point for environmental ethics in particular, escaping the charge of anthropocentrism as well as avoiding the dangers of naturalism. What organises the category of things with moral standing in an account like Midgley's is not the relation of resemblance to rational, adult humans, nor, on the other hand, capacity for membership in the biotic community: we can have duties to artifacts on Midgley's view.[22] Rather, to be morally considerable is to be a thing to which duties can be owed, and to be a possible object of duty is to be *fragile* or *vulnerable* or *destructible*. These are not concepts that apply only or primarily to humans: they apply, as the concept of *member of the biotic community* does, to human beings among other things. This much is consistent with the thinking that underlies opposition to extensionism; but it also allows for a view of objects of duties that reinstates the familiar individuals recognised as objects of duty in conventional morality.

Now to say that fragility is the basis for moral standing or moral considerability is not to give a complete normative ethics, nor to adjudicate in conflicts where duties to human beings conflict with duties to islands and forests or, differently, duties to defend human beings against fragile but *dangerous* things, like the HIV virus. Perhaps it will remain a question in the fragility-based ethic exactly *when* the vulnerability of animals and forests gives a decisive reason for ignoring or sacrificing human welfare. But asking exactly *when* the vulnerability of nature is a compelling reason is quite different from asking sceptically whether it can *ever* be a compelling reason. In other words, the fragility-based ethic does not feed scepticism about whether animals and forests have moral standing, but, on the contrary, arrests it. In doing so, it may be returning to, rather than making an advance on, moral common sense. After all, it is not as if the very idea of protecting forests at the expense of human interests is out of bounds to ethical theory, or even out of bounds to pre-theoretical ethical thought, once considerations about the connection between destruction and justice are in play. Sometimes it is the other way about: the difficulty is to find principles that justify *cutting down* the forest. Midgley puts the point very effectively:

> Scruples about rapine have been continually dismissed as irrational, but it is not always clear with what rational principles they are supposed to conflict. Western destructiveness has not in fact developed in response to a new set of disinterested intellectual principles demonstrating the need for more people and less redwoods, but mainly as a by-product of greed and increasing commercial confidence.[23]

On Midgley's assumptions, the wrong of rapine can certainly trump the welfare of the timber companies, since, on her assumptions, there is so little to be put in the moral balance on the other side.

Nor must the question of whether duties to the environment ever outweigh others be left for consideration on a case-by-case basis. Certain *principles* seem relevant, some of them familiar from the literature on paternalism. Large-scale damage is worse than small-scale damage; irreversible damage provides stronger justification for intervention than reversible damage; long-term reversibility is worse than short-term reversibility. Thus, evidence of large-scale, irreversible damage would justify interventions on behalf of the forest and against the foresters more readily than evidence of just *any* damage. Evidence of irrecoverable and ruining loss to the most vulnerable employees in the timber company from not felling the redwoods would be more weighty morally in favour of felling the forest than evidence of big but not ruinous damages to the timber company itself. And so on.

Of course, the question of whether the destruction of forests or islands *can* count for more than some kinds of human welfare is not the question of whether it *ought* regularly to count for more, and an environmental ethic that only allowed questions to be asked on behalf of islands and forests, and that rarely called for greater efforts on behalf of forests and islands, would seem hollow and disappointing. There is no reason to think, however, that the fragility-based ethic *only* allows the questions to be asked. It can also answer them, and to the advantage of islands and forests. After all, in many of those cases what is good for the forests and islands will also be good for people. As for cases of conflict, where the imperative of avoiding destruction or damage where possible demands actions for people at the *expense* of islands (or at the expense of fragile but dangerous viruses), it is unclear that that must always be unjustifiable or expressive of a bias. Whether it is depends on a number of things, including the facts about people and islands. It may be that fragility favours taking action for humans because there are more ways of being damaged or injured as a human than there are of being damaged as a forest or tree; or it may be that this isn't so. But if members of one species are more fragile, or more vulnerable than members of another, then it doesn't seem to be a matter of bias to take it into account.

It might be thought that what is wrong with fragility as a basis for environmental ethics is not the possibility of its undervaluing the fragile things other than humans in nature, but an error about destruction. For is it true *in general* that destruction is a bad thing? Certainly it is not true universally. If you like building houses of cards, you probably don't mind knocking them down and starting over again; and surely you do nothing wrong if you knock down your own house of cards. There are demolition derbies: surely they are harmless enough if no one gets hurt? Uninhabitable buildings are torn down to make way for habitable ones: isn't this a kind of destruction that, on utilitarian assumptions, say, might be not only permissible but obligatory? And this is to say nothing of the cycles of regeneration and destruction in nature itself. So isn't the bad or wrong of destruction exaggerated? In a way this line of thought is shallow. To say that destruction needs a justification is compatible with saying that sometimes the justification exists; and there are kinds of destruction or damage that are explicably good, as when many cars are crashed in order to produce a safer car; or when stitches dissolve when a wound has healed. The principle that was introduced with the concept of fragility was that, other things being equal, destruction is wrong. Another way of putting the point is by saying that destruction is prima-facie unjust or something of the sort. But there is surely a sound thought needing formulation in this area which the quibble about permissible destruction does not affect.[24]

The fragility ethic does not imply that we have duties to the whole of nature. In particular, it does not imply that we have duties to parts of nature that are impervious to us or forever inaccessible to us. So it fits in with a view of nature that is not earth-centred, and that does not overdraw the human threat to nature. Human beings are certainly a threat to life and wilderness on earth; but we are not public enemy number one in nature, and we must certainly be, by cosmic standards, one of the puniest dangers to it in existence. Indeed, we are pretty fragile ourselves, and a suitable collision of the earth with a big enough piece of space debris could wipe out very large numbers of our species. If there are intelligent beings on some other planet who know about our fragility, and who are in a position to prevent our destruction at no great expense to themselves, I hope they realise that they have duties to *us*.

Finally, the fragility-based ethic may do better than other formulations of environmental ethics with respect to more abstract considerations. An important such consideration is that fragility is not biased towards individuals rather than species or ecosystems. Again, as a possible basis for an environmental ethic, the concept of fragility may be able to remove a metaethical source of anthropocentrism that embarrasses the land ethic in Callicott's hands. Here what is in question is the dispute in metaethics over subjectivism and objectivism, that is, over whether value is discovered or conferred. Callicott clearly harnesses his case for the land ethic to a kind of ethical subjectivism, and so to a view that puts the source of the value of nature not in soils, waters, grasses and so on, but in consciousness of those things, including human consciousness:

> It is my view that there can be no value apart from an evaluator, that all value is as it were in the eye of the beholder. The value that is attributed to the eco-system is, therefore, humanly dependent or (allowing that other living beings may take a certain delight in the well-being of the whole of things, or that the god may) at least dependent upon some variety of morally and aesthetically sensitive consciousness.[25]

Is this not to elevate a certain form of conscious life over life in general and nature in general, as if the Benthamites were right in a way, and a certain refined sort of sentience was necessary for moral value after all? Callicott anticipates this objection (which calls in question the depth of his deep environmentalism) but thinks it can be met with a distinction:

> It is possible that while things may only have value because we or (someone) values them, they may nonetheless be valued for themselves as well as for the contribution they make to the realisation of our (someone's) interests.[26]

But this only reopens the question that separates the deep from the shallow environmentalists: namely the question of whether there is a *reason* drawn from facts about forests and islands to value forests and islands. What *else* can it mean to value them 'for themselves'? If the answer is that there *is* a reason, then the reason, whatever it is, identifies a value that forests or islands may have even if we lose our aesthetic and moral consciousness. It tells us what that sensitivity is a sensitivity to. There are many possible ways of filling out the answer. It may be to do with the 'independence' of islands or forests; with their grandeur; with their organisation; with their abundance; with their health or vitality. And each of these ways of spelling out what natural things are valued for when they are valued independently of their impact on our interest is also a way of indicating the aspect under which damage to these things can be understood. The connection between the basis of value in something external to us and the concept of damage makes the fragility-based ethic less subjectivist and (because some subjectivity is human) less anthropocentric than the land ethic, or at least the land ethic in Callicott's hands. The general approach is compatible with Rolston's placing value in the form or life of a species,[27] and it is compatible, too, with many other standard suggestions made in the environmental ethics literature about the basis of the value of nature.[28]

The fragility-based ethic departs from traditional moral theories as well as from the land ethic. Is the need for such a theory evidence that the problem of grounding duties to islands and forests is anomalous? Yes. We said in chapter 2 that it was sufficient for anomaly that a problem seemed to require a departure from traditional theories. Yet a departure in the form of a fragility ethic is a much less radical departure than the land ethic. Its arguments from fragility to the wrongness of destruction are arguments from 'justice' in a sense that is accessible to ordinary understanding and that has content in common with the justice treated by traditional moral theories. But the arguments are not exactly Kantian, not utilitarian at all, and not obviously Aristotelian either. So the kind of anomaly we have been discussing does not tend to drive one in the direction of anti-theory; although it supports scepticism about the ability of traditional theories to solve a problem, it does not throw doubt on the ability of any theory to solve the problem, and nor is the conceptual apparatus used particularly exotic.

Although forests and islands may not have rights, people have duties not to injure or destroy or damage the vulnerable, and, forests and islands and the rest of the biosphere being vulnerable, we have a duty to be careful with these things in particular. This qualifies as a deep environmental ethic because it makes damage to nature prima-facie wrong without any reference to the effects of that damage on people. The fragility-based ethic is not extensionist; rather, it tries to find a common source for duties to creatures and objects of quite different kinds. Because of the range of objects of duty it discerns and the kind of basis for those duties, it is not anthropocentric. On the other hand, it is not biological, because the concept of damage or vulnerability is not. Damage may consist of being less able to live, less able to act in one's own right, being less fit for a certain purpose or use; or of losing beauty. Damage to natural objects will be only one kind of damage among others that at first sight needs to be avoided. But the fact that it is only one kind of damage among others and not pre-eminent damage is a good thing: it allows the duties that flow from the need to avoid damage to nature to be co-ordinated with duties of other kinds.

From Deep Environmentalist Theory to Practice

Although the fragility ethic indicates the form of reason that we have to leave forests intact and islands undevastated, it is vague about which agents, if any, have prime responsibility for preventing destruction or damage, and its stress is on a pattern of omission rather than active benevolence or protection. In other words, when it comes to saying what should be done, and by whom, it is not very definite. The question of what should be done is often posed by environmentalists against the background of a belief in an imminent, if not present, crisis or emergency, of which the signs are dramatic climatic change, increasingly widespread shortages of such necessities as clean water, and, in some places, large-scale devastation of terrain through nuclear or chemical contamination, or through large-scale engineering projects, such as dam construction or the diversion of rivers. In the rich West, a high-consuming life-style centred on the personal automobile is often said to be responsible for a disproportionately high level of the damage and depletion of resources that constitutes the emergency. Since many people who enjoy this life-style do not appear to be aware of its effects on the environment, or perhaps doubt that its effects are all that severe, or perhaps do not care about the effects, whatever they are, there is no prospect of an early change in their behaviour, still less the kind of concerted change that would make a difference.

Suppose that the effects of this behaviour really do constitute the emergency that some claim. Or suppose that the effects are less than catastrophic but still bad enough to justify much less consumption or much more restricted use of the automobile. How is the reduced consumption and the reduced use of the automobile to be brought about? By a choice on the part of individual westerners to consume less, recycle more, go back to the land, or change styles of life in thoroughgoing ways? What if too few make choices of this kind to make a difference? If the change will not come by individual choice, should it be required by legislation? In the West, that will depend on persuading voters and their representatives to agree to self-denial, which is unlikely to be popular. Should it be by mass campaigning of the sort undertaken by the large environmental pressure groups? By direct action against the worst trespassers against nature, sometimes thought to be timber companies or road-building or dam-making enterprises? And if by direct action, then direction of what sort? Should it stay within the law, no matter how big the perceived threat? May the direct action extend to violence and sabotage? If it may, morally speaking, should people engage in violence in sabotage as part of a campaign of open disobedience, or, if it prevents enough animal suffering and saves enough trees, can it be covert? Not many of these questions can be answered here. I shall confine myself to asking what we should think about violent, direct action to protect whales or seals from hunting, or to prevent the destruction of a certain animal and plant habitat in the course of road construction.

Shouldn't an environmental ethic that is deep stand up for the kinds of direct action just described? And if it should, mustn't it conflict with the weighty principles that condemn violence, or that require it to be minimized? We are back to the question of the justifiable expense to human welfare of protecting the environment or of damaging it much less in the future than we do at present. The question of direct action may seem to have an added edge if the background theory of ecological emergency is taken seriously. Justifiable expenses are reasonably set high in times of emergency. So *if* there is an ecological emergency now, is direct action relatively easy to justify?

The requirements of emergency

Some people do think direct action justified. Dave Foreman, founder of the radical environmental group Earth First!, was arrested in 1989 and charged with conspiracy to sabotage two nuclear power plants and a manufacturer of triggers for nuclear bombs. He was not always an environmental radical, having once worked as a lobbyist in Washington for an environmental pressure group. But disillusioned by what he took to be the ineffectiveness of political persuasion, he eventually became a believer in direct action. He explained his beliefs in an interview in *Mother Earth News* in 1985:

> Species are going under every day. Old-growth forests are disappearing. Overgrazing continues to ruin our western public lands. Off-road vehicles are cutting up the countryside everywhere. Poisons are continually and increasingly being injected into the environment. Rain forests are being clear-cut. In short, the environment is *losing* . . . everywhere. And to try to fight such an essential battle with less than every weapon we have available to us is foolish, and, in the long run, suicidal.[29]

What Foreman seems to be describing is the losing side in a war, a losing side that can use all the help it can get. But it is not true in other wars that just any weapon turned against the enemy does some good, if only just a little. A single shot that kills one enemy soldier can alert the enemy army to resistance that it quashes, and that could have kept on going and done more damage to the enemy army if the single shot had never been fired. In the case of the war against the environment, local small-scale efforts at defence risk being counterproductive as well. They can actually contribute to a set-back, because they alienate the support that could make action at the level of *institutions* more likely.

It cannot both be the case that damage to the environment amounts to a global emergency, and that it isn't urgent to mobilise institutions, the bigger and more powerful the better, for the (so-far-losing) side. But if that is right, then the impression made on those who do not share environmentalist's values, still less environmentalist activist's values, can be very important. So long as the crisis is as big as the activists say it is, political action on the environment's side in the war against it is necessary: an institutional policy of non-injury to, or protection of, the environment needs to be given effect. But then the question of what activism is permissible is the question of what activism, if any, is compatible with mobilising the institutions, and not the question of what action, taken locally, is the most authentic expression of the pro-environment partisans. In other words, *not* using every available weapon may be necessary if one takes the environment's side in a war waged against it.

The point is both accepted and rejected by Foreman in a passage from the 1985 interview in which he speaks up for 'monkey-wrenching': any technique for destroying or disabling machines that pose a threat to the environment:

> I'm convinced that monkey wrenching can be one of the most effective ways of protecting our few remaining wild places. If a sufficient number of sincere individuals and small groups around the country were to launch a serious campaign of strategic monkey wrenching – a totally defensive effort to halt the continued destruction of wilderness – it would in fact cause the retreat of industrial civilization from millions of acres of wildlands.[30]

'If a sufficient number of sincere individuals and small groups were to . . . launch a serious campaign': this describes the result of a political campaign of mobilisation, not an extra-political alternative to it. It is easy to miss this, if one is fixated by the little that would be required for an *individual* act of monkey-wrenching, namely the quiet spiking of a tree (to disable a saw) in a wilderness area. But the fact that if a lot of committed people did a little thing, a big effect would be created, does not make it straightforward to get a lot of people to do the little thing – spiking the tree – still less organising the serious campaign of strategic monkey wrenching. It would take conventional political means, namely, speaking, writing, and setting a public example. If the conventional political means made a sufficient number of people into full-blown activists, why wouldn't the same means make for sufficient numbers of activists for a powerful conventional political campaign in favour of the environment, directed at governments? The irony is that Foreman both assumes that a sufficient number of independent activists can spontaneously rise up and spike trees in their localities, and yet also appears to criticise conventional political efforts to save the environment as naïve and ineffectual. Conventional political effort is required for radicalism just as much as staid legislative action.

The point is not simply that political mobilisation is difficult but necessary by Foreman's own lights; it is that the deep discrepancy between deep environmentalism, which is not widely subscribed to, and shallow environmentalism, which probably is, is a big obstacle in the way of taking what deep environmentalism must agree is the most effective action on behalf of the environment, namely strictly enforced political policies. Either deep environmentalism needs to be more widely believed, which may be a matter of political campaigning, if that is more effective in winning support than direct action, or else, because of the urgency of the emergency, common cause may have to be made with shallow environmentalists, who may deny that trees or even whales have intrinsic value. Either way, the fact that direct action and deep environmentalism are made for one another does not by itself add up to a case for direct action of any kind by deep environmentalists. Like the isolated shot in war between human armies, it may express dedication to a just cause and yet advance the cause not at all.

The answer to the factual question of how direct action does affect public opinion, then, should matter as much to environmentalists who think that we are in a global emergency as the philosophical question of whether an environmental ethic, or normative ethics in general, justifies direct action to protect trees or whales independently of emergency. It is to this second and more general question that I now turn.

General justification of direct action

It is sometimes claimed that direct action on behalf of the environment can be justified in consequentialist terms if civil disobedience in general can be.[31] Although civil disobedience has quite a lot to be said against it, namely the utility of law-abidingness, it is not impossible that by publicly breaking the law and accepting the penalty, the good produced can outweigh the disutility of public law-breaking. Similarly, although it is normally wrong to interfere with the lawful activities of road-builders and sawyers, and to destroy property that they need to carry out their work, it is not impossible that the good produced can outweigh the bad of road-building and cutting down forests. Martin,[32] who has explored this line of thought, claims that many empirical questions about the consequences of direct action need to be answered before the possibility of a consequentialist defence is turned into an actual defence, and he claims, plausibly enough, that more would have to be done to justify monkey-wrenching as a means of preventing road-building than would need to be done to justify lying in the path of bulldozers.

There do, however, appear to be cases where the consequences of non-violent direct action by environmentalists are good, and, incidentally, where more than the goodness of the consequences seems to provide the justification for what is done. In a brief history of the actions of what became the Greenpeace organisation,[33] Bob Hunter describes undertakings that appear to be morally successful as well as successful in bringing favourable attention to the environmental movement. The immediate predecessor of the Greenpeace organisation was a group of environmentalists based in or near Vancouver, Canada, who all belonged to the local chapter of the Sierra Club. They formed themselves into the Don't Make a Wave Committee, with the aim of mobilising opposition to underground nuclear testing by the US Atomic Energy Commission at Amchitka Island in the Alaskan Aleutians. The Don't Make a Wave Committee believed that the testing could create a damaging tidal wave, and aggravate the very strong natural seismic activity in that part of Alaska. After a student protest in September 1970, which took the form of a blockade of a border crossing between Canada and the US near Vancouver, the committee hit on the idea of making a protest by stationing a ship at the site of a nuclear test. The idea drew support from organisations that were normally antagonistic to one another, such as the Vancouver Real Estate Board and the then socialist New Democratic Party. With the co-operation of a ship-owning fisherman who was willing to risk the voyage to Alaska as well as the dangers of standing by close to the site of a nuclear test, the protest sailing got under way in September 1971. It attracted enormous publicity, got the endorsement of the then Canadian Prime Minister, and put the American government in the embarrassing position of having to postpone its tests. After forty-two days, the ship, named Greenpeace while chartered by the committee, had to return to Vancouver. A replacement ship was prevented by bad weather from getting to Amchitka before a nuclear test could be successfully carried out. But by then the question of whether the testing should be prevented on environmental grounds had reached the US Supreme Court, which allowed the test to go ahead by only one vote. This near-victory was turned into the real thing by what happened next: the US Atomic Energy Commission closed its site on Amchitka and turned the island into a bird sanctuary. Immediately after this decision became known, the Greenpeace Foundation was established.

The action of the Don't Make a Wave Committee was not just an extremely effective way of making an environmentalist point: going by

Bob Hunter's account it seems to have been a complete moral success as well. Prima facie, it appears to have done all of the following: publicised a serious environmental threat world-wide; removed that threat; attracted financial support from tens of thousands of British Columbians through the purchase of bumper stickers and buttons; attracted high-level political support; precipitated a legal challenge to the Amchitka testing on environmental grounds; led to the creation of a bird sanctuary; created a valuable campaigning organisation; set a model for other successful protests against nuclear testing; revolutionised environmental campaigning while involving members of pre-existing environmental organisations, for example the Sierra Club; hurt no one; destroyed or damaged nothing; violated no law except a tariff regulation enforced by the US Coast Guard at Akutan island.

This list of good things is not complete: it leaves out the good of the good people involved, notably Captain J. C. Cormack who put himself, his forty years of experience at sea, and his halibut boat at the disposal of the protest. Some of the good of the Amchitka protest is the good created by any open, mass-based piece of public, political activity that involves co-operation between people who disagree about many other things, and that creates good will both between the people directly involved, and between them and a wider public. But it seems that there is also, in addition to all of these things, the good of returning Amchitka Island and the Aleutians to the peaceful places they were before their remoteness recommended them as places where nuclear testing could be carried out. After Amchitka, damage to the *site* of underground testing, as much as damage caused elsewhere by the after-effects of the testing, became important. It became important before there was an articulate theory to explain why or whether it was morally important.

A Residual Anomaly

Nearly thirty years after Amchitka there are many different approaches to justifying morally a requirement of environmental protection. Not all of these approaches are satisfactory, and if Callicott's version of the land ethic were the best theoretical grounding available, one would have to conclude that moral theory was not up to the task of explaining the moral importance of environmental damage, at any rate in the same sense of 'moral' as slavery has long been taken to be morally important. A fragility-based ethic does make sense of this sort of moral importance, without multiplying senses of 'moral'. Following Midgley, we can say that it is unjust to damage the environment *and* harm the human helpless, and in saying this we use only a single sense of 'unjust'. Although the fragility-based ethic is non-standard, and the problems it solves are anomalous, the concepts it uses are neither exotic nor new-fangled: the pre-theoretical associations of the concept of justice may inspire it.

But there is more to environmental ethics than the imperative of not damaging or not harming the environment. There is also the value, whatever it is, of living in greater harmony with the environment. This value is not reflected in every experiment in living that benefits the environment. Thus it is possible to sell one's car, connect one's house to an electrical supply generated by the wind or the sun, shun the products of factory farming, and do all of these things because one feels that otherwise one is contributing to a way of life that is damaging the planet. But it is also possible to do these things without leaving the suburbs of a large city, in which the only green spaces are public parks and private gardens. The measures taken by the suburban householder may be required and motivated by justice; but they do not fit into a life that seems attuned to the special value of wilderness or of the seasons or that seems to be affected by awareness of the natural cycles built into, say, agriculture. Although the suburbanites show consideration for the environment, the suburban life may not, from the point of view of deep ecology, give nature its due. The problem should not be exaggerated: since even residents of the suburbs and city-dwellers can be mobile and divide their time between wilderness and office blocks, it is not impossible for the value of fitting into nature to be acted upon some of the time even by people with addresses in Manhattan. But there is a clear sense in which this way of life, combined with scruples about how much and which things one consumes and how one travels within the city itself, is a less thoroughgoing application of an environmental ethic than the ethic of returning to nature.

Is the more thoroughgoing application of the ethic also morally better? I believe that this is quite a difficult question, and one that, as far as I can see, will be hard to pursue with the resources of traditional theories *or* those of the fragility ethic. Here is where the otherwise outlandish frameworks that deep ecologists have proposed may come into their own. That is, the idea of living in greater harmony with nature seems intelligible if imprecise, and adherents of deep ecology have definite visions of how it might be given effect and why it matters morally. But justifying the life more thouroughgoingly lived in nature and regulated by nature is not the same as giving a full environmental ethics, and the apparatus of deep identification with nature that may illuminate the value of harmonising with nature is obscure and unsuitable for co-ordinating justice to islands and forests with other forms of justice.

Is the value of greater harmony with nature moral value? The option of saying that it is not remains open, but it seems a desperate measure. Ways of life that seem dedicated to nature rather than to minimising harm to nature, such as ways of life described by some bio-regionalists,[34] do seem to be a way of taking *further* what is recommended by the fragility-based ethic of duties to nature. These ways of life first of all require people to find out what taking up residence in a certain place demands of the place: its watershed, its plant and animal populations and so on. And then the form of practical problem is *how to fit in*, how to live and let live, with respect to all the life of the place. If one goes in for bio-regionalism one seeks more than a truce between one's way of life and the lives of the other populations there: one seeks to harmonise. Since this calls for more than minimising harm; since it subordinates one's convenience to other things; since it is highly other-regarding, bio-regionalism seems to be morally more exacting and not just more exacting in some morally neutral way than the ethic of being environmentally conscious in the suburbs. It seems a way of living better rather than a way of roughing it.

A distinction that seems to be sensitive to the idea that bio-regionalism takes the fragility-based ethic *further* morally is that between the obligatory and the supererogatory. Applying this distinction, one might say that when one lives scrupulously in Manhattan (and perhaps lobbies for a highly enlightened environmental policy) one discharges one's obligations to nature, but when one embraces bio-regionalism one does something more: still something right, but more than is required by morality. But it is odd to find a use for the category of the supererogatory here, since in its central employments it usually involves benefit to someone other than the agent. The bio-region probably does not benefit from the migration of city-dwellers who want to be thoroughgoing in their relation to nature, and it is not the good effect on the bio-region that makes bio-regionalism morally more thoroughgoing than Manhattan scrupulosity. It is rather that respect for nature is much more the centrepiece of one's life than a constraint on it. A better model for thinking about the matter may be provided by the analogy between bio-regionalism and a life dedicated to religion – say lived in a Christian religious order – versus Manhattan scrupulosity, which would have a counterpart in a secular life constrained by the Bible. There is a sense in which the full-time religious life takes further the morality of a Christian secular life, but does it take it further in a way that adds moral value? The answer 'Yes' to this question does not seem absurd, but I do not know how moral theory can deliver it without assuming some sort of religious inspiration for morality or some sort of moral core to religion. I am not sure that this is better than *stipulating* the answer is 'Yes'. The versions of deep environmentalism I criticised for obscurity and for failing to fit into normative ethics may turn out to have a role in answering *this* question, even if they are not needed to justify the value of protecting the environment. But to say they have a role is to say that there is a gap to be filled by moral theory: it may be that the environment is the source not only of the anomaly for which the fragility ethic is required, but another in addition.[35]

PART **THREE**

Conclusion

7

The Significance of Anomaly

Even in areas where traditional moral theory has been criticised for failing to recognise distinct moral problems for what they are, anomaly is more elusive than one might have expected. Although radical feminists and radical environmentalists often claim that a fresh start has to be made in moral theory if the problems they are concerned with are to be addressed and solved, it is hard to agree that a lesbian ethic or a theory of one's obligations to wilderness and wildlife has to be arrived at *de novo*. On the contrary, some of the analogies between the oppression of women and the oppression of cultural and racial minorities or the economically impoverished are explained by traditional theory in ways that lesbian ethics takes for granted or appropriates. And some of the principles that are intended to have consequences specifically for behaviour in lesbian communities turn out to look like special cases of principles that apply to other, or more inclusive, communities. Thus, even if violence within lesbian relationships lacks some of the background that makes violence within heterosexual relationships objectionable, it is implausible to say that the phenomena have nothing in common, or that one sort of violence might be relatively innocuous, because practised in a relatively wholesome wider community, while the other violence is wholly abhorrent, because expressive of the deep tendencies of heterosexual misogyny. It is more plausible to say, and lesbian ethics has resources for saying, that the violence of some lesbians against lesbians has something in common morally with other sorts of violence.

Something similar can be said in reply to radical environmentalists who claim that a moral justification for protecting wilderness would have to draw on a radically new ethics or be guilty of being anthropocentric. This point of view makes sense if orthodox normative ethics has written into it a contempt for, or indifference to, the non-human or the inanimate. What was argued in the last chapter is that this isn't so: the concept of justice has no such contempt written into it. Admittedly, philo-sophical work sometimes needs to be done to free the concept of justice of some theoretical associations that disable it for environmental and animal ethics. Midgley calls attention to the (for her purposes) unwanted associations of justice with the social contract in recent theory; and in reminding us that the concept of justice has not always had these associations, even in moral theory, she teaches an important lesson: namely, that quite a lot of things have been dreamt of in western moral philosophy, and that nothing utterly gleaming and shiny and freshly manufactured has to be invoked to rescue *nature*, of all things, for ethics. Deep ecologists are impressed by how the traditional thinking of native peoples fits nature: their admiration might also be awakened by the history of bad old rationalist philosophy, if it were only given a chance.[1]

Anomalies Reviewed

Significant anomaly has only been revealed in one of the places the critics of theory lead us to expect it, and even then the non-standard theory that was outlined in response to it was not particularly exotic. Although the question of what we may justly do to forests or islands needs a non-trivial departure from Kantianism, utilitarianism and probably also from Aristotelianism, the departure does not take us out of the territory the other theories occupy. The justice that the fragility ethic connects with a duty to preserve forests is related to the justice that demands the protection of the weak from the strong. So although there is anomaly where the environmentalists claim there is, it is manageable anomaly.

Small-scale prima-facie anomaly has *also* emerged in each broad area of application of moral theory – business, politics, the treatment of women, and the treatment of the rest of nature by human beings – covered in the last four chapters. Chapter 3 considered business and moral theory. In particular, it considered a tension between the narrow interests pursued by business and the wider interests represented by morality. Business is typically pursued for the profit of those who own or run a business; yet there are cases where morality gives reasons for owners and managers to do things that are unprofitable. When this happens it is unbusinesslike to be ethical and unethical to be businesslike. Such cases do not show that the very idea of business ethics is incoherent. But they do point to a sort of highly contingent connection between doing business and promoting interests beyond a business. Business typically aims at the profit of those who manage or own an enterprise; it aims indirectly, if at all, at the good of the people lower down in the business, and indirectly, if at all, at the public good. Medicine, law, political office-holding, policing, on the other hand, all aim at things that are *part* of the public good: health, justice, safety. So they appear more elevated than business, morally speaking. This is the background for what I called in chapter 3 the 'moral condescension of theory to business'. Nevertheless, the dualism involved in the role of business person is sometimes overcome. Certain exemplary business people manage to *fuse* business practice with ethics, rather than to be ethical despite the demands of business. They make their business practice seem (anomalously) superior to the typical run of activity of those whose professions are connected definitionally to the public good. No role morality, and no obvious application of theory to business, seems to capture successfully the moral value of what these exemplary business people do. On the contrary, given the moral condenscension of theory to business – reasonable given what business is typically like – even very upright business people are likely to count for less morally than relatively ordinary pursuers of morally much more creditable professions, such as medicine. This problem over valuations may be an anomaly, though a modest one.

Chapter 4 considered political office-holding as a scene of anomaly. The leading candidate for anomalous phenomenon was dirty hands. Dirty hands *looks* anomalous, because, in order to apply to it, moral theory seems to have to speak paradoxically. It has to resort to talk of the need to do wrong in order to do right. Either that, or it seems to be compelled to multiply spheres of morality, endorsing the Machiavellian claim that political life is subject to a set of moral rules quite different from that of private morality. This is no better than speaking paradoxically, since the politicians' rules conflict with those of ordinary morality, and seem to call for wrongdoing, even from the Machiavellian point of view. There seems to be a utilitarian way of dispelling the paradox, namely by saying that if dirty-handed action maximises the public welfare, it is not a matter of doing wrong in order to do right. It is a matter instead of having to do something that, while normally wrong, has good enough consequences to be right in the circumstances. In chapter 4 I agreed with the conclusion of utilitarianism – that dirty-handed action might be justifiable if the consequences of omitting that action are very bad – but I insisted, contrary to utilitarianism, that theory had also to bear out the impression that doing the justifiable thing had something morally to be said against it even when it clearly does more good than rival courses of action. The key to the proper treatment of dirty hands is the idea of choosing in the face of moral conflict. When a dirty-handed action is being contemplated in a utilitarian framework, there is always something to be said against it: the action will be of a type that a rule of rule utilitarianism says is normally prohibited because of its disutility. But what is normally wrong to do may not be avoidable in an emergency. And this may be all the more true in relation to public officials in a public emergency: those in power are in power to, among other things, prevent injury to those they have power over. A big threat to public safety excuses a lot, even summary execution or mass disinformation, if there is no other way of meeting the big threat. Nevertheless, the word 'excuses' in this connection is used advisedly: there is something wrong to excuse, though that thing is worth doing overall. It is an evil, but, in the circumstances, a lesser evil than allowing the injustice to go unprevented or unmitigated.[2] A formulation along these lines captures simultaneously the idea of doing wrong and doing right on balance, only without any air of paradox.

Dirty hands is one prima-facie anomaly for moral theory; another is political partisanship: knowingly pursuing the lesser public good because of one's connections to a constituency. Unless there are institutional means of discounting for the narrowness of one's constituency's interest, it does not seem right for a representative to defend the interests of a constituency *just* because it is his. The connection between partisanship and dirty hands emerged when the excusing power of democracy was considered in relation to dirty hands. The problem about partisanship looks like the dualism in business ethics, and seems to give rise to an analogous, but again small-scale, anomaly.

More problems for theory emerged from the treatments of feminism and environmentalism in chapters 5 and 6. There was the anomaly of apparently defensible double standards in lesbian ethics, and there was the problem of making out as moral the added value of behaviour in harmony with nature as opposed to merely considerate of nature. The first question I want to consider is whether these and the anomalies of chapters 3 and 4 have anything in common, something that might be characteristic of anomaly in general. I shall claim that they all arise in the course of bumping up against the limits of the narrow area of normal application of the precepts of common-sense morality. This narrow area of application is not the artifact of theory, something theory imposes on ordinary moral thought for the sake of revealing the system in it; it is something inherited from pre-theoretical moral training.

Do Anomalies Have Anything in Common?

Let us return to one of the first things that was said about moral theory in chapter 1, namely that it organises the everyday precepts of personal morality. It organises, by trying to find a common justification for, after partially refining, precepts acquired in ordinary moral training. 'Don't lie'; 'don't steal'; 'don't break promises'; 'don't hurt others' – these are typical of the precepts in question. They are the sort of precepts that might be taught to children in the light of their actual violations of those precepts; there are others – 'don't kill', for example – and precepts of sexual morality that might also be taught in the course of one's child-hood or early adulthood, but probably often in the absence of experi-ences in which the precepts would have direct application. And there are further precepts, for example, 'don't trade shares on the basis of inside information' or 'don't represent one client in a dispute with another client' that do not belong to everyday morality because they are addressed only to members of a certain profession, or only to people involved in a certain line of business. Now one common source of anomaly might be this distinction between precepts for everyone and precepts for occupants of special professional roles: perhaps it is not pos-sible to draw the justification for the professionals' precepts from the justification for the non-professionals' precepts. This diagnosis might fit business and politics and perhaps more of professional morality, but it does not fit anomalies in the area of the environment or women.

A suggestion that comes closer to identifying a common source for our anomalies once again starts from the precepts that we acquire through moral training. These precepts, it might be thought, are primarily intended for private life or for personal morality, behaviour outside a public or social role; anomaly crops up where moral theory has to justify precepts that go beyond personal morality. This suggestion is more general than the first, and it allows anomaly to flow from the demands added by public life (including political life) to personal life. It also allows anomaly to flow from the demands of a particular profession, since professional life is part of public life. Anomalies might arise from the intelligibility of more and less inclusive understandings of the public sphere, some of them mutually conflicting (for example, the public as made up of adult aristo-cratic males, the public as made up of adult, rational white males, regard-less of wealth and birth; the public as made up of all rational adults, regardless of race, sex, wealth and birth; the public as made up of human beings, regardless of rationality, age, sex, wealth, etc; the public as made up sentient creatures, regardless of biological species; the public as identical with the biotic community). Unfortunately, while the variety of possible understandings of 'the public' appears to collect together the general areas we have been considering in the last four chapters, it understates the challenge to theory coming from these areas. For one thing, both environmental ethics and feminist ethics get us to think twice about some of the precepts of *personal* morality. It is not as if these remain unproblematic, and as if anomaly only arises when one gets *beyond* the personal sphere. The land ethic gets us to think twice about eating meat; and feminism insists on the political nature of sex and marriage. Lesbian ethics might justify dishonesty with men as a form of self-defence against the aggression of men.

Instead of the distinction between ethics for everyone and ethics for professionals, or slack in the theory of the private/public distinction, a certain way of understanding the difference between the normal and the abnormal in moral questions may be a key to identifying a common source of anomalies, at any rate those we have already encountered. It is plausible to maintain that when moral theory attempts to justify the precepts of ordinary or everyday morality, certain background assumptions are already in place about the normal scope of application of the precepts, and about the circumstances in which the precepts will normally be applied. Anomaly may arise when there is evidence that some of the background assumptions do not in fact hold; or when moral reasons are given for thinking that the background assumptions shouldn't be made.

An extremely important example of a challenge to a background assumption, extremely important both to the history of ethics and to my preoccupations in this book, is Hobbes's challenge to the idea that the precepts of morality oblige no matter what and no matter when. As soon as behaving morally means risking one's safety, Hobbes maintains, people are not obliged to behave morally. One is told to tell the truth, keep promises and so on, on the understanding that most of the people one tells the truth to and makes promises to – most people – are not one's enemies. Different precepts apply when what is in question is how you should behave in bandit country, or when you are caught behind enemy lines in a war. Different precepts also apply when you know you stand in the way of what an unscrupulous and determined person wants most. In all of these cases, self-defence or self-preservation may require departures from ordinary morality.

Anomalies and war-zones

Many anomalies or would-be anomalies that have emerged in preceding chapters are associated with the belief that there is a war where everyday morality assumes there is security. Radical feminists say that there is an undeclared war of men against women, and that it takes the form of routine rape, child abuse, and wife-battering. This is the background against which we should understand the anomaly identified in chapter 5. In other words, heterosexual life is supposed to be a war-zone, and separatist lesbian communities are places of refuge from this war. They are not neutral areas, but pockets of partisan support for the victims of the war declared by men. The reason it is possible for women in those places of safety justifiably to reserve their beneficence for fellow lesbians, while directing hostility to men, and keeping heterosexual women at arm's length, is that there is a war on, and that it is dangerous to consort or help people who might belong to the enemy.

Radical environmentalism makes use of a similar line of thought. In chapter 6, Dave Foreman, the environmental activist, was quoted as saying that violent direct action against foresters and roadbuilders might be justified because 'the environment is *losing* . . .' everywhere. Foreman is naturally interpreted as saying that the environment is losing a *war* being waged against it, and losing on all fronts. Of course, radical environmentalism needs to challenge other background assumptions of everyday morality in order to justify the violent defence of wilderness; but that does not take away from the point that the assumption of war makes it easier for people to suppose that the conditions normally assumed to hold by ordinary morality have lapsed.

Opponents of a rigorous business ethics often represent commercial competition as a facsimile of war, and reject as Utopian any attempts to extend the precepts of ordinary morality to business. This preference for war imagery and the rejection of utopianism can now be seen to be tightly connected: everyday morality resists extension to business, because business is a war-zone. In chapter 3 I rejected the idea that business was a war-zone, arguing that the analogy between war and commercial competition is routinely overdrawn, and that there is a misleading analogy within an analogy in the form of the idea that bankruptcy is a form of death. For present purposes that misleadingness is beside the point. The point is that in business as elsewhere, war is supposed to cancel the conditions for the operation of ordinary morality.

It is a short step from the businessmen's war among competitors to a government's war against domestic terrorism and the cold war involved in making one's country's interests prevail over another's, a cold war that is supposed to justify routine deception, broken promises, and, less routinely, assassination in the course of the overthrow of an unfriendly regime. Here again the postulation of a war-zone assists a certain form of apologetics, sometimes a sound apologetics, for dirty hands. Chapter

4, in which these matters were discussed, did not exploit the concept of war, but the broader one of a public emergency. If there is any idea that could justify departing from the normal conditions of applying moral precepts, it is that of emergency.

Normality and abnormality again

Does war or emergency or the lapse of security give us a connecting link between anomalies? No. It does not even give us a connecting link between all of the anomalies discussed in this book. I think it *does* have a bearing on the anomaly of justifiable separatism and partisanship in lesbian communities, but it is too narrow to explain the bifurcation of private and public morality in chapter 4, and it does nothing to throw light on the source of the added value of harmonising with nature that proved puzzling in chapter 6. Finally, war suggests a pseudo-anomaly in business ethics, and does nothing to explain the anomalous value of fusions of business and ethics. To encompass the full range of genuine anomalies, we need a more comprehensive notion of what is taken as the normal case in both basic training in, and systematic justification of, the precepts of ordinary morality. Background security is just one aspect of the normal case; there are others. The more departures there are from assumptions built into the normal case, the greater the scope for anomaly.

The normal case for moral training and moral theory alike is the application of precepts of individual conduct, albeit sometimes the conduct of individuals in groups. The normal case again is the case where the individual is considering his or her conduct outside a professional role – but not necessarily outside any role. (Family roles may be assumed to be understood normally; and questions about what one ought to do can arise within them.) In the normal case the practical question raised by the agent is 'May I do this?', or 'What should I do?' and the precept prescribes a course of action in the circumstances that is normally beneficial to the agent and those around him, or that gets the agent out of a conflict between course of action he would like to pursue. The question 'May I do this?' does not come up in just any circumstances. If there is no choice about how to act or no time to deliberate, the case is abnormal. It is abnormal, too, if the question of what I should do or what I may do is raised in conditions of great danger. The standard question concerns the permissibility of doing something particular in the circumstances of an agent. The question, 'How should I live?' or 'What should I live for?', though it certainly belongs to moral theory, is not the question raised in the normal case. Some of the anomalies before us arise where the practical question is not the normal one, for example where it mentions, or is raised within the confines of, a professional role; others arise from disagreements with moral theory about which background conditions for the 'May I do this?' are normal.

We have already identified aspects of the normal case that are called in question in lesbian ethics. If there really is a war of men against women, or perhaps of male-dominated heterosexuals against lesbians, then normal background security is absent, and the idea that women normally have the same obligations of justice to everyone, or that lesbians do, is certainly questionable. At the same time, the otherwise anomalous phenomenon of a morally valuable partisanship, that is, of morally valuable discriminatory practices, or of morally valuable separatism and of double moral standards for insiders and outsiders, makes sense – but against what it assumes controversially is really the normal background or action – a war of aggression against women. Notice that an ethic of caring also raises critical questions about the normal case. For example, it challenges the idea that the primary medium of moral thought is general precepts or principles, and that moral thinking often takes the form of subsuming cases under principles. Perhaps the ethic of caring also challenges the idea that principles of *justice* are foremost among moral principles. But these are not particularly unsettling challenges to theory, since the things that the caring ethic prefers to precepts, namely ties of sympathy or trust, also carry with them a picture of the normal case. In the normal case there is background security, and expressing the preferred sentiments does not normally backfire or do harm to the agent; the primary objects of the trust or sympathy are particular individuals with whom the agent enjoys personal relationships and so on, and the agent is not forced to put one personal relationship ahead of another. It is open to even non-caring ethics, such as those of Rawls or Kant, to say that this sort of case (benevolent or at least non-hostile treatment of someone one knows personally against a peaceful background) is normal or standard in at any rate basic moral training. There can even be agreement between caring and non-caring ethics that the use of reason is not essential to moral behaviour in the normal case – again, at any rate in *basic* moral training. It may be that conditioning is the active ingredient or that sentiment is. The use of reason may become the norm when moral training passes beyond the basic, that is, when training becomes reflective and, for example, addresses moral conflict in private life, or when it asks a moral agent to try to get a purchase on moral decision-making from the angle of the *public* good.

If the normal case bears primarily on the application of precepts of individual conduct, albeit sometimes the conduct of individuals in groups, then it should be unsurprising that the ethics of government office should challenge moral training, and challenge moral theory suited to the justification of the moral precepts transmitted by that training. It should be unsurprising in particular that the problem of dirty hands should pose a challenge. Moral theory in combination with democratic theory can rise to this challenge, I suggested in chapter 4, but not without inheriting the moral difficulties there may be in democratic partisanship. These difficulties, which arise for the whole range of roles and offices in private life, have to do with arriving at a balance between the right of certain narrow interests – personal and sectional – to be given respect when they compete with the demands of a full impartiality.

Lesbian ethics is a reasonably predictable location for anomaly, and so is the ethics of political life. The view from behind the lines of the war of men on women is abnormal, and the tensions between the impersonal demands of office and the demands of personal relations are formidable. When it comes to the environment, anomaly is once again unsurprising. In the normal case moral precepts govern relations between people. I think it is also plausible to say that they govern relations between people and their dependents, where this includes household animals. Certainly it is very common to include the treatment of household pets in the moral training of even young children. The idea that ethics is *exclusively* a matter of relations between humans is not taken from pre-philosophical thinking about ethics. All the same, the precepts of ordinary morality do not standardly apply to relations between people on the one hand and forests and islands on the other, even when those precepts include precepts about justice. If abnormal subjects of just treatment are to be accommodated at all, a particularly general theory of justice needs to be arrived at for the purpose. Midgley's is a gesture in the direction of such a theory. It is a non-standard theory, but it exploits features of a concept of justice that are already present in ordinary thinking about justice towards people, features that are obscured by certain heavily-discussed theories of justice. So the question of *how* non-standard a theory hers is, is a good one.

In chapter 6 I asked the question whether moral theory could concede added moral value to ways of life that not merely tried to avoid harm to the rest of nature but that are designed to *harmonise* with the rest of nature. I claimed that moral theory was not able to say that the added value of harmonising with nature was moral value, and this was an anomaly. In this connection I drew an analogy between the life lived in harmony with nature and the religious life. Both sorts of life, I said, were ways of taking further lives that were led with *moral* scruples. And perhaps the relevant sense of 'taking further' should register somehow in added moral value. It is possible that there is no anomaly here after all, because most moral theories bear not just on what one must do to conform with moral requirements, but also on ideals that one should aim at, and ways of perfecting oneself. Perhaps I am making too much of the connection between moral training and following moral requirements, and not enough of the link between moral training and living up to certain ideals or following certain examples in the course of trying to perfect oneself. In Kant, for example, there are duties of virtue as well as duties of right, duties about adopting certain ends rather than meeting the requirements of right. Part of the difficulty for moral theory posed by the thoroughgoing ecological life is the difficulty of giving a systematic theory of virtue in Kant's sense, where this tells one not only what not to do, but what ends to adopt. The difficulty is compounded if the question of which ends to adopt is raised with the expectation that there be a single substantive (i.e. not merely schematic) end that organises all the others one ought to have in life. But there is of course also a problem of making *moral* sense of trying to harmonise with nature – of incorporating *ecological* content into a moral theory of perfecting oneself. Perhaps only the second problem points to anomaly. Or perhaps, as I suspect, the normal case of the application of precepts of morality and moral theory is in the part of theory that Kant calls the theory of right, and the question of what ends to adopt, let alone what overarching end in life to adopt, is itself abnormal, and one that theory does not address very effectively. Either way, a theory of what made the life lived in harmony with nature morally valuable would be a non-standard theory.

I have been suggesting that the question of the value of the ecologically conscious life is in several ways removed from the 'May I do this?' or the 'What should I do?' of the normal case. The question of the value of exemplary ethical behaviour in business is similarly recherché. Part of what is at stake is the value of the supererogatory. When Aaron Feuerstein's employees were shielded at Aaron Feuerstein's expense from the normal commercial consequences of a devastating factory fire, there is no question that he went beyond what was required of him by morality. Unifying the values of the obligatory and the supererogatory is difficult for theory. But in Feuerstein's case there is the further twist that it was supererogatory and done for the sake of keeping the business going. It was not supererogatory and done *despite* the demands of business, but done *because* of the demands of business, at least as Feuerstein understands business. His act and perhaps his way of doing business generally, overcomes the dualism of practical reason – the dualism of promoting a narrow welfare and promoting a broad welfare – in business ethics. It is not true that Feuerstein overcomes the dualism to the extent of making his goals in business directly serve the public interest generally. But he does overcome it in the sense of not making profitability a condition of beneficence in business. Here the source of anomaly is a double departure from the normal case. The questions Feuerstein asked arose within a business role; but Feuerstein's way of answering these questions shows that he plays that role abnormally and up to a point reinvents that role.

Anomaly and atrocity

If anomaly arises when theory geared to the normal case is asked an abnormal question, or challenged about what it assumes to be normal, then it is a relatively straightforward matter not only to represent the different anomalies already encountered as specimens of the same thing, but also to explain why questions from areas of applied ethics *not* so far considered might give rise to anomalies. Atrocity is a good example. Here the difficulty for theory is not that of calling an atrocity wrong. It is the difficulty of capturing in its explanation of why an atrocity is wrong the *enormity* of the wrong sometimes committed. It is natural for theory to have difficulty with this question if its primary task is that of saying why the things we are accustomed to think of as right, and which we transmit through moral training, really are. More explicitly, theory will have difficulty with atrocity if the following is true. There is a pre-theoretical morality. We learn it as children by being weaned away from doing what we like. Our elders tell us after we have done a prohibited thing that we mustn't do it again, and when we have taken in enough to be able to ask ourselves or others whether something not yet on the prohibited list is also prohibited and why, we can start to be told that something is prohibited because it's another case of something already agreed to be prohibited. This is the beginning of theory, and maybe of wisdom as well. We are able to think about what we do, and we ask that some sort of pattern be imposed on prohibitions, when they are added to in moral training. Suggestions about why all of the prohibited things are wrong, or why bunches of them are, are proto-theory. Out-and-out theory is developed where there is consciousness of different ways in which bunches of prohibitions (and, indirectly, permissions) can be justified, and when the different methods of justification are themselves the subject-matter of reflection.

Now if moral theory develops in this way from shared customs of child-rearing, and if the main method of extension of moral thought is by correction for prohibited action, then theory is importantly constrained by the range of childhood misdemeanour corrected for in moral training, and by the range of adult wrongdoing that is common in adult experience. If theory has these roots, and if it is mainly justifying requirements that people come unthinkingly to conform to, it is out of its element when faced with large-scale evil. 'Because it hurts' or 'Because it's not the truth' quickly become reasons that unify classes of prohibited acts. But 'because it hurts' massively understates the objection to torture; and a violation of a requirement of respect cannot do justice both to racism *and* to genocide. Even utilitarianism, which is well able to track the difference that numbers of people killed make to the wrong of killing, or that the intensity of pain makes to the wrong of inflicting it, is unequal to saying how meticulous organisation adds to the crime of exterminating the Jews or the way the operation of the whim of an all-powerful individual makes a Stalinist reign of terror more terrible. Understatement of the reasons why an atrocity is wrong in moral theory is naturally traced to a preoccupation in theory with species of wrongdoing much closer to the permissible than atrocity. What moral theory treats as normal is a pattern of human action and disposition that needs channelling or smoothing out, but that is basically benign. Radical evil is foreign territory.

The Significance of Anomaly

I turn now from the source and range of anomaly to its significance. If anomalies are what they are only relative to the normal case, and if its picture of the normal case is something moral theory inherits from moral training, then, notwithstanding the way that training over time has internalised some theory, it is really pre-theoretical lore as much as theory, or pre-theoretical lore as the raw material of theory, that anomaly calls into question. It is not some philosophical craving for generality about right and wrong, or some philosophical contempt for the culturally and temporally parochial that makes scrupulousness in business, ruthlessness in politics, solidarity among lesbians, and bioregionalist blending with one's surroundings hard for theories to do justice to; it is the way that in real life norms derived from special roles and from unusual kinds of solidarity can disturb what ordinary moral training reasonably takes for granted. The disturbance rubs off on theory; it is not produced by theory. On the contrary, it is the clash of certain sorts of practice with pre-theoretical assumptions that may be at the bottom of anomaly. These practices clash with theory because of what theory takes over from the pre-theoretical.

The existence of anomaly shows that moral theory has limitations, even though some of these limitations are inherited. Sometimes theory says conflicting things in answer to the same question – the question of the permissibility of doing wrong for the public good, for example; sometimes it is guilty of understatement; and sometimes it is reduced to silence where its saying *anything* would be welcome. Some of its limitations arise from the way in which, if I am right, it extends and rationalises a scheme of moral training that corrects for everyday wrong-doing, according to the standards of a given community and a time and place. This training is at the source of the intuitions we have not only as moral agents, but as readers and writers of applied ethics in some parts of the rich, English-speaking world. Whatever the limitations of theory, they exist alongside a formidable capacity to answer practical questions, from the most childlike 'May I do this?' to questions as sophisticated as 'What is the fairest system of health-care rationing?' or 'Is it better on balance to forgive the debts of the most indebted under-developed countries or reschedule them?' The claim that moral theory has a formidable capacity to answer practical questions, however, is not the claim that moral theory has the capacity to answer most of them uncontroversially or wisely.

I am speaking of answers delivered by moral theory. But it is in a way fraudulent to suggest that the answers are being spoken with a single voice coming from a unified theory. For most of the purposes of this book, three theories have been in question – utilitarianism, Kantianism and an Aristotelian theory of flourishing – and these three theories come in more than one version, not all of them mutually compatible. Isn't this incompatibility being glossed over? Isn't it even being concealed in a theory-by-theory and question-by-question approach to the testing and criticism of moral theory? The incompatibility has certainly not been concealed. In the case of dirty hands it was positively highlighted. Is the conflict troubling?

Orthodox utilitarianism and orthodox Kantianism are antagonistic to one another, and to the idea of a plurality of moral theories. Each ortho-dox theory comes with a claim to be as comprehensive as its rival, and arguments for one theory often work by exposing the ineradicable defects of the competition. Over and above this, utilitarianism and Kan-tianism often conflict at the level of arguments about their overarching principles or values. Thus, classical utilitarianism says that maximising happiness is utlimately all that matters, and that other things that matter are either part of maximising happiness or the same as maximising hap-piness. Classical Kantianism denies this, and sometimes calls on people to do things that decrease the sum of happiness. Surely they cannot both be right? And if they cannot, how can successful *applications* of either theory count in favour of a moral theory in general? The incompatibilities between the standard theories, as well as their pretensions to comprehensiveness and exclusive correctness, can surely not be ignored or tolerated in a defence of theory? If they cannot be shown to be merely apparent,[3] mustn't a defence of theory take the form of a defence of just one specimen of theory – either one of the rival standard theories we have at the moment, or else a unitary successor to the rival theories?

Not necessarily. The fact that a partial or limited theory solves some problems is surely evidence for the viability of theorising, even if the partial or limited theory is not the only one in the field, or if illumination comes from other partial accounts. On the other hand, nothing I have said up to now is supposed to exclude the *possibility* of a unitary successor theory. Such a theory may well be arrived at one day. But I am sceptical of a programme of unification that consists of making just one of the currently standard theories prevail over the others. Chapters 3 to 6 provide evidence that different standard theories come into their own in response to different moral problems. A fight between the three standard theories that left just one standing would not acknowledge these different strengths. So one is led to consider a different form of unification: one that takes components from the three theories and ends with a single theory. A certain body of literature already tries to combine consequentialist and deontological material,[4] and there is a growing recognition that deontology and a version of virtue theory go together.[5] Perhaps these tendencies point the way to a unitary theory. Or it may be that the classical forms of the standard theories are revised so as to drop their claims to comprehensiveness. The conflict between Kantianism and utilitarianism might be narrowed, if utilitarianism were reinterpreted as an ethics for actions originating at government house only.[6]

Moral theory may speak in more than one voice because different aspects of practical questions are (as yet) only captured by different theories. But the significance for normative ethics of difference or conflict between theories should not be overdrawn. There are more than three voices of moral theory, but there is a remarkable amount of speaking in unison. One doesn't have to be a Kantian to think that lying is wrong, or an Aristotelian to admire courage. If there were not this widespread agreement – which is prima facie a strength of theory – there couldn't be the suspicion that moral theory simply regurgitates a bourgeois common sense about right and wrong. If there weren't this agreement, there would not be such a thing as 'puzzles' for theory; there would be too much disorder and disagreement for that. It is true that there are areas of enduring controversy. There isn't a settled conclusion in theory about whether euthanasia is right, for example, or whether abortion is. Nevertheless, there is much agreement between subscribers to different theories about what arguments a satisfactory answer would have to address, and this agreement can unite even those who disagree about the rights and wrongs of abortion or euthanasia. Indeed, this is why it often seems to professional writers of applied ethics as if the discussion of these topics has got bogged down, and as if the same ground has been traversed from every possible direction. The capacity of different theories to refine the relevant issues, even where it does not settle controversy, is surely not valueless. So to speak of the limitations of moral theories is not necessarily to speak of the limitations of so many ungainly pieces of apparatus with no power to illuminate.

Acknowledging the limitations is consistent with believing that they are not numerous enough or big enough to disable moral theorising: the last four chapters establish the elusiveness of anomaly far more convincingly than its existence. Not only has anomaly proved to be rarer than one might have expected, given the attention paid in this book to movements of thought in feminism and ecology that are strongly critical of orthodox moral theory; anomaly has also turned out to be smaller than it might have been expected to be. Even radical feminism and radical environmentalism are compatible with, if not committed to, a lot of orthodoxy about equality and about the need to avoid hurting the vulnerable. So the existence of anomalies such as those that have emerged in this book is perhaps better evidence of the strength of theory than of its limitations.

Anomalies arise, if at all, theory by theory, and practical question by practical question. A particular practical question that utilitarianism has a lot to say about, like dirty hands, may be hard to formulate in ways that come naturally to virtue theory; and violations of duties to oneself that Kant treats in detail may not arise as moral issues according to utilitarianism, because the effects of those violations can be so local. Limitations of one theory, then, are not limitations of theory in general, and the effort of identifying anomaly may make the criticism of moral theory in general less facile than the highly general line of objection one gets from Williams, and, in different ways, from MacIntyre and Rorty and Baier. Paying attention to anomaly may also prompt a re-evaluation of applied ethics. Among philosophers, even moral philosophers, applied ethics is often looked down upon. It may attract people to the study of philosophy and keep up student numbers. It may attract the interest of academics in other disciplines. It may be thought relevant enough to be supported financially with sponsorship and endowments. But intellectually, so the criticism goes on, applied ethics is puny, and articles about abortion or corporate social responsibility have more in common with letters to the editor in newspapers than the rigorously argued papers of philosophers of language or philosophers of mind. Admittedly, not all of moral philosophy is tarred with the brush that is applied to applied ethics. The critics sometimes concede that metaethics may raise questions of real philosophical value, that is questions that really belong anyway to the philosophy of language and the philosophy of mind; but, they say, applied ethics does not and cannot.

This line of criticism is unstable if it is combined with the view that the renewal of normative ethical theory since the 1970s has been philosophically respectable, for the *application* of normative ethical theory is an important source of evidence of the adequacy of a normative ethical theory. Applied ethics is not always explicitly or rigorously engaged in the testing or refinement of a full-blown normative ethical theory, but this is a central and familiar task of applied ethics, and it is philosophically respectable if normative ethical theorising is. What is more, it may only be by trying and failing to apply normative ethical theory that one understands the theory one is criticising well enough to identify its limitations in ways that supporters of theory cannot dismiss as ill-informed or part of an intellectual programme with an anti-theoretical agenda. The radical critics of orthodox moral theory may turn out to be in the right; but their criticism often seems naïve or ill-informed to those supporters of a particular theory who consider it a strength for it to extend to gender and green issues. Often the literature produced by the radicals takes as decisive a pattern of objection that seems to mainstream theorists to be irrelevant or confused. Unless the critics' objections are directed only to those who already share their views, their generality or lack of detail seriously undercuts their force. For example, the dismissal of theory as hopelessly patriarchal or anthropocentric on the strength of its heavy reliance on principles or principles about persons is no more compelling than the dismissal of the *criticism* of theory as man-hating or human-hating. It is different if the critics burrow into the theory and find anomaly at the end of the tunnel. Then they are in a position to show other users how an apparatus malfunctions, not just to confirm non-users in the belief that they needn't bother with the apparatus in the first place. But the approach of burrowing and criticising from the inside has its dangers: one can, despite oneself, find *light* at the end of the tunnel. One can be won over to the use of the apparatus one has suspected is defective, or wished were defective.

I am saying that an improved criticism of theory will result from the effort to apply theory to breaking point. But something else may result as well. This is the conviction that, for the time being, we cannot afford to do without the whole range of established theories we have, their limitations notwithstanding. The idea that an argument in the abstract against impersonal morality should make anyone give up utilitarianism or Kantianism is as strange as the plan of narrowing down the so-called methods of ethics to one or two by purely abstract argument alone. So long as we ask the range of practical questions we do and try to unify the answers, we are going to be in the market not only for as many ethical ideas as possible, as Williams says, but a variety of ethical theories as well. Anomaly may make us suspicious of the theories that have been handed down by moral philosophy. It may even convince us that there is something badly wrong with all of them. But it can no more show us that the established theories are non-starters than it can show that they answer no questions worth asking. The theories answer a *vast* number of questions worth asking. Their silences and hesitations are forgivable.

Notes

1: Moral Theory and Anti-theory

1 For discussions of the shortcomings of some stock applications of stock principles to clinical practice in medicine, see B. Hoffmaster, B. Freedman and G. Fraser (eds) *Clinical Ethics: Theory and Practice* (Clinton, NJ: Humana, 1989). In the same vein, see all of the articles in the Fall 1990 number of *Journal of Medicine and Philosophy* (vol. 15). For more recent discussions, see L. W. Sumner and J. Boyle, *Philosophical Perspectives on Bioethics* (Toronto: University of Toronto Press, 1996). Critics of moral theory in medical ethics sometimes exaggerate the abstraction of moral theory and mistake the aspiration to justify for a wish to generate practical conclusions mechanically, by deduction alone. See e.g. B. Hoffmaster, 'The theory and practice of applied ethics', *Dialogue* 30 (1991), pp. 213–34. As Hoffmaster is particularly critical of the view of theory given in chapter 1 of Beauchamp and Childress's *Principles of Medical Ethics*, it is perhaps worth calling attention to a paper in which Beauchamp explicitly anticipates and rejects an interpretation like Hoffmaster's of this textbook. See T. Beauchamp, 'On eliminating the distinction between applied ethics and ethical theory', *The Monist* 67 (1984), p. 518. I have no quarrel, however, with Hoffmaster's claim that applications of theory are often insensitive to practice and context in ways that make medical ethics look like a sterile subject.

2 For an attempt by a supporter of theory in medical ethics to conciliate the critics of moral theory, see N. Daniels, 'Wide reflective equilibrium in practice', in Sumner and Boyle, *Philosophical Perspectives*, pp. 96–114.

3 I say 'proto-theory', because the principles appealed to in justification may not be basic but intermediate, and roughly conceived or articulated. Or the agent may have only a partial grasp of the precepts subsumed by a higher-order principle. On the importance of partial grasp and partial reference to theories for reaching agreement in negotiations and deciding cases at law, see Cass Sunstein, *Legal Reasoning and Political Conflict* (New York: Oxford

University Press, 1996). Larry Lessig impressed upon me the importance of Sunstein's idea of incompletely theorised agreements.

4 Sometimes the theories have suggested further prescriptions and prohibitions, as well as mechanisms for applying these in unobvious ways to cases. F. M. Kamm distinguishes between 'low theory' – pursuing questions in applied ethics on the one hand – and 'high theory', such as Ross's theory or general statements of utilitarianism. See her 'High theory, low theory and the demands of morality', *Nomos* 37 (1995), pp. 81–107.

5 Not all of these applications of theory have gone unquestioned. For constructive criticism of the whole field of applied ethics from a broadly Pragmatist angle, and with much attention to detail, see A. Edel, E. Flower and F. O'Connor, *Critique of Applied Ethics* (Philadelphia: Temple University Press, 1994). Edel *et al.* emphasise the ways in which discovery and innovation are crucial to moral enquiry (see their ch. 10).

There is a big literature on the moral and intellectual significance of applying moral theory. See chs 1–9 of E. Winkler and J. Coombs (eds) *Applied Ethics* (Oxford: Blackwell, 1993). Another good collection of articles is in the *The Monist* 67 (1984). Other recent papers include James Brown, 'On applying ethics', *Philosophy* 22 (1987), pp. 81–93; D. Marquis, 'The role of applied ethics in philosophy', *South Western Philosophical Review* 6 (1990), pp. 1–18; and James Young, 'The immorality of applied ethics', *International Journal of Applied Philosophy* 3 (1986), pp. 37–43.

6 For the interpretation of Aristotle adopted in the following paragraphs, I am indebted to M. Burnyeat, 'Aristotle on learning to be good', in A. Rorty (ed.) *Essays on Aristotle's Ethics* (Berkeley: University of California Press, 1980), pp. 69–92.

7 As before, I mean moral theory in the sense of a normative ethical theory articulated by philosophers. Such a theory may improve a public rhetoric otherwise dominated by sceptics about morality or by the fanatically partisan. For a discussion of how moral theory may improve upon, without condescending to, ordinary moral rhetoric, see my *Moral Theory and Capital Punishment* (Oxford: Blackwell Publishers, 1987), ch. 1. Moral theory along the lines described there is not a deductive apparatus shielded from debate or from second thoughts that arise when the theory is tested in practice. On the other hand, it does articulate principles that are supposed to apply universally or at least generally, and that are supposed to justify the conclusions of practical deliberation.

8 For more on the more that might be needed, and on the difficulties of coming up with a satisfactory account in this connection, see James Griffin, *Value Judgement: Improving our Ethical Beliefs* (Oxford: Clarendon Press, 1996), pp. 87ff. Griffin's book came into my hands too late for me to make proper use of it. Some of its themes are close to those of this book.

9 My account will concentrate on varieties of this scepticism in Anglo-American philosophy; for a treatment that takes into account positions derived from French philosophy, and theorists writing in English who are

sympathetic to the Continental tradition, see D. Furrow, *Against Theory* (London: Routledge, 1995).

10 For one recent attempt at a systematic treatment that is alive to the disunity of 'anti-theory', see Robert Louden, *Morality and Moral Theory* (New York: Oxford University Press, 1992), ch. 5. See also Furrow, *Against Theory*, ch. 1. Important articles in anti-theory are collected in S. Clarke and E. Simpson (eds) *Anti-theory in Ethics and Moral Conservatism* (Albany, NY: SUNY Press, 1989).

11 For an account of the Enlightenment influence from someone who is not *quite* an anti-theorist, see C. Larmore's *Patterns of Moral Complexity* (Cambridge: Cambridge University Press, 1987) and his later collection of essays, *The Morals of Modernity* (Cambridge: Cambridge University Press, 1996).

12 Louden questions the claim that Aristotle lacks a theory, and questions the claim that the theory he put forward justifies the criticisms of the anti-theorists.

13 See especially Baier's 'Theory and reflective practices' in her collection *Postures of the Mind* (London: Methuen, 1985), pp. 207–27.

14 See, e.g., *After Virtue* (London: Duckworth, 1984).

15 See, e.g., 'Morality and pessimism', in Hampshire's *Morality and Conflict* (Oxford: Blackwell Publishers, 1983).

16 See, e.g., J. L. Mackie's *Ethics: Inventing Right and Wrong* (Harmondsworth: Penguin Books, 1977).

17 See Baier, 'Doing without moral theory?', *in Postures of the Mind*, pp. 239–40.

18 See J. J. C. Smart and Bernard Williams, *Utilitarianism: For and Against* (Cambridge: Cambridge University Press, 1973) and Williams, *Moral Luck* (Cambridge: Cambridge Univerity Press, 1981).

19 Susan Wolf, 'Moral saints', *Journal of Philosophy* 79 (1982), pp. 419–39.

20 Bruce Ackerman, *Social Justice in the Liberal State* (New Haven: Yale University Press, 1980).

21 'Theory and reflective practices', in *Postures of the Mind*, pp. 212ff.

22 Judith Jarvis Thomson, 'In defense of abortion', *Philosophy and Public Affairs* 1 (1971). Thomson wants to move the debate about abortion beyond the impasse that is reached when one side insists, and the other denies, that the foetus has the same moral status as an adult human being, and so she *concedes* to her opponents their claim that the foetus *is* equal in status, marking the concession with a discussion of a case in which a talented adult, a violinist, is dependent for his survival on being connected by tubes for nine months to a woman who is kidnapped to act as a sort of life-support machine for him. Thomson's claim is that if the woman does not consent to act as life-support machine, she is not morally obliged to continue being one, notwithstanding the fact that the violinist will die if she discontinues, and notwithstanding the fact that the violinist is not party to her being kidnapped and forced into service as life-support machine. Even if something far less than nine months' confinement were needed to keep someone alive, the touch of Henry Fonda's hand on a fevered brow, say, there would be no *right* on the

part of the one in need against Henry Fonda, Thomson claims. It might be rather decent of Henry Fonda to go out of his way to touch the fevered brow; it might be extremely generous, of the kidnapped woman to act as a life-support machine for nine months for the violinist; but no right to life would make these actions necessary, even though the purported right to life is that of a fully fledged human being, with full human rights.

23 If conscientious contraception fails and a woman becomes pregnant, according to Thomson, the woman is no more obliged to carry the pregnancy to term than an owner of a house that takes every precaution against the entrance of people-seeds (seeds that grown into people when they take root) is obliged to offer hospitality to a people-seed that penetrates the house's defences and takes root in the carpet.

24 Cora Diamond, 'Losing your concepts', *Ethics* 98 (1987–8), pp. 255–77.

25 *Ethics and the Limits of Philosophy* (Cambridge: Harvard University Press, 1985), p. 117.

26 Theory and reflective practices', p. 217.

27 For a survey of some of the relevant claims in this area, see Louden, *Morality*, pp. 90–2. See also Stanley Clarke, 'Anti-theory in ethics', *American Philosophical Quarterly* 24 (1987), p. 239.

28 See Alan Donagan, *The Theory of Morality* (Chicago: University of Chicago Press, 1977).

29 John McDowell, 'Virtue and reason', *The Monist* 62 (1979), pp. 331–50.

30 For a survey of various versions of this objection, see Louden, *Morality*, pp. 95–8.

31 'Theory and reflective practices', p. 224.

32 In *Contingency, Irony and Solidarity* (Cambridge: Cambridge University Press, 1989).

33 Near the beginning of his *A Short History of Western Ethics* (New York: Macmillan, 1966) Alasdair MacIntyre writes,

> It is not that we have first a straightforward history of moral concepts and then a separate and secondary history of philosophical comment. For to analyse a concept philosophically may often be to assist in its transformation by suggesting that it needs revision, or that it is discredited in some way, or that it has a certain kind of prestige. Philosophy leaves everything as it is – except concepts. And since to possess a concept involves behaving or being able to behave in certain circumstances, to alter concepts, whether by modifying existing concepts or by making new concepts available or by destroying old ones, is to alter behavior. So the Athenians who condemned Socrates to death, the English parliament which condemned Hobbes' *Leviathan* in 1666, and the Nazis who burned philosophical books were correct at least in their appreciation that philosophy can be subversive of established ways of behaving. Understanding the world of morality and changing it are far from incompatible tasks. (pp. 2–3)

34   T. Nagel, *The View from Nowhere* (New York: Oxford University Press, 1987), ch. 8.

35   There are critics who combine a dislike of apriorism with a dislike of generality, and who are attracted instead to a kind of moral anthropology as a basis for some moral claims. For an approach along these lines to the theory of justice, see Michael Walzer's *Spheres of Justice* (New York: Basic Books, 1983).

36   I have already criticised one version of the programme of naturalising ethics in my *Scientism* (London: Routledge, 1991), ch. 7.

37   See O. Flanagan's 'Ethics naturalized: ethics as human ecology', in L. May, M. Friedman and A. Clark (eds) *Mind and Morals* (Cambridge, Mass.: MIT Press, 1996). Page references in brackets are to this volume.

38   Flanagan follows Paul Churchland, *A Neurocomputational Perspective: The Nature of the Mind and the Structure of Science* (Cambridge, Mass.: MIT Press, 1989), who calls it the problem of normativity.

39   Churchland, *A Neurocomputational Perspective*, pp. 301–2, quoted by Flanagan, p. 31.

40   O. Flanagan, *Varieties of Moral Personality* (Cambridge, Mass.: Harvard University Press, 1991), p. 32.

41   'How moral psychology changes moral theory', in May *et al.*, *Mind and Morals*, p. 49.

42   A much more moderate naturalism than the scientistic naturalism I have been considering here has been proposed by James Griffin, in *Value Judgement*. Griffin insists (ch. 7) that utilitarianism overdraws our capacities for impartiality and for calculation; deontology makes mysterious how we come to discover moral norms with an authority of their own; and virtue theory calls for a balance in our respect for different values that matter to human flourishing, but does not tell us in any more than the barest and preliminary way how that balance is to be achieved. So all of the standard theories have gaps in their answers to the question how agents are to live according to the values they use to systematise norms. Griffin thinks that 'common-sense morality' contains elements of all of the values the standard theories use to systematise norms; but it is not systematic itself. It is naturally eclectic, affected as it is by human limitations and by the accretions of child-rearing and political conventions (ch. 6, esp. p. 97). As will perhaps be obvious, I find Griffin's distinction between a wholesome and unambitious common-sense morality on the one hand, and a philosopher's doubtful systematisation on the other, highly questionable. Philosophy is one of the formative elements of common-sense morality as we now have it, not something external to it with systematising ambitions.

43   'Whose agenda? Ethics vs. cognitive science', in May *et al.*, *Mind and Morals*, pp. 69–88.

44   Ibid., p. 80.

45   In 'Losing your concepts'.

46   Scepticism about the claim that theory involves conceptual loss is also in order when the claim comes from MacIntyre. According to MacIntyre

moral theory since the Enlightenment has done away with the very thing – some teleological conception of human nature – that is needed to give viable moral theory and practice a focus. Viable moral theory and practice is focused on the virtues. But the expression of this claim of MacIntyre's in *After Virtue* is accompanied by a big chunk of text that conjures up in people supposedly deprived of it a grasp of quite a lot of thinking that comes from the defunct conception of virtue. MacIntyre's rhetorical strategy makes it difficult to believe that we have lost a concept or concepts outright. The most he can apparently mean is that a concept that ought to be in the foreground of ethics has been driven into the background, both in our culture and in the moral theory that the culture has spawned. In any case, there are many modern advocates of virtue theory. So one can be forgiven for asking why virtue theory cannot be considered one *more* moral theory of modern times rather than a conception that has been displaced or obliterated by moral theory of modern times.

47   This is the objection made by Iris Young, as I understand her, in *Justice and the Politics of Difference* (Princeton: Princeton University Press, 1990), ch. 4.

2: Theory versus Theories

1   *Ethics and the Limits of Philosophy* (Cambridge: Harvard University Press, 1985).
2   Ibid., p. 93.
3   See 'A critique of Utilitarianism', in J. J. C. Smart and B. Williams, *Utilitarianism: For and Against* (Cambridge: Cambridge University Press, 1973). For the parallel criticism of Kant, see Williams, *Moral Luck* (Cambridge: Cambridge University Press, 1981).
4   *Ethics and the Limits of Philosophy*, p. 112.
5   Ibid., p. 116.
6   Ibid., p. 115.
7   Ibid., pp. 66–70.
8   Ibid.
9   Ibid., pp. 113–14.
10   Ibid., p. 102.
11   Ibid., p. 112.
12   Ibid., p. 76.
13   Ibid., p. 99.
14   Ibid., p. 103.
15   For the notion of wide reflective equilibrium, see Norman Daniels, 'Wide reflective equilibrium and theory acceptance in ethics', in Daniels (ed.) *Justice and Justification* (Cambridge: Cambridge University Press, 1997), pp. 21–46.
16   *Ethics and the Limits of Philosophy*, p. 117.
17   Ibid., pp. 114–15.

18 Michael Tooley, 'Abortion and infanticide', *Philosophy and Public Affairs* 2 (1972), pp. 37–65. Tooley argues that that new-born infants, like foetuses, are too conceptually impoverished to have the desires that confer a right to life, and that therefore abortion and, within temporal limits, infanticide, are both permissible.

19 *Ethics and the Limits of Philosophy*, p. 115.

20 Williams's critique of theory has generated a big literature. For recent reactions rather different from mine, see e.g. A. Gibbard, 'Why theorize how to live with each other?' and a response by T. M. Scanlon, 'Moral theory: understanding and disagreement', both in *Philosophy and Phenomenological Research* 55 (1995), pp. 323–56. See also T. Nagel, *The Last Word* (Oxford: Clarendon Press, 1996), pp. 112–15 and Warren Quinn, *Morality and Action* (Cambridge: Cambridge University Press, 1993), pp. 134–49.

21 *The Structure of Scientific Revolutions* (Chicago: Chicago University Press, 1962).

22 Whether a problem is a mere puzzle or anomaly may not initially be clear; and the classification of a puzzle as an anomaly can be overturned if some refinement or reinterpretation of a theory makes a result or observation that was not easy to accommodate initially into a straightforward consequence or prediction of a theory. So perhaps every anomaly has to be taken as a so-far recalcitrant puzzle rather than one that is bound to defeat, or has already defeated, a theory.

23 See Jonathan Glover's attempt to limit utilitarianism with constraints that preserve autonomy in *Causing Death and Saving Lives* (Harmondsworth: Penguin Books, 1977).

24 See Michael Slote's 'Virtue ethics' in M. Baron, P. Pettit and M. Slote, *Three Methods of Ethics* (Oxford: Blackwell Publishers, 1997), pp. 191ff.

25 London: Allen & Unwin, 1986.

26 See James Griffin, *Well-being* (Oxford: Clarendon Press, 1986); see also Wayne Sumner, *Welfare, Happiness and Ethics* (Oxford: Clarendon Press, 1996).

27 On the contrary, I think that deception and coercion are important for theory not so much in connection with the relief of hunger, but in connection with improving the quality of life beyond a bare minimum. In other words, it seems to me that in the ethics of economic development, as opposed to, say, outright famine-relief, there is plenty of application for a principle making it obligatory to avoid coercion and plenty of application for a principle making it obligatory to prevent deception. Indeed, it may be that these principles prove their worth in association with a more complex account than O'Neill seems to have in mind of who are the relevant victims and perpetrators of deception and coercion in development matters. The victims of coercion are likely to be the poor, as O'Neill suggests, but the victimisers are not just of institutions of the rich world, but the elites of the poor world. In the case of deception, on the other hand, those immediately on the receiving end may quite often be the public of the rich countries, and in particular those sections sympathetic to the poor in the poor

countries, rather than the public of the poor countries themselves. The side-effects of the deception in the poor world may of course be worse than the deception suffered in the rich world, but they may be side-effects all the same. The immediate targets of deception are likely to be located outside the poor world.

28 See O'Neill's 'Constructivisms in ethics', in *Constructions of Reason* (Cambridge: Cambridge University Press, 1989).

29 See *Towards Justice and Virtue* (Cambridge: Cambridge University Press, 1996).

30 Ibid., p. 166.

31 Ibid., p. 167.

32 Oxford: Oxford University Press, 1991.

33 See Part Three of Thomas Pogge's *Realising Rawls* (Ithaca, NY: Cornell University Press, 1989).

34 The remainder of this paragraph summarises pp. 19–28 of Daniels's *Just Health Care* (Cambridge: Cambridge University Press, 1985).

35 Ibid., p. 28.

36 '[M]eeting health care needs may have a definite *tendency* to promote happiness. This tendency may be all the utilitarian needs to guide public policy, and it may give us an explanation of why health care is thought so special. I have no conclusive response to this position: it is a generalised version of the view that health care is special because it reduces pain and suffering, which much of it no doubt does' (p. 27). See also p. 49.

37 Ibid., p. 27.

38 Ibid., p. 33.

39 Ibid., pp. 47–8.

40 For a treatment of pain as an objective reason for action in a basically Kantian framework, see T. Nagel, *The View from Nowhere* (New York: Oxford University Press, 1987) ch. 8.

41 Ibid., p. 20. In addition to doing justice to the widely held beliefs about the importance of health care, an adequate account is also subject to two constraints on the justification of a principle of fair equality of opportunity.

3: Business, the Ethical and Self-interest

1 The appearance of overridingness has been questioned by Philippa Foot. See Essays 11, 12 and 13 in her *Virtues and Vices* (Oxford: Blackwell Publishers, 1978).

2 Elaine Sternberg, *Just Business* (New York: Little Brown, 1994). Elizabeth Valance, *Business Ethics* (Cambridge: Cambridge University Press, 1995).

3 'What's wrong with business ethics?', *Harvard Business Review* 71, 3 (1993), pp. 38–48; see p. 38.

4 *Ethics and Excellence* (New York: Oxford University Press, 1992).

5   'Armchair applied philosophy and business ethics', in C. Cowton and R. Crisp (eds) *The Theory and Practice of Business Ethics* (Oxford: Clarendon Press, 1998).

6   For more on the sources outside business for ethical standards that business people acknowledge as having authority, see T. Sorell and J. Hendy, *Business Ethics* (Oxford: Butterworth-Heinemann, 1994), ch. 1.

7   Ibid.

8   *Harvard Business Review* 46 (1968). I refer to the *HBR* revised and abridged reprint, 1-391-298 (1992).

9   Ibid., p. 1.

10 Ibid., p. 2.

11 Ibid., p. 7.

12 Norman Bowie's *Business Ethics: A Kantian Perspective* (Oxford: Blackwell Publishers, 1998) makes the case at book length.

13 I myself think there is a lot of intuitive appeal in the idea that morality is tainted by self-interest and that moral value is the highest value. I think these intuitions are sometimes at work when people recoil from at any rate a simple form of utilitarianism. So it may not be good enough that some moral theory says what Stark wants it to say. That moral theory may run afoul of intuitions that Kant exploits and that seem more compelling than the theory that departs from them.

14 See Milton Friedman's 'The social responsibility of a business is to increase its profits', reprinted in T. Beauchamp and N. Bowie, *Ethical Theory and Business*, 5th edn (New York: Prentice Hall, 1997), pp. 56–61.

15 'A stakeholder theory of the modern corporation', *Business Ethics Quarterly* (1994); reprinted in Beauchamp and Bowie, *Ethical Theory and Business*, 5th edn, pp. 66–75.

16 Ibid., p. 73.

17 Ibid.

18 Ibid., pp. 67–8.

19 Ibid., pp. 68–9.

20 Or it is soluble if something can be done to solve certain problems of cultural narrowness and the bias in stakeholder theory towards big business. See the last section of the article on which most of the preceding sections of this chapter have been based: my 'Beyond the fringe? The strange state of business ethics', in M. Parker (ed.) *Ethics and Organizations* (London: Sage, 1998), pp. 15–29.

21 See *Leviathan*, chs 13–15.

22 *The Methods of Ethics*, 7th edn (Indianapolis: Hackett, 1991).

23 Ibid., bk. 2, ch. 5.

4: Politics, Power and Partisanship

1   There is still controversy about the killing in Gibraltar in 1988 of three people believed to have been members of the IRA and believed to have been

on the point of carrying out a terrorist act against the British military. After being shot the three were found to be unarmed.

2 See M. Walzer, 'Political action: the problem of dirty hands', *Philosophy and Public Affairs* 2 (1973), pp. 160–80.

3 For details, see my *Hobbes* (London: Routledge, 1986), ch. 9.

4 See *Leviathan*, ch. 31.

5 *Innocence and Experience* (Cambridge, Mass.: Harvard University Press, 1989). See also 'Public and private morality' and the title essay in Hampshire's *Morality and Conflict* (Oxford: Blackwell Publishers, 1983). Hampshire's 1996 Tanner Lectures return to the themes of these works.

6 See pp. 172ff.

7 Ibid., p. 177.

8 Ibid., p. 140.

9 Ibid., p. 154.

10 Ibid., p. 68.

11 Ibid., p. 170.

12 Ibid., p. 68.

13 Ibid., p. 66.

14 Ibid., p. 170.

15 Ibid., pp. 138ff. See also Hampshire, *Morality and Conflict*, p. 148.

16 *Morality and Conflict*, pp. 8–9.

17 Ibid., p. 165.

18 See the essays 'Morality and pessimism' and 'Public and private morality', in *Morality and Conflict*.

19 'Morality and conflict', p. 152 of Hampshire's book.

20 See Dennis F. Thompson, *Political Ethics and Public Office* (Cambridge, Mass.: Harvard University Press, 1987), ch. 1.

21 See T. Nagel, *Equality and Partiality* (Oxford: Oxford University Press, 1991), chs 2 and 6.

22 'Their own interests' in this formulation is admittedly vague, and ambiguous (but I believe excusably so) between each person voting in the interests of that person or each person voting in interests shared by other voters in a constitutency. Both are natural interpretations of self-interest. Empirical studies of the influence of self-interest in voting preferences and opinions associated with these sometimes overdefine self-interest for the sake of testability, and then find that political opinions reflect self-interest less frequently and to a smaller degree than one might think. This may be what happens in the 1990 study by D. Sears and C. Funk, 'Self-interest in Americans' political opinions', in J. Mansbridge (ed.) *Beyond Self-interest* (Chicago: University of Chicago Press, 1990), pp. 147–70. Self-interest, in their account, is the response to measurable material short-term impact by the survey respondent or his or her family.

23 I think these issues come under Sears's and Funk's heading of 'ambiguous severe threats' which do measurably mobilise self-interest in even their narrow sense. See Sears and Funk, 'Self-interest', p. 160f.

24 For a survey and discussion of some relevant empirical studies, see Tom R.

Tyler, 'Justice, self-interest, and the legitimacy of legal and political authority', in Mansbridge, *Beyond Self-Interest*.
25 *Equality and Partiality*, p. 61.
26 Ibid., pp. 12–13.

5: Feminism and Moral Theory

1 Susan Moller Okin, *Justice, Gender and the Family* (New York: Basic Books, 1989), pp. 108–9.
2 See Will Kymlicka, *Contemporary Political Philosophy* (Oxford: Clarendon Press, 1990), pp. 246ff.
3 See the essays by Shanner, Purdy, Overall, Sherwin and Morgan in L. W. Sumner and J. Boyle (eds) *Philosophical Perspectives on Bioethics* (Toronto: University of Toronto Press, 1996).
4 *Science, Morality and Feminist Theory*, supple. vol. 13 (1987) *of Canadian Journal of Philosophy*, pp. 265–84.
5 Ibid., p. 266.
6 Ibid., p. 277.
7 Ibid., p. 279.
8 'Relational rights and responsibilities: revisioning the family in liberal political theory and law', *Hypatia* 11 (1996), pp. 4–29; see p. 22.
9 Ibid., p. 19: 'An ethic of care that values the efforts of continuous care and help must find a place in any account of family lives and in any just family law.'
10 See N. Noddings, *Caring* (Berkeley: University of California Press, 1984); S. Ruddick, *Maternal Thinking* (Boston: Beacon Press, 1989).
11 Joan Tronto, 'Beyond gender difference to a theory of care', *Signs* 12 (1987–8), pp. 644–63. See also Claudia Card's opening essay in her collection, *Feminist Ethics* (Lawrence, Kan.: University of Kansas Press, 1991).
12 *In a Different Voice* (Cambridge: Harvard University Press, 1982), p. 58.
13 Ibid.
14 Ibid.
15 Ibid., p. 72.
16 Some do not even feel that they have to abandon philosophy or the western ideals of reason. I have in mind Sara Ruddick in particular, whose attachment to these things does not prevent her from stating and defending a nonstandard theory in her book, *Maternal Thinking*.
17 *Moral Voices, Moral Selves: Carol Gilligan and Feminist Moral Theory* (Cambridge: Polity Press, 1995).
18 At one point Nancy Chodorow rather than Gilligan is credited with responsibility for the shift. See pp. 67ff.
19 See 'What do women want in a moral theory?', 'The need for more than justice', 'Hume, the women's moral theorist?' and 'Trust and antitrust', all in Baier's *Moral Prejudices* (Cambridge, Mass.: Harvard University Press, 1995).

20 L. Brown and C. Gilligan, *Meeting at the Crossroads: Women's Psychology and Girls' Development* (Cambridge, Mass.: Harvard University Press, 1992), pp. 18–19. Quoted by Hekman, *Moral Voices*, p. 20.

21 Hekman, *Moral Voices*, pp. 1–8.

22 Ibid., p. 21.

23 Ibid., p. 30.

24 See Hekman, *Moral Voices*, ch. 2.

25 And perhaps shouldn't (in view of the excesses of naturalism considered in ch. 1 of this book).

26 Ibid., p. 25.

27 Ibid., pp. 26–7.

28 Ibid., pp. 38ff.

29 Ibid., pp. 40–5.

30 See e.g. p. 57.

31 Hekman not only fails to show that Gilligan breaks the mould of the philosophical sort of moral theory; she undercuts the claim of a Gilligan-inspired theory to be distinctively feminist (I believe), because she seems to think that the controlling concept of such a theory will be 'difference'; this, as she acknowledges, applies to race and class as much as gender.

32 'The need for more than justice', esp. pp. 28ff., in Baier, *Moral Prejudices*.

33 For the importance of relative power in a feminist approach to medical ethics, see e.g. Laura M. Purdy, 'Good bioethics must be feminist bioethics' and Christine Overall, 'Reflections of a sceptical bioethicist', in Sumner and J. Boyle, *Philosophical Reflections on Bioethics*.

34 Baier, *Moral Prejudices*, p. 30. See also 'What do women want from moral theory?', p. 6, where Baier claims that standard moral theories – theories geared to the concept of obligation – falter in their treatment of obligations to the young. Baier's alternative to the concept of obligation is trust, a relation of Gilligan's care. See also 'Unsafe loves', where love of progeny is 'put at the center of the cluster of kinds of love', *Moral Prejudices*, p. 49.

35 The problem is acknowledged by feminist moral theory. See Debra Shogun, 'Feminist ethics for strangers', in Debra Shogun (ed.) *A Reader in Feminist Ethics* (Toronto: Canadian Scholars' Press, 1992), pp. 169–82.

36 Up to a point, the same is true of Sarah Ruddick's theory of the maternal virtues in *Maternal Thinking*. Ruddick thinks that certain demands encountered in the practice of mothering can, if met there, provide a model for meeting the demands of peace-making and peace-keeping. Although clearer than Gilligan, Ruddick is open to the scepticism about the worth of caring in a patriarchal society that has been developed by feminists such as Hoagland. See the following section.

37 See Marylin Friedman, 'Beyond caring: the de-moralisation of gender', *Canadian Journal of Philosophy* 13 (1987), pp. 87–110.

38 See Sarah Hoagland, 'Some thoughts about caring', in Card, *Feminist Ethics*, pp. 246–64.

39 The pioneer of the approach is often taken to be Mary Daly. See her

Gyn/ecology: The Metaethics of Radical Feminism (Boston: Beacon Press, 1978). For the normative ethics, revolving round what Daly calls the 'volcanic virtues', see *Pure Lust: Elemental Feminist Philosophy* (Boston: Beacon Press, 1984).

40   Hoagland, 'Some thoughts', p. 259. 'Amazons love to explore, hunt, and gather things away from cities. Mothers are city-bound and over time take pleasure only in seeing their abdomens grow.' See also Marylin Frye's comments on the need to invert the American white southern valuation of ladies over women, 'A response to *Lesbian Ethics*', in C. Card (ed.) *Adventures in Lesbian Philosophy* (Bloomington, Ind.: Indiana University Press, 1994), p. 57.

41   *Lesbian Ethics: Toward New Value* (Palo Alto: Institute of Lesbian Ethics, 1988).

42   Hoagland, 'Why *lesbian* ethics?', in Card, *Adventures in Lesbian Philosophy*, pp. 199–207.

43   Judy Grahn, *Another Mother Tongue: Gay Words, Gay Worlds* (Boston: Beacon Press, 1984), p. 34. Quoted in Hoagland, *Lesbian Ethics*, p. 66.

44   Hoagland, *Lesbian Ethics*, pp. 111ff.

45   Ibid., p. 112.

46   Ibid., pp. 154–6.

47   Ibid., pp. 157–64.

48   Ibid., p. 126.

49   Barbara Houston, 'In praise of blame', in Card, *Adventures in Lesbian Philosophy*, pp. 144–62.

50   K. Martindale and M. Saunders, 'Realising love and justice: lesbian ethics in the upper and lower case', in Card, *Adventures in Lesbian Philosophy*, pp. 163–85.

51   Frye, 'A Response', in Card, *Feminist Ethics*.

52   Ibid., pp. 57–8.

53   Hoagland, *Lesbian Ethics*, p. 267.

54   See Houston, 'In praise of blame', p. 154. I agree with Houston, though, that there are many questions about 'intelligibility' as an alternative to blame that Hoagland does not answer.

55   Hoagland, *Lesbian Ethics*, e.g. p. 9, p. 13.

56   Ibid., pp. 10ff.

57   For a review of this periodical, see Card in *Adventures in Lesbian Philosophy*, pp. 210–13.

58   'Violence and cruelty among lesbians: the legacy of men's violence against girls', *Lesbian Ethics* 5, 3 (1996), pp. 40–51.

59   Ibid., p. 43.

60   Ibid.

61   Ibid., p. 45.

62   Ibid., p. 46.

63   Ibid., pp. 48–9.

64   Ibid., pp. 49–50.

65   Ibid., p. 48.

66 Linda Strega, 'A Lesbian love story or ... When Lesbian community works', *Lesbian Ethics* 5, 2 (1995), pp. 3–13.
67 Ibid., p. 9.
68 For arguably defensible double standards about stealing, see C. E. Atkins, 'Towards an ethics of stealing: thoughts on oppression and theft', *Lesbian Ethics* 5, 3 (1996), pp. 105–8.

6: Environmentalism and Moral Theory

1 See John O'Neill, 'The varieties of intrinsic value', *The Monist* 75 (1992), pp. 119–37.
2 Perhaps Paul Taylor's *Respect for Nature* (Princeton, NJ: Princeton University Press, 1986) can be understood as an attempt to adapt Kant's notions of respect and membership in a kingdom of ends to the demands of environmental ethics. Still, fidelity to Kant does not seem to have been a desideratum of the account, and there are more departures from than echoes of Kant.
3 I refer to the reprint of this article in R. Elliot (ed.) *Environmental Ethics* (Oxford: Oxford University Press, 1995), pp. 29–59. This version of the paper has a preface written in 1994, in which Callicott modifies some of the conclusions. The paper originally appeared in 1980.
4 Aldo Leopold, *A Sand County Almanac* (New York: Oxford University Press, 1949), pp. 224–5. Quoted in Callicott, 'Animal liberation', p. 39.
5 Callicott, 'Animal liberation', pp. 51–2. In the preface to the 1994 version of his paper, Callicott says that the land ethic indicates that vegetarianism is required, but the ground for this claim is to do with the ill effects of large-scale farming (see p. 30), and does not appear to me to tell against the small-holder who keeps and butchers a few pigs or chickens.
6 Ibid., pp. 49ff.
7 Ibid., pp. 52–3.
8 Ibid., pp. 40–9.
9 Ibid., p. 48.
10 Ibid., p. 49.
11 Although the claim that we consume too much needs careful treatment. An excellent discussion is by M. Sagoff: 'Do we consume too much?', unpublished Ruffin Lecture in Business Ethics, delivered at the University of Virginia, April 1997. See also B. Norton, 'Sustainability, human welfare, and ecosystem health', *Environmental Values* 1 (1997), pp. 97–111.
12 For a view of extinction and preservation of species closer to the mainstream of environmental ethics, see Holmes Rolston, 'Duties to endangered species', *Bioscience* 35 (1985), pp. 718–26.
13 For an argument that they are, see Elliot Sober's, 'Philosophical problems for environmentalism', in Elliot, *Environmental Ethics*, pp. 233ff.
14 Users of the strategy include Peter Singer in *Practical Ethics* (Cambridge:

Cambridge University Press, 1979); Tom Regan in *The Case for Animals* (London: Routledge, 1984) and Paul Taylor in *Respect for Nature*.

15 'Deep ecology: a new philosophy of our time?', *Ecologist* 14 (1984), p. 7.

16 See Arne Naess, 'Identification as a source of deep ecological attitudes', in Michael Tobias (ed.) *Deep Ecology* (San Diego: Avant Books, 1985). See also Freya Matthews, *The Ecological Self* (London: Routledge, 1991).

17 See e.g. Val Plumwood, 'Nature, self and gender: feminism, environmental philosophy, and the critique of rationalism', in Elliot, *Environmental Ethics*, pp. 158ff. Other critics include Richard Sylvan (a.k.a. Routley), 'A critique of deep ecology', *Radical Philosophy* 40–1 (1985) and Jim Cheney, 'Ecofeminism and deep ecology', *Environmental Ethics* 9 (1987), pp. 115–45. For Fox's reply, see his 'The deep ecology-ecofeminism debate and its parallels', *Environmental Ethics* 11 (1989).

18 Onora O'Neill's own treatment of duties to the environment is not based on a duty of non-injury alone, but on a social virtue as well. See her *Towards Justice and Virtue*, (Cambridge: Cambridge University Press, 1996), pp. 203–6. This makes her treatment more anthropocentric than might be wished, as she admits (p. 203n).

19 'Duties concerning islands', reprinted in Elliot, *Environmental Ethics*, pp. 89–103.

20 Ibid., p. 95.

21 Ibid., p. 96.

22 Brennan urges a distinction between duties regarding, and duties to, things, and seems to suggest that there are no duties to artifacts like works of art. See his 'The moral standing of natural objects', *Environmental Ethics* 6 (1984), pp. 35–56.

23 Midgley, 'Duties concerning islands', p. 98.

24 There is perhaps a bigger issue over whether, when so much weight is put on fragility, conservation rather than innovation is overvalued; but it is not immediately obvious what the relative values of conservation or innovation are, or whether the fact that the choice of fragility as a basis for an environmental ethic raises this question is a criticism of that choice.

25 Callicott, 'Animal liberation', p. 45.

26 Ibid.

27 See Rolston, 'Duties to endangered species', pp. 60–75.

28 For an argument from an unusual angle for objective value in nature, see Holmes Rolston, 'Disvalues in nature', *The Monist* 75 (1992), pp. 250–78.

29 Quoted in Michael Martin, 'Ecotage and civil disobedience', in Peter List (ed.) *Radical Environmentalism: Philosophy and Tactics* (Belmont, Calif.: Wadsworth, 1992), p. 256.

30 Quoted in Martin, 'Ecotage and civil disobedience', p. 260.

31 This is the main thesis of Martin, 'Ecotage and civil disobedience'.

32 Martin, 'Ecotage and civil disobedience'.

33 'Taking on the Goliaths of Doom', reprinted in List, *Radical Environmentalism*, pp. 136–41.

34 For an engagingly down to earth and definite account, see Jim Dodge,

'Living by life: some bioregional theory and practice', in List, *Radical Environmentalism*, pp. 108–17.

35 There are environmental ethicists who may say that this anomaly is contrived, because *ecofeminism* does away with facsimiles of the obligatory/supererogatory distinction. See Plumwood, 'Nature, self and gender'. See also List, *Radical Environmentalism*, ch. 2. See also A. Brennan (ed.) *The Ethics of the Environment* (Aldershot: Dartmouth, 1995), pp. 275–364. According to this view, an ethic of care explains the value of protecting the environment as well as the value of living in harmony with it. But I think that ecofeminists assume a success for the ethic of care in its home area of explaining what is wrong with normal relations between men and women, when, as chapter 5 indicated, nothing like that is accepted by all feminists. Adding the problems of environmental ethics to the problems of women seems to me to put a crushing weight on an ethic of care.

7: The Significance of Anomaly

1 It must be admitted that Spinoza and Hegel are sometimes exempted by some ecologists from the critique of traditional philosophy. But Midgley shows that one doesn't have to revive metaphysical substantial monism to bring philosophy into the service of deep environmentalism.

2 The overall treatment is not unlike Hampshire's, but stripped of his scepticism about theory. Hampshire makes use of two pre-theoretical ideas: that of choosing the lesser evil – applicable wherever the utilitarian says that if a thing is right overall it is right full stop – and the idea of its being a requirement of justice to prevent or minimise great evils. Combining the two ideas, it can sometimes be a requirement of justice to commit (a relatively small) injustice in order to act against a much greater evil than injustice.

3 For an example of an attempt to think through the compatibility of Kantianism with utiitarianism, see R. M. Hare, *Sorting Out Ethics* (Oxford: Clarendon Press, 1997), Part III.

4 I have in mind work by Nagel and Scanlon among others. Thomas Nagel represents consequentialist considerations and deontological considerations as emerging at different stages in the articulation of a political theory. See his *Equality and Partiality* (Oxford: Oxford University Press, 1991), ch. 2, and T. M. Scanlon, 'Rights, goals and fairness', reprinted in S. Scheffler (ed.) *Consequentialism and its Critics* (Oxford: Oxford University Press, 1988), pp. 74–92.

5 See Onora O'Neill, *Towards Justice and Virtue* (Cambridge: Cambridge University Press, 1996). See also M. Baron, P. Pettit and M. Slote, *Three Methods of Ethics* (Oxford: Blackwell Publishers, 1997), pp. 33ff.

6 See the title essay in R. Goodin, *Utilitarianism as a Pubic Philosophy* (Cambridge: Cambridge University Press, 1995), pp. 3–27.

Index